Object-Oriented Defect Management
of Software

HOUMAN YOUNESSI

ISBN 0-13-060928-5

Prentice Hall PTR
Upper Saddle River, NJ 07458
www.phptr.com

Library of Congress Cataloging-in-Publication Data
A catalog record for this book can be obtained from the Library of Congress.

Editorial/Production Supervision: Carol Wheelan
Acquisitions Editor: Victoria Jones
Marketing Manager: Debby vanDijk
Manufacturing Buyer: Maura Zaldivar
Cover Design: Anthony Gemmellaro
Cover Design Direction: Jerry Votta
Interior Series Design: Gail Cocker-Bogusz

© 2002 Prentice Hall PTR
A division of Pearson Education, Inc.
Upper Saddle River, NJ 07458

ISBN 0-13-060928-5

Pearson Education LTD
Pearson Education Australia Pty, Limited
Pearson Education Singapore, Pte. Ltd.
Pearson Education North Asia Ltd.
Pearson Education Canada, Ltd.
Pearson Educación de Mexico, S.A. de C.V.
Pearson Education—Japan
Pearson Education Malaysia, Pte. Ltd.

TABLE OF CONTENTS

CHAPTER 2   Defects and Defect Management in an Object-Oriented Environment   41

v

Dedication

I dedicate this work to those whom I love most, to my family.

PREFACE

If you selected this book to learn more about testing of object-oriented programs, you are about to get more than you bargained for. As the title implies, this book discusses defect management of object-oriented software systems. This latter activity goes beyond merely testing object-oriented code in many respects.

First, we will be discussing defect management, of which testing is only one type. Defects can potentially be injected into our software systems at any stage of the software process. If left unchecked and undiscovered, they would manifest themselves as errors or "bugs" when the final executable is set into operation. Testing—exercising the executable in the hopes of making it fail—can uncover many of these defects. However, there are other techniques that do not require the executable code to be available and instead rely on examining various artifacts of the process. We could call these *static techniques* to contrast with the former, which we might call *dynamic*. In this book, I discuss in detail both the static and the dynamic approaches to defect management.

Second, testing is the removal of defects at the last, or nearly last, available opportunity before the product is to be used. It can thus be argued that taking an approach based on testing of code alone, a strictly corrective approach, is contrary to the very axiom of software engineering. We also need preventive approaches. Software engineering—in its entirety—can in fact be viewed as the process of managing defects in a software product. This claim may sound controversial at first, but in reality it is not so at all. Look at it this way: Any activity we perform as part of our software process is targeted toward either preventing defects from being included in our product or identifying and removing of those that have been already introduced. This in turn implies that defect management techniques are not uniquely applied to code, but can also be employed in relation to every activity of the software engineering process. In this book, I cover defect management techniques relevant to all stages of the software engineering process and not just techniques that deal with code. Additionally, both the corrective and preventive approaches are considered.

Third, this book is about managing defects in an object-oriented environment. This does not mean, however, that all defect management techniques that are introduced in this book are exclusive to object orientation. Conversely, however, every technique I cover is useful in an object-oriented context, although it may not have been originally developed for that domain.

Finally, given the recent ascent of the Unified Modeling Language™ (UML) and the Rational Unified Process™ (RUP)[1] to the level of having been accepted as standard means of modeling and conducting an object-oriented process respectively, we have made every attempt to be compatible with both when logically possible.

Given these characteristics, this book might be used in many fashions. It is targeted to professional software engineers, researchers in object technology and in defect management, and postgraduate students in software engineering. It may be used as a textbook for an advanced course (masters and Ph.D. level) in object-oriented defect management or as supporting material for advanced courses in object-oriented software engineering. It may also be used as training material in a professional industry-based course in object-oriented defect management.

In bringing this book to you, I owe a debt of gratitude to many people. Particularly:

- To all my teachers, students, and colleagues from whom I have learned what I know so I could write this book.

- To my wife and best friend, Sheyda, whose support and understanding has made this book possible.

- To my son, Z. Daniel Younessi, whose technical assistance has proved invaluable in producing the text and the artwork herein.

---

[1]The Unified Modeling Language and the Rational Unified Process are both trademarks of the Rational Corporation.

- To the professionals at Prentice-Hall, especially Ms. Victoria Jones, Ms. Carol Wheelan, and Mr. Mike Meehan, through whose efforts this book has been published.
- To you, the reader, who gave me reason to write it in the first place.

It is my most sincere wish that you will find this book of use.

Houman Younessi
South Windsor, Connecticut
October 2001

Chapter 1

SETTING THE SCENE

Software, Software Engineering, and the Software Engineering Process

The profession of software engineering, like any other engineering profession, is concerned with building of artifacts; in this case, of software. When professionals build things they usually aim to produce the highest quality artifact possible utilizing the minimal amount of resources necessary to achieve this aim; anything else would be wasteful. Paying attention to what is done, how it is done, who does it, under what conditions, and what tools are utilized becomes paramount. In other words, process becomes important and its quality underpins the quality of the product being produced.

Software engineering is therefore the collective term applied to attempts to produce the highest quality product possible, of often complex and large software systems, on a reasonably sustainable and repeatable basis with minimal resource expenditure. To do so, software engineering has relied and continues to rely on three principal approaches and a number of other disciplines. The three principal approaches are:

- Improving the management of the software development process;
- Establishing a rigorous foundation for software development; and
- Technology support.

In discussing the relationship between the quality of a product and the process that yields such a product, it is possible to postulate that the external quality attributes of a product can be deemed as functions of process attributes. This, in turn, implies that a software process must have a methodological dimension and a technological aspect (Haas et al., 1994). Furthermore, there is also an undeniable organizational dimension (Humphrey, 1989) that pervades any actual instantiation of a specified software process. Therefore, for our purposes, I define a software process as the organization of technologies and methods utilized within a particular context by an entity to produce a software product.

This definition captures the most current understanding of the term and differs from those that equate a software process and a development methodology, in that the latter implies that the mere adoption of a software development methodology is sufficient for ensuring increased software quality (Sauer & Lau, 1994). Such a definition fails to explain, for example, why a given formal methodology succeeds in one situation or organization and not in another.

Although I believe the stated definition is workable, I recognize that the dimensions cited may not be exhaustive or entirely orthogonal.

In fact, most current definitions for process, if not explicitly, at least implicitly recognize the existence of all the three dimensions mentioned in this definition. It has been asserted (Humphrey, 1989; Younessi & Henderson-Sellers, 1997) that the three major areas of concern enumerated earlier support the notion that the process of software development relies on these three major elements:

- People and organizational influences (hence the need for improved management);
- Methodology (hence the need for rigor and formality); and
- Technology (hence the need for tool and technological support).

Hence, I present the preceding definition. In the same article Younessi and Henderson-Sellers (1997) further asserted that it is the balance of elements from these three dimensions that defines a process and leads to the recognition of a specific level of process quality.

A Constructive[1] Approach to Software Engineering

The process of constructing software is not monolithic, nor should it be considered as such. Building of software can be thought of as assembling of a group of carefully selected techniques that together produce the software artifact being built and any intermediate products required. This "Lego™"[2] approach to software construction allows us to concentrate on specific techniques, maybe even a variety of techniques, that are suitable for achievement of a particular task. We can then define what that technique is, how it is applied, what products it generates, what resources are required, how it interfaces with other techniques and even sometimes how effective it is and under what conditions. This approach allows a degree of comparative analysis between individual techniques and is the one I use in this book.

In fact we can take this approach one step further and envisage the software engineering process as a collection of activities, the end result of which yields the software product. Activities can therefore be considered as being composed of a collection of tasks. A task can be thought of as a unit of work for the conduct of which we might have one or several techniques, yielding one or several work products. This constructive approach is, incidentally, the essence of a number of the modern software processes such as the Object-Oriented Process Environments and Notation (OPEN; Graham et al., 1997), as shown in Figure 1.1.

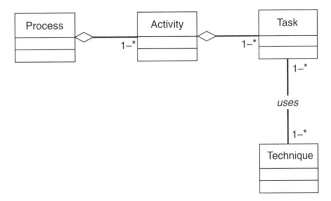

Figure 1.1
OPEN's core relationships as an example of a constructive approach.

---

[1]The adjective *constructive* refers to the way techniques are put together purposefully and in accordance with some rules to construct a process.
[2]Lego™ is a trademark of The LEGO Group A/S.

The Process of Constructing Software

It seems that there is in any construction project, whether it is a quilt, a fighter jet, a house, or a piece of software, a number of activities that have to be performed. These are, at a minimum, the following:

- Finding out about the problem that this construction needs to solve.
- Coming up with one or several alternate solutions to this problem.
- Actual construction of the solution artifact.
- Evaluation of the suitability of the artifact and its ability to solve the problem.
- Delivery for use in the field.
- Continuous assessment of suitability and artifact maintenance.

In our discipline we refer to these activities as follows:

- Requirements elicitation, analysis, and specification (sometimes called requirements engineering).
- Design and design specification.
- Implementation.
- Verification and validation.
- Delivery and installation.
- Maintenance.

Current software process frameworks such as OPEN (Graham et al., 1997) and the Rational Unified Process (RUP; Jacobson et al., 1999) recognize this fact and thus allow for planning a software process instance that contains tasks to realize each and every one of these activities. As mentioned before, however, there are a variety of tasks that can be attributed to each of these activities. For example, testing may be a task selected as part of the verification and validation activity for a particular project. *Mutation testing* (Budd, 1980) might be the technique used to accomplish this task. Alternatively (or in conjunction), we might select inspection as another task within the verification and validation activity. The technique of Strauss and Ebenau (1995) might be used for accomplishing this inspection task.

In a later discussion, we shall see that looking at the software engineering process from this perspective has a distinct advantage in terms of what we intend to do in this book. It would allow us to look at each activity, task, and specifically each technique as a means of managing *defects*, defined as any shortcoming in a software product deliverable.

The definition of a software process is also paradigm-based, meaning that the choice of tasks and techniques to achieve each software engineering activity depends on an overall way of thinking, a philosophical perspective, or a paradigm. For example, choosing a transformationally based paradigm (which assumes that a problem situation, the solution to the problem, and thus the software system that delivers that solution can all be adequately modeled in terms of a series of changes to some inputs by a number of transformations to generate certain outputs) would require the selection of certain modeling techniques (e.g., a flowchart) that would be inappropriate if we had taken a causal paradigm, which assumes that a system can be adequately modeled based on state transitions. Thus the choice of a paradigm plays a central role in the selection of the tasks and techniques that are to be completed, which, in turn, would define our defect management effort with respect to each. Our paradigm in this book is object-oriented.

Object Orientation

Much has been written about the object paradigm in the past decade. It has in fact become clear that object orientation has emerged as the dominant paradigm of software engineering. With its roots in the world of program construction, it has more recently become pervasive throughout the software process. We now have object-oriented analysis techniques; design methods; techniques for specification, formal or otherwise; verification and validation; metrics; and much more. There are now even full software process definitions and frameworks such as OPEN (Graham et al., 1997) and RUP (Jacobson et al., 1999) that take an object-oriented perspective. But what is object orientation and why is it important?

Understanding the Object Paradigm

When asked to describe the essence of object orientation, many would present concepts such as classification, inheritance, polymorphic behavior, and reuse. Interesting and important as these concepts might be, they are secondary by-products of object orientation. The essence of object orientation lies elsewhere and relates to how we perceive and model systems, whether they are of a problem, a solution, or an implementation of a solution.

Creating models is therefore central to the construction of object-oriented systems. Most simply stated, a *model* is a mapping from one domain into another (Ross & Wright, 1992). This means that we cognitively translate what we see as relevant from one environment into another, given a particular purpose and abstraction level. For example, if our purpose is to identify how many chairs there are in a room, then a chair observed in the room may be mapped into the domain of positive integer numbers. If our purpose is to know the colors of furniture in this room then the mapping may be into a constructed set of colors (Allen & Yen, 1979).

Speaking from a cognitive psychology standpoint, a model is what is captured and communicated from our understanding of the situation presented in one domain (often the real world) into another, using a particular language of communication, or a modeling language (Eysenck & Keane, 1990). On this basis, most models (those that attempt to map what is externally perceived through our energy-activated sensory organs) are described as at least a double mapping. The first mapping is from the environment (the real world) into our cognition; that is, forming a mental model (this is also called *perception*). The second mapping involves using our cognition as a means of creating another model of what it has perceived, this time for the purpose of communicating our perception to others (e.g., a blueprint or an object diagram when used as a medium between the designer and the implementer) or to ourselves at a later time (e.g., a note in our scratch book, or a diagram to remind us of what transpired at the client interview; Eysenck & Keane, 1990; Martin & Odell, 1995). Sometimes, however, the first of these mappings might be absent (e.g., when we attempt to create a model of a Gorgon).

Modeling is therefore closely related to the activities of perception and communication. Consistent with this, and a large number of other definitions (Bruner, 1957; Checkland, 1981; Gibson, 1966; Gregory, 1980; Neisser, 1976; Preece et al., 1995), modeling may be defined as the acquisition, retention, and communication of those views of the situation that are, at the time, relevant to the observer.

In relation to the issue of the various views of "reality" previously discussed, it has also been observed throughout the centuries (Aristotle, 1924; Descartes, 1911; Plato, 1974, 1989) that knowledge of structures, processes, and sequences in which events occur are all necessary for comprehending the real world, which is in turn a prerequisite for modeling some aspect of it. This is of particular relevance when there is an absence of a priori knowledge in terms of the future utility of the model to be constructed. An example may clarify the intention here.

Assume that a model of a system is being created in such a way that we would use it, in the future, to answer questions of this type: Of what is X composed? Given this a priori knowledge of the future use of the model, it is

[handwritten margin notes: Object orientation combines: 1. object model 2.]

probably sufficient to provide a model that c[...]
that exist in the system (objects) and their int[...]
called *structural models* or *object models*. I[...]
accomplished in this system, then a model that concentrates on inputs, processes, and outputs might be the one of choice. These models are known as *process models* or more correctly as *transformational models*. An a priori interest in knowing when or in what sequence we do things would likely lead to a model of states, events, and sequences, which is usually called a *dynamic* or *sequential model*.

However in the absence of any a priori knowledge of the intended utility of a model, the modeler has no choice but to provide all three models and clear evidence of their mutual interrelation. This is what we do when we become observers of some situation. Our cognition registers not only objects, but also changes and sequences.

Traditional modeling languages and paradigms of software engineering usually concentrated on one such aspect and were, as such, limited in their ability to yield general models. For example, a data model principally captures the structure of the situation and lacks transformational or causal detail. A flowchart captures the transformational details but lacks important structural and causal detail, and a state diagram or state machine captures sequential information but lacks structure and transformation details.

Object technology combines these three perspectives. In fact, this ability to provide such a rich model that does not depend on any specific modeling view is one of the greatest strengths of object orientation. By capturing and putting together the relevant details of the situation from all three perspectives, object orientation "encapsulates" reality into modules, as we perceive it. In other words the object-oriented paradigm allows us to view the system in terms of elements that our perception is most comfortable with as it (our perception) has also absorbed, encapsulated, and modeled the situation using the same abstractions. This in turn means that the proximity of an object-oriented model and how we actually perceive the world (the system) is maximized. This is the concept of *encapsulation*, which allows us to perceive objects in the world from the perspective of a given relevance and thus identify all those objects that have these same characteristics. This in turn leads us to the concept of types. Those encapsulations that have from a particular point of relevance the same or similar characteristics can be perceived to belong to the same type. Each member of a type is called an *object*.

For a system (the world) to operate, its objects have to establish relationships with each other and communicate. This is also the case in an object-oriented model of any reality. This means that as part of the causal model of a situation we identify and decide on those interactions of relevance that give the system of our intent a particular meaning. That is, we extract from the infinite

[handwritten margin notes: Previous attempts to modeling - data - flowchart - state machine Encapsulation - structure of situation - transformational details - sequential information]

number of interactions possible between objects only those that we perceive as relevant and model those, as we did with the objects themselves. This means that a given object would react to a request by another object that calls on its service. This is the message-passing model, and along with encapsulation, it is the very essence of object orientation.

In fact, we can perceive object orientation as the implementation of the client–server model at the micro (individual object) level. This means that Object A, which has as part of it a service x, might be called by Object B, which needs the service x of Object A. Object B is the client and Object A is the server.

A powerful paradigm, object orientation would bring forth both opportunities and challenges for the software engineering practitioner. The following is a discussion of some of these opportunities.

Comprehensive Model Generation

A well-developed object-oriented model is multidimensional. It depicts the encapsulated and combined structural, transformational, and causal–sequential aspects of the situation being modeled. Given this multidimensionality, it can be argued that an object-oriented model of a particular situation would contain more information than one that is developed along only one of the three dimensions previously mentioned. It stands to reason, therefore, that given the same level of granularity of view and accuracy, the object-oriented model would be capable of answering more questions about the situation modeled than say each of an Entity-Relationship (ER) diagram or a Data Flow Diagram (DFD), a flowchart, or a state machine representation individually. In general, and particularly in terms of the objectives of this book, this quality represents a great advantage because if system functionality should be maximally modeled, then omission of any one of the three dimensions would be an absolute omission that would detract from the information content of the model. We will see later that such an omission can be classified as a defect and is thus of interest to defect management.

This, however, does not mean that object-oriented products are necessarily and invariably of higher quality than their traditionally developed counterparts just because we can be more comprehensive through the object-oriented process. It does mean that taking an object-oriented approach provides the potential for more information to be available up front and greater ease in communication of information. This in turn would tend to work toward clarity and observability in the project, which can contribute positively to the product quality.

Seamlessness

Another great advantage of object orientation is seamlessness. In developing software systems, as mentioned earlier, it is necessary to go through three interrelated activities. The observer or analyst must develop an understanding of the problem situation that is in need of improvement; such an understanding, when acquired, must then be recorded and communicated. A model of the problem situation therefore must be constructed. Once the relevant professionals in the software development process are made familiar with at least a sufficiently large portion of the problem situation (often using the model obtained), it is possible to propose solutions to the problem. The mental images arrived at as a workable solution must then be modeled so they can be communicated with those who have to build the product. This is called a *design model*. Ultimately, this design has to be constructed in program code. This is a third model, a model of the solution that is executable. Applying the object-oriented paradigm to the development of software systems, we can use the same modeling elements to develop all three of these models. In other words, we use the same abstractions, the same vocabulary, and the same grammar to tell each of the three stories. This is the language of objects, classes, inheritance, aggregation, states, transitions, message passing, and the like. Given the comprehensive nature and multidimensionality of the paradigm, as already discussed, the same language can model all three situations. After all, a model is a model.

Permitting More Complex Systems to Be Constructed

The power of abstraction and the multidimensionality inherent in object orientation has allowed us to tackle more complex and convoluted problem situations than had been possible before. In the absence of object technology, many software applications utilized today, graphical user interfaces, the World Wide Web, and many other products would be out of reach in terms of our ability to provide adequate design models to realize them.

Promoting Distribution

In the object paradigm we model the world in terms of communicating objects. This, as mentioned before, implies the implementation of the client–server model at the very low level of the individual object. This capability, in conjunction with the concept of encapsulation, allows for construction of modules at multiple levels of abstraction (object and class, packages, packages of packages, subsystems, etc.) yet still maintains the message-passing paradigm between these encapsulated abstractions. It is easy to see how such organization would naturally support distribution. In fact, given such an architecture, putting various of these elements in different memory spaces (e.g., different machines) would be a matter of providing the mechanism for locating server objects in remote memory spaces by client objects. In a nonencapsulated system, providing for distribution is far more difficult.

Promoting Reuse

Much has been written about the potential afforded by object orientation in terms of reuse. Understanding the potential for reuse at the code level is easy. Component objects are one form of such reuse. Components are specific, often already compiled individual objects (instances of classes) that are designed and implemented to deliver a very specific service as described by its contract. They are the software equivalent of the integrated circuit (IC) chip. They may be put together, possibly with some additional new objects, to compose an application.

Abstract, often generic, extendible classes arranged in libraries are tools or building blocks to construct an application. They are usually not application oriented (i.e., interrelated to compose an application), but instead are utility oriented (i.e., interrelated, usually hierarchically, to be used across a number of application domains to address a specific type of need). Class libraries are usually passive; they are just a set of classes interrelated through inheritance without any control flow or message passing between them. They do not do anything, but they can be used to build things that do things. Java foundation libraries, graphical user interface (GUI) libraries, and so on, are good examples.

It is possible in object orientation to extend the potential of reuse to beyond just that of code. Analysis and design patterns and application and design frameworks can all arguably be examples of none-code reuse opportunities afforded by the adoption of this paradigm.

It is important to note that reuse, particularly code reuse, has an implication for defect management. Components and class libraries are written by others, often in software process situations that are vastly different from the one used in your organization. Defect management standards other than yours may have been applied in their construction. In short, they may not be at the same level of quality as your product. If they exceed yours, in general, you are winning. If they lag yours, then you must be careful. Additionally, how you interface such products with your home-written software becomes important. For software to be reliably interfaced with the host system it has to have certain characteristics (e.g., it has to have a clearly and correctly defined contract). Such characteristics must be extant if our testing of the adequacy, robustness, and correctness of the interface is to be effective.

Finally, reusable software obtained from a third party might often be used by many organizations other than yours. This affords the opportunity for you to become aware of some of the product's problems and defects without having to discover them yourself. This would have a positive impact on your defect management effort.

On the other hand, some of the challenges that come with the adoption of this paradigm are covered in the following sections.

A Change in Process Is Required

Although the activities to be completed to produce a software system are largely the same irrespective of the paradigm used, how we conduct them is remarkably different. This means that the tasks and techniques utilized are often not those used when producing software in the traditional (nonobject-oriented) fashion. The realization that different tasks and techniques are required is important, but the issue goes deeper than this. There is also a corresponding shift in the proportion of time and effort expended on the different activities. There will be changes on all three dimensions of methodology, technology, and context, and the process will be remarkably different.

A Change in Attitude Is Necessary

With any change in paradigm comes a corresponding necessity to change certain attitudes. The contextual changes necessary in the process are particularly remarkable. There must be an understanding, for instance, that there is likely to be proportionally more time spent on analysis and design and less on coding than in a traditional development environment, particularly initially. There must be a change in attitude in terms of how software engineering staff productivity is evaluated and how they are rewarded. It is important to realize that Rome was not built in a day; it will be some time before the new paradigm is well established and yields positive results of the magnitude expected. New roles are needed (e.g., reuse manager) and some roles might be eliminated.

Resource Issues

An important challenge in migrating to the new object paradigm is that of human and technological resources. Obtaining skilled personnel, appropriate tools and technologies, and even training and consulting in the area can be a major challenge.

Defect Management

Abstraction, modularity, and message passing, which are the basic tenets of object orientation, create both opportunities and challenges in defect management of object-oriented systems. We have already alluded to some of the opportunities in preceding sections. In this section I deal with some of the more significant challenges.

The implication of many studies, books, and other works on object technology has been that the use of the paradigm during analysis and design assists with comprehensiveness and completeness and thus drastically reduces the potential for the inclusion of defects of omission from the specification and design. Defects of omission are also usually positively impacted, or so it seems. Thus, it appears that as far as defect management is concerned, the object paradigm has a positive impact on the defect situation during the analysis and design phases and the defect content of analysis and design models. However, research based on data collected by Jones (1997) from several hundred projects states that object-oriented analysis and design have higher defect potential and it is harder to identify and remove defects from object-oriented analysis and design models than it is from traditionally composed design artifacts and models! This finding is counterintuitive and may be related to the differences in how we identify a defect in an object-oriented model as opposed to a non-object-oriented one. Also, it may have to do with the differences in overall maturity of the extant techniques of design defect identification between the two paradigms and possibly even the level of experience of the people completing or evaluating these artifacts who participated in the study. Nevertheless, if independently confirmed using robust empirical research techniques, this finding could somewhat alter the way we look at object technology.

Specifically, abstraction and modularity might assist in clarity and visibility. Encapsulation, the way we arrive at abstraction and modularity in object-oriented systems, thus helps avoid global declarations, amorphous programming, and so on. At the same time, however, it can introduce some challenges. For example, as a consequence of encapsulation, it becomes difficult to examine the current state of an object, a task that must be done easily during testing. Additionally, as control is distributed in an object-oriented system, even if the state of an individual object is obtained and examined, overall system state, being distributed, is hard to examine. Inheritance, a useful by-product of encapsulation, and particularly multiple inheritance, also creates opportunities for defects to escape detection or introduction of defects that are hard to test out. Polymorphic behavior, dynamic binding, and proliferation of interfaces all can contribute to problems in testing object-oriented code.

The first three of these challenges are management issues, the last is both technically and management oriented. It is this aspect that is the focus of our attention in this book.

Defect Management

Developing high-quality software, in whatever paradigm, is not an easy task. But what makes such development so difficult?

To begin with, the concept of quality itself is enigmatic. Davis (1994) acknowledged that the notion of quality in relation to a software product often means different things to the different stakeholders involved with the development and use of the product, and these notions may be contradictory. In other words, quality is not absolute and depends on the purpose or viewpoint for which it is being assessed.

As an example from another domain, to determine the quality of a bottle of wine, it is first necessary to determine the purpose for which the bottle is being purchased. These could include the following:

- **To enjoy with a meal.**   Here it is necessary to know the type of meal being served, the time of day of the meal, the season, and the ambient temperature, among other considerations. Once these are known, a number of criteria will be used to decide on the wine to be consumed.

- **To take to a party.**   One needs to know whether one is likely to be the only person drinking the wine or will be sharing. If one is to share, who will be there? What will their taste be in wine?

- **To impress a guest or a host.**   One needs to know about the recipient's level of knowledge of wine, his or her current financial situation, socioeconomic background, taste in wine, and so on.

Having determined the purpose and the issues that need to be considered relating to that purpose, only then will a person be in a position to use specific criteria to choose a particular bottle. To enjoy the wine with a meal, assuming a good knowledge of wine, the criteria might be region, style, bouquet, color, acidity, and price. Otherwise the choice might be made on the basis of producer, attractiveness of label, and price. A wine to be taken to a party is probably selected using similar criteria, but price and style probably play a more significant role. If the purpose is to impress, criteria to use will be price, rarity of vintage, and possibly packaging. Having decided on the criteria of assessment, what constitutes a good price or an appropriately rare vintage or good color? Some decisions are easily made. For example, it is a matter of simple numerical comparison to choose a bottle with a lower price, but such determination is hard when concrete measurements are absent, say in the case of bouquet. Even if measurable, such assessments are highly personal and culturally based. For example, a price of $50 for a bottle may be low for one person and unreachably high for another. Determinations of this nature, especially those that do not fall into a universally accepted scale, are based on the assessor's past history (social status, experience, place of birth, education, financial status, and a myriad of other influences).

Accordingly, we recognize that determination of the quality of an artifact is heavily culturally based.

It should be noted that in our example the choice of a bottle of wine is often not solely made on the measure of one criterion. Assessment usually means weighing up merits and levels of a number of criteria that are important for assessing the quality for a given purpose. It is also conceded that despite all of this, there are wines that are just "better" than others, seemingly irrespective of purpose.

First, a better wine, it seems, is one that is rated highly by the majority of assessors on the majority of criteria. Note however that being a better artifact does not mean that it is always the artifact of choice. If you cannot afford to drink the wine, you will never know if it is a quality wine. Without experiencing the artifact, definitive discussion of quality is meaningless.

Second, the rule of majority or authority often creates an aura of desirability or popularity around a certain product, often irrespective of its internal properties as assessed by the person experiencing it. We can identify wines that we acknowledge as being of high quality (because of our respect for experienced wine judges) but that we dislike.

The preceding observations indicate to us that quality is determined through assessing the appropriateness of a product for fulfilling a given purpose, and is evaluated by (in order):

- Determining the purpose for assessment;
- Recognizing the premises for determination;
- Determining the criteria for assessment;
- Measurement against such criteria; and
- Weighing up measurements against each other in view of the premises.

This view of quality is in accord with the popular definition of quality as fitness for purpose. It tacitly recognizes that the selection of purposes, viewpoints, and criteria, and the process of determination of quality are multifaceted. However, there is more to quality than just fitness for purpose. For example, is it not possible that many solutions to a problem be equally fit for the purpose, but still vary in quality due to their structure and form? Is "spaghetti code" that implements all of the functionality required in a specification as good as software that reaches the same level of meeting the functionality requirements but is highly modular, with high cohesion and low coupling, is internally well commented, and follows a consistent style? Additionally, does the amount of resources consumed in—in other words the efficacy of means of—arriving at the solution a consideration in determining quality?

A wider discussion of quality and its implications and specification is required. We do this in the following section.

Specifying Quality

In presenting the contents of this section, we follow the lead of Dromey and McGettrick (1992), who provided a critique of the existing definitions for the concept of quality and suggested a "constructive" approach that is suitable for use with respect to designed systems such as software.

Views of Quality

Quality may be viewed from many different perspectives. Garvin (1988) provided a classification of views of quality on the basis of the "metaphysics" of the term. He concluded that quality may be viewed from five distinct perspectives:

- The transcendental view;
- The user view;
- The manufacturing view;
- The product view; and
- The value-based view.

The transcendental view is the ethereal notion that you'll know it when you see it. In other words, quality is a notion that we all strive for and achieve in all our endeavors. Various levels are recognizable but not necessarily measurable. Elegant as it may be, this definition is useless to any notion of assessment and measurement of quality, or the construction of methodologies to do so.

The user view is grounded in product characteristics that meet the user's needs. This view takes an evaluative view and examines the product in terms of meeting user requirements. This view is therefore the one adopted by Crosby (1979), who has put forth one of the most influential and well-publicized definitions of quality: Quality is conformance to requirements.

The manufacturing view is the most popularly held view of quality (Kitchenham & Pfleeger, 1996). In a survey reported in *IEEE Software* a number of years ago, nearly 50% of respondents held a view of quality most aligned with the manufacturing view, and more than 67% held a view that included the manufacturing view (Kitchenham & Pfleeger, 1996). This view considers the process of construction of the artifact and assesses to what degree the product is developed "right" the first time. The aim seems to be quality control and the efficacy of the construction process as measured by the extent of rework required.

The product view is a look at the product from the perspective of the "construct" of the product itself; that is, the product's internal and inherent characteristics. It was the second most popular view held by the respondents of the survey just mentioned (more than one-third of the respondents). This view is in line with the Bauhaus principle of fitness-of-form. Provided that we can establish a relationship between internal characteristics of a product and how it performs, this definition provides at least a partial inroad into the problem of quality measurement because it is a lot easier to measure internal product attributes than external product behavior (Fenton, 1991). This is a concept that we further discuss later in this section and it is one of the important elements of this work.

The value-based view relates the concepts discussed in the previous section. It deals with the multiplicity of views of various stakeholders and the fact that there is not one view of quality that is always right. It is in line with the fitness-for-purpose definition and another influential definition of quality that states: "Quality is all the features that allow a product to satisfy stated or implied needs at an affordable cost" (ISO 8402).

Agreeing with the principle of multiplicity of views at the core of the value-based view, and as such also with Dromey and McGettrick (1992), we believe that a multifaceted definition is required to be utilized as a basis for the construction of methods for the measurement of product quality.

Dromey and McGettrick (1992) provided arguments that lead us to the following definition of quality: Quality of a product depends on the measures of fitness-for-purpose of the solution and fitness-of-form of the design of the product. The quality of a process depends on the measure of the efficacy of means by which the process builds products of quality.

Taking such an approach to quality has the following advantages:

- Fitness-for-purpose is in line with many of the most popular definitions of quality given (e.g., that of Crosby and that of ISO). It provides a functional, user, and in itself a multiperspective view of quality.

- Fitness-of-form is in line with the product view of software and permits a constructive approach to measurement of quality.

- Efficacy of means highlights the importance of process and brings to the forefront the manufacturing view of quality.

These three elements together cover nearly 100% of all views of (at least) the respondents to the survey previously mentioned, and together subsume virtually all other definitions of quality with the possible exception of some transcendental definitions, as the former will by necessity fall into one of the categories already mentioned.

This definition is going to be the basis of our work in this book. Using this definition, we evaluate software products of interest from a perspective that includes both the fitness-for-purpose and the fitness-of-form considerations. We also propose ways of utilizing the concept of process efficacy as a means of relating product quality to process quality. In this discussion we refer to the fitness-for-purpose considerations of products as *external quality attributes* and to the fitness-of-form considerations as *internal quality attributes*.

Internal Quality and External Quality: Form Complements Function

In any designed process, it is the quality of the product on which the producer's external reputation is ultimately going to rest. In the context of software quality, it is therefore imperative to focus initially on software product quality.

Software is largely a commercial product, and as such it is subject to market orientation (Kotler, 1997). Market orientation necessitates (nonexclusively) a customer view of product quality. The quality of a software product, at least from a commercial viewpoint, is largely assessed through consideration of a set of attributes, which must be external and customer-oriented. These attributes orient the determination of the quality of a product to the fitness-for-purpose argument presented in the previous section.

However, as we mentioned earlier, this is not the full story. The developers, and also more recently, savvy customers, also demand good form and efficacious means of development. So what attributes do we select to evaluate the quality of a product? Similarly, given the product, how do we measure the efficacy of the process that has yielded such a product?

Software Product Quality Attributes

From the perspective of their orientation toward the fitness-for-purpose consideration on the one hand and the fitness-of-form consideration on the other, software quality attributes may be grouped into the following two categories:

- External quality attributes
- Internal quality attributes (Fenton, 1991)

External Quality Attributes

External attributes are those that can be measured in relation to the context or the environment in which the product persists (Fenton, 1991). For example, modularity (internal) and reliability (external) are both attributes of a software product. However, the average customer is likely to be far more interested in the reliability of software he or she will receive than whether proper abstract data types have been developed to increase the modularity of the product.

Consistent with recent apparent consensus arrived at among investigators and practitioners, and as reflected through IEEE standards, external product attributes of importance relate to the following:

- Functionality (How closely does the product meet the requirements as stated or implied in the requirements document?)
- Reliability (What is the likelihood of failure-free operation?)
- Usability (What is the extent to which the product is convenient and practical to use?)
- Maintainability (What is the level of ease with which software can be corrected, adapted, or enhanced to fit an altered set of requirements?)

It should be noted that a number of attributes including reusability, efficiency, and cost-effectiveness conceivably might be added to this list. We have not included them for reasons enumerated next.

Reusability measures the degree to which components of a software product can be used in constructing other software of similar utility. This is largely an internal product attribute. (It is also in most cases of greater concern to the developer than to the customer.)

Efficiency measures the degree to which software makes good use of the hardware resources available to it. Efficiency may be absorbed into the concept of functionality, as the resource utilization requirements of a software system usually feature prominently in a requirements document.

Cost-effectiveness has at least two distinct meanings when viewed as a software quality attribute. First, it may represent a measure of the level of efficacy and economy by which available resources were or are being utilized in the process of creating a software product. This is clearly a process attribute that, for the moment, lies outside the scope of our discussion. Second, it may represent the extent to which the price paid for a software product is recouped through effective and productive utilization of the product in the organization. In this context, the effectiveness becomes a function of other external attributes of software quality, such as reliability and functionality, and also of how intelligently the customer has put the product to use. The cost part becomes a function of the cost-effectiveness of the process, and also the marketing decision made about the level of profit to be made by the software vendor. In our opinion, this is not a direct and external product quality attribute.

However, on occasion there are some internal attributes (attributes that represent the extent of fitness-of-form), to an extent identifiable and measurable and utilized by "informed" customers, which may be predictive of important external attributes (fitness-for-purpose) of software that are generally harder to measure statically. Reusability and modularity are good examples of such internal attributes.

Customer-Oriented Quality Assessment

As previously mentioned, ultimately, responsible product marketing dictates customer orientation. (This is not meant to imply, however, that customers cannot be educated in what they can expect, or converted to concur with possibly more appropriate or realistic alternatives set forth by a vendor, or for that matter that the views, requirements, restrictions, and abilities of a vendor are not also important.) Accordingly, product attributes assessed to determine the quality of a product must be meaningful to, and in line with, the quality aspirations of the customer. For example, from the external attributes mentioned earlier, reliability is a good example of a customer-oriented attribute, whereas reusability is a developer-oriented one. As such, whereas customers are critically conscious of the reliability of software, they are likely to be largely unconcerned with the degree of the reusability of the components making up the source code. (We concede an exception in the case of general management, as stakeholders in internally developed software, holding an interest in the overall economics of a company's IT department.)

Using the foregoing criteria, we have investigated and classified a variety of product attributes as follows:

- Important customer-oriented external product attributes:
  - Functionality (including efficiency);
  - Reliability; and
  - Usability.
- Important developer-oriented external product attributes:
  - Maintainability (discussed later); and
  - Reusability.

As per our earlier discussion, we recognize that informed customers may, on occasion, identify and establish links between developer-oriented quality attributes and customer-oriented ones. In such cases the former attributes also become important to the customer. A good example of this is maintainability.

Assessing Product Quality

Another popular definition of quality is "absence of defects" (Crosby, 1979). In this section we put forward an argument that this definition is also in accord with the one we have provided and that the perspective it provides will assist in the construction of a bridge that will lead us toward a model that relates internal measures of software to external characteristics and to the measures of process quality.

We mentioned that the fitness-for-purpose argument holds that all external attributes of software relate to how the system is seen to satisfy some need. As such, any measure of an external quality attribute would be a measure of the expectation that the software must do what it is supposed to do. Thus we can say that if a product does not do what it is supposed to do, it has failed in some respect. We therefore define a *failure* (for the moment) as an instance of lack of fitness-for-purpose.

Similarly, we said that fitness-of-form argues that internal characteristics of the software must have been designed satisfactorily. In other words, the software must also be what it is supposed to be. If the software does not satisfy this condition, we can say it has failed, or has a failure. This new notion necessitates the separation of the two concepts of failure due to function on the one hand, and failure due to form on the other. We therefore define the former as *operational failure* and the latter as *structural failure* in accord with the definitions of operational and structural failure in all other fields of engineering (Ditlersen & Madsen, 1996).

Products fail because they are defective, or in the course of operation they develop defects. Software, however, does not wear (Pressman, 1995) in that given no change in requirements, it does not develop defects as a result of utilization, unlike a mechanical device that eventually yields to metal fatigue. Therefore it is only the former category of failures (those designed into the product) that are of importance in the case of software. It is logical to assume that these failures that are designed into the product are all results of some omission, mistake, or error by someone in the development team. Therefore, the concepts of defects and failures are very closely linked. It is thus important to manage defects in the course of software development if high quality is desired.

In the next section we first provide an overview of the current situation of software engineering in terms of our ability to manage defects, and then build a model that relates the three perspectives of importance mentioned in our definition of quality.

Defect Management as a Means of Ensuring Quality

Although the situation has improved recently, there has traditionally been substantial confusion with respect to defect prevention and defect removal terminology. Beizer (1991) equated the terms *bug, glitch, error, slip, fault,* and *oversight,* among others, as referring to some shortcoming in software. Ghezzi et al. (1992), although distinguishing between defects and failures, equated defects with faults, errors, and bugs. Similarly, a number of authors (Ghezzi et al., 1992; Hetzel, 1988; Humphrey, 1995) explicitly stressed the need to distinguish between debugging and testing, implying the existence of confusion between the two terms. Hetzel (1988) stated that "a number of early papers on 'testing' actually concern 'debugging' " (p. 4). Even when distinguished from debugging, different authors have defined the activity of testing variously. Hetzel (1988) defined testing as "the process of establishing confidence that a program or system does what it is supposed to" (p. 4). On the other hand, Myers (1979), in a still widely cited work, defined testing as "the process of executing a program or system with the intent of finding errors" (p. 7). An opposite view to that of Hetzel, this supports the famous assertion by Dijkstra (in Dahl et al., 1972) that program testing can be used to show presence of bugs, but never their absence. A discussion of the differences between the two definitions just given and Hetzel's defense of his own is provided in Hetzel (1988). This argument, which revolves around the assertion that Myers's definition is too narrow and implies application of testing only after a program has been written, in fact highlights another point of confusion. Hetzel, in attempting to mount a defense of his view, confuses (a) product testing versus product acceptance and (b) defect identification (e.g., black box testing) and defect propagation prevention (e.g., design inspection).

Similarly, in another older but very influential work, even today, Goodenough and Gerhart (1975) defined a "successful" test as one that does not uncover any deficiencies, whereas Myers (1979) and others (e.g., Beizer, 1991) define a successful test exactly the opposite way; that is, one that does uncover at least one deficiency.

Under these conditions it is necessary to explicitly enumerate the definitions that pertain to our subsequent work. Effort has been expended to arrive at a consistent, popularly recognized set of such definitions. The set presented next is derived to be consistent with current prevalent definitions, particularly those of

Ghezzi et al. (1992), Humphrey (1995), and Sommerville (1995). The wording and the taxonomy presented based on these definitions are, however, my own.

We start by restating that a software program can be viewed as three distinct entities, with the distinctions between them regarded as critical:

- **The source code.** When viewed as source code, a program may be regarded as a very precise (formal), yet intermediate model of the requirements developed through progressive refinement of an initially ambiguous and less formal model of a possible solution (design model). This is done by constraining the modeling syntax and the ultimate transfiguration into a modeling language that is executable (the target programming language). As such, source code can be deemed as a formal model of the requirements, but it is often popularly referred to as software, as in "I am writing software."

- **The executable.** Probably the most nebulous of the three manifestations, the executable is another formal and intermediate model of the requirements translated into a syntax that can be executed on the target machine architecture. At this stage it might be considered an integral and indistinguishable part of the system architecture that is to ultimately provide an execution of the solution sought. This too is often referred to as software; for example, "Give me a copy of that software," or "Let's load the software."

- **The execution.** This is the solution provided through running of the program-executable code on some hardware. In other words, the execution is a model of some virtually constructed environment created to satisfy the intended requirements (hopefully the one understood in common between the producer and the client). Arguably, this virtual environment is the true software product. This too is referred to as software, as in "Our software would not let us do that."

With this observation of the multiplicity of software in mind, we now attempt to provide definitions for some common terms in this area.

Failure

[handwritten: - some quality expectations are not met -> some functional or non functional requirements are not met]

We mentioned earlier that software product quality was best discerned through the external product-quality attributes such as functionality and reliability. Therefore the recognition that such quality expectations are not being met with respect to a particular product is identified through these means. We term such shortcomings *failures*.

A failure is said to have occurred when the software product does not satisfy expectations (Ghezzi et al., 1992; Sommerville, 1995). This might take the form of an incorrect result, nonprovision of a result, presentation of an unexpected system state, or a user perception of a poor interface.

Not all failures are directly related to software source code or an executable. In fact, what was just described is best termed *system failure*, with *software failure* being a specific case. For example, a failure observed as the presentation of an erroneous result might be traced to the executable. Another failure caused by an interruption in the power supply is not. In our discussion, we only consider the failures of the former type. An exceptional case must be highlighted in that the way the software is to behave under certain specific environmentally caused failures (e.g., power interruption) might be specified. Lack of fulfillment of such requirement should still be considered an omission (lack of functionality).

In fact, software failure itself may be divided into two categories: operational failure, when the software does not do what it is supposed to do with regards to some external quality attribute, and structural failure, when the software is not what it is expected to be. An example of the former might be a division by zero resulting in a reliability failure. An example of the latter might be a maintainability failure, such as the nonprovision of a class header. Note, however, that this is manifest in the source code, but does not propagate to the executable and beyond.

failure is a general term

Fault — *is a executable failure*

A *fault* is an incorrect state entered by a program executable (Ghezzi et al., 1992) or an incorrect transformation undergone; for example, the result of a division by zero with the exception not being handled. Faults are characteristics of the executable code and only result in failure when they are executed with a valid set of data causing transition from a valid state or resulting in the provision of incorrect output. Faults do not necessarily cause software failure, which is also impacted by how the software is used. Reliability (related directly to failures) is a function of executable faults as well as how the system is executed. The complex relationship between executable faults and execution reliability has been studied by a number of investigators (e.g., Littlewood, 1990; Mills et al., 1987).

defect ⟹ bug ⟹ fault
bug ⟹ fault *⟩ failure*
error ⟹ defect

Defect

— in a software process that leads to generation of a source code that leads to a fault

A *defect* is an imperfection in the software engineering work product that requires rectification (Humphrey, 1995). Some of these defects cause the generation of an executable that contains a fault (e.g., some code that makes the value of a variable x to equate to zero for $y = 3$ when the intention is to make $x = y$).

Bug

— a defect in a source code, that might cause a fault

A defect that causes the generation of a fault is called a *bug*. This implies that some defects do not generate faults. One such defect might be the provision of a comment on the wrong line or in the wrong section of the source code. A bug is also sometimes called an *error* (e.g., in the context of compiler reports). This is not the case in our terminology, as the term has a separate meaning described next.

Error

— in any stage of a process that result in a defect

In our terminology, an *error* or a mistake is a commission or omission at any stage of the software process by a software engineer that results in a defect (Humphrey, 1995).

Operational Failure in Software

Operational failures in software can manifest themselves in the form of shortcomings in the external quality characteristics of software that deal with what the system must do. The important ones we mentioned were functionality, reliability, and usability. Maintainability and some other attributes not included in this work, such as reusability, mainly deal with structural failure.

Functionality

We define *functionality* as the extent to which the software product under utilization accurately implements the operations required of it as defined in the requirements specification. This is in line with the definition provided by ISO 9126. In other words, functionality is the degree of faithfulness in the implementation of requirements, either stated or implied (Younessi & Grant, 1995). Missing functionality therefore naturally detracts from operational quality.

failures ⟶ *operational*
⟶ *structural*

A precise and universal measure of functionality is not available, but functionality is usually estimated as the coverage demonstrated during acceptance and in-field utilization of the functional behavior of the system in comparison to the specified requirements. A highly functional system therefore has a high proportion of its specified required functions demonstrably implemented.

To estimate the degree of functionality, therefore, one needs two artifacts: the specification and the final product. There is also a tacit assumption that the specification itself is complete and reflects all the requirements explicitly. Unfortunately this assumption is not safe, as it has been shown that a large portion of problems encountered during system acceptance and subsequently is due to incomplete specification of requirements; that is, the existence of tacit requirements (Lauesen & Younessi, 1998).

Putting the issue of completeness aside for the moment (we discuss later that these failures can also be traced back to defects, not necessarily in code but instead requirements or architectural design), we concentrate on the issue of the implementation and its extent and accuracy of coverage of the explicitly stated requirements.

Correctness is a very significant relationship between functionality and an internal characteristic of the software product. To assess whether a software product is functionally defective, it is usually assessed against its specification. Deviations from the specification would then indicate the defect areas. These are usually one of two types.

Defects of omission are those deviations from the specification that lead to some intended function not being implemented; for example, a software product cannot display the result of a calculation or query due to the omission of a print function, although the specification requires it.

Defects of commission are those deviations from the specification that, although functionally implemented, fail to operate properly. They provide incorrect or unexpected results despite the provision of valid inputs; for example, the print function from the previous example has been implemented but prints the address of x rather than its value.

The relationship specified between the external quality attribute of functionality and the internal software characteristic of correctness implies that omissions and commissions do introduce defects into the software that can manifest themselves as shortcomings in functionality, or to use a better term, functional failure. These defects we term *defects of functionality* or *F-type* defects. Removing F-type defects should logically improve the functionality of the software.

Reliability

Reliability has been defined as the fundamental statistical measure of failure-free operation (Sommerville, 1995).

Assuming functionality as given, the failure-free operation referred to in this definition differs from that in the omission and commission defects already mentioned. We introduce the term *transitional failure* to define those failures to meet the specification when the system makes a transition from one state to another. Under such circumstances, although the operation or functionality required has not been omitted from implementation, the system still (often only under certain circumstances) produces unexpected results as a consequence of making the transition into an invalid state. For example, we have a transitional failure when a statement makes a division by zero calculation when given certain values of a variable x although the basic formula for the calculation is present and in accordance with the specification.

It is important to distinguish between functional failures of commission when dealing with functionality and those of the transitional type discussed here. The distinction is that although the former produces a wrong result, the state of the system after the production of such a result is expected to be valid and correct (e.g., printing the address rather than the value of a variable). In the case of operational failure, the result may or may not be correct (it usually isn't), but the state after the operation is unexpected, invalid, and incorrect (e.g., dividing by zero when attempting to print the value of a variable).

Reliability can then be expressed as the probability that a software product will not produce a transitional failure when utilized in its operating environment for a given period of time.

Based on this, we can define *R-type* defects as those that lead to transitional failures or failures in reliability. Many authors and practitioners include the F-type defects of commission in the same group as R-type defects, but we maintain their separation.

Usability

Usability is the extent to which the product is convenient and practical to use. This property of software products is usually evaluated by conducting a usability evaluation against a usability specification often organized in terms of some attributes (e.g., learnability, adaptability, etc.; Dix et al., 1993; Preece et al., 1995; Shneiderman, 1992). The extent of conformance to such a specification is therefore taken as the usability of the system. In this sense, evaluating usability is similar to evaluating functionality. The implication is that omissions and commissions of certain types do introduce defects into the software that

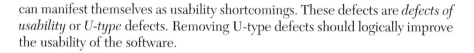

can manifest themselves as usability shortcomings. These defects are *defects of usability* or *U-type* defects. Removing U-type defects should logically improve the usability of the software.

Structural Failure in Software

Structural failures in software can manifest themselves as shortcomings in the external quality characteristics of software that deal with what the system must be. The important one we mentioned was maintainability. We also provided reasons why some other attributes that relate to structural failures, such as reusability, have not been included in this study.

Maintainability

Maintainability is defined as the degree to which software can be corrected, adapted, and enhanced to fit an altered set of requirements (Basili, 1990; Ghezzi et al., 1992; Lano & Haughton, 1994; Lientz & Swanson, 1980).

In the context of software product quality, Sommerville (1995) highlighted that the aim in measuring maintainability is not to arrive at a cost of making a particular change or to predict whether or not a particular component will have to be maintained. As the preceding definition suggests, the aim is to determine the ease with which the software program may be refitted into a new situation. Sommerville, among others, also asserted that all product-quality-focused definitions and measures of maintainability are based on the assumption that maintainability of a program is related directly to its complexity of design. On the other hand, it can also be argued that maintainability relates to the quality of the supporting documentation.

These considerations suggest that preventing or identifying and removing these design defects in software that would lead to maintainability problems (what we call *M-type* defects) would improve the maintainability of the product, at least in an absolute sense. Identification and removal of defects (in the sense of our definition) in the documentation also can be argued to have the same effect.

Other Potential Attributes

Despite what was presented earlier regarding the adequacy of the preceding attributes of product quality, one might still wish to add other attributes (e.g., reusability). Doing so is consistent with our framework and what will proceed from it in terms of the future models that are to be built in the context of this work. What needs to be done, however, is the following:

- Arrive at a concise definition for the attribute to be added.
- Ensure relative orthogonality with existing attributes. In fact, recognition of a defect as more than one type is generally permissible (e.g., a denominator that may be evaluated to zero when this is not part of the specification is both a reliability defect and a functionality one). This permissibility requires a proviso that the defect classification scheme supporting the model recognizes this fact and the measurement model knows how to deal with such overlaps. In our work here, such nonorthogonality is permitted.
- Define the types of defects that might contribute to failures impacting the newly introduced attribute within a defect classification scheme that forms the basis of defect management activities relating to the process by which the product is built or evaluated (e.g., *E-type* defects for reusability).

Achieving Quality Goals

The preceding concerns and observations have led to the understanding that goal setting, establishment of criteria, and—most important—measurement are critical in achieving quality goals. In terms of software, such considerations have given rise to much research and practice targeted toward the determination of goals and purposes for software development projects, determination of software product-quality criteria, and software product and process metrics. Beyond that, a number of approaches and paradigms have been based on the premises that (a) measurement is a necessary element of quality determination, (b) measurement must be made against specific criteria that have (c) been themselves selected in accordance with a specific purpose or goal. The Goal, Question, Metric (GQM) paradigm put forth by Basili and Selby (1987) is a good example of such effort.

In terms of goals for IT development, Curtis (1989) identified the following seven reasons (neither orthogonal nor exhaustive) why organizations develop software and information technology:

- An alternative system would not cope;
- Cost savings;
- The provision of better internal information for decision making;
- The provision of competitive customer service;
- The opportunities provided by new technology;
- High-technology image; and
- Change in legislation or regulations.

Any one of these reasons, or any combination of them, might be the context that can be used to determine the purpose or the goal with respect to which quality is to be assessed.

As noted by Davis (1994), the purpose of a system may be viewed differently by different individuals in an organization. For example, the purpose of a particular information system may be, according to the CEO of the firm, to provide a strategic alliance between the firm and the manufacturer of the system or the firm and its customers. To an administrative officer, the purpose of the system may be to assist with his daily administration. In a scenario like this, it is quite possible that the CEO would consider the system as fulfilling its purpose, yet the administrative officer, forced to battle with a poorly designed user interface, might not share this opinion.

The enigmatic nature of quality has contributed to considerable confusion in the investigation of improving software quality. The basic hurdles are as follows:

- It is very difficult—if not impossible—to meet an undefined target. As mentioned earlier, software quality is very subjective. Despite many years of research in the field, there is still no universally agreed definition of software quality, let alone a standard measurement system with consensus validity and suitability. This makes defining and communicating a particular level of quality exceedingly challenging, resulting in what is ultimately a futile exercise of shooting in the dark.
- Views differ as to what represents quality. This again is a consequence of the multiplicity of perceptions of the various stakeholders as to what is a quality product. These perceptions are impacted not only by technology, economics, and negotiating position, but also by culture, philosophy, and the psychology of the stakeholders. Determining what represents quality therefore becomes akin to searching in the dark.

- Products and processes are not clearly related in a theoretical context. Neither researchers nor practitioners have yet established a direct, explicit, well-understood relationship between the characteristics of the development process to be employed and its capability for yielding a product of a given quality. In this sense, software development resembles stabbing in the dark. This is despite the existence of the Software Engineering Institute Capability Maturity Model (SEI CMM [Humphrey, 1989]) and many other approaches created to the same end (e.g., El-Emam et al., 1997; Koch, 1993) that provide mechanisms to assess the maturity and capability of software processes. The models are essentially reductionist in nature and are generally mappings of many aspects of organizational and process characteristics (in the case of CMM) into a linear scale of discrete values. They are fundamentally comparative in nature. Most (e.g., the CMM) do not explicitly consider the assessment of product quality from diverse human perspectives. Much further research remains to be done in all these areas.

Research into software and software process quality may be categorized into the three streams of product focus, the link between product and process, and process focus, which are discussed next.

Product Focus

Adherents of this view are of the opinion that as the product is the main artifact of software development, to ensure a high-quality product, one must concentrate solely on those features of the product that directly impact quality and ensure that these features are implemented adequately. Extremists within this category would be of the opinion that the research into process and process improvement is nonessential, as process quality does not impact product quality (Bach, 1995; Sanders, 1997).

This stance, at least in its extreme form, is unwarranted. As a practitioner and researcher in this field, I have very frequently encountered arguments put forward by the proponents of this camp (e.g., Bach, 1995; Sanders, 1997) that: There exist many organizations that possess a very well-developed "process" yet continue to fail to produce high-quality software. Therefore, the argument continues, there is no relationship between product quality and the software development process.[3] Convincing on the surface, this argument breaks down on closer scrutiny of their definition of the term *process*. As we said earlier, a software process is the collection of technologies, methodologies, people, and organizational influences that are utilized to produce software products. It is, however, a common error that a software process is often equated with the methodology utilized (e.g., the Booch method; Booch, 1991) or the notation used (e.g., Unified Modeling Language [UML]; Rumbaugh et al., 1999). As this latter more restricted definition ignores the influence of technology and people, a variety of shortcomings or strengths demonstrated within a software development activity can no longer be explained adequately, giving rise to the preceding question and others like this: Why is it that Companies X and Y use the same "process" yet produce vastly different results in terms of product quality?

The answer might be that the software development technologies utilized (e.g., Computer Assisted Software Engineering [CASE], PSEE, compilers, static analyzers, etc.) might differ between the two firms or that the organizational aspects are not comparable. For example, it may be that employees at Company X are better trained or more experienced than those at Company Y or that they may employ more stringent verification and validation procedures than those in effect at Company Y. Therefore, the correct way of asking this question is: Why is it that Companies X and Y use the same *methodology* (e.g., both use SADT), yet one produces a vastly superior product to the other?

Why is it that our introduction of CASE as a means of process improvement did not have a significant effect? The answer to this may be associated with other aspects of the process such as inadequacy of staff training in utilization of technology introduced, with training planning being an important organizational aspect of a relatively mature process (Paulk et al., 1993).

Why did our ability to build high-quality software diminish significantly when X left the team, although we have not changed the process? The answer is that although the methodology may not have changed, the process obviously has, through the departure of X, which has altered the organizational context. This is a common feature of immature software development firms within which expertise is resident in individuals rather than the organizational procedures and hence not within the process.

All—or at least the vast majority—of the issues just enumerated would be resolved if we expand the definition of the software process to encompass the technological and organizational aspects. This is consistent with the bulk of informed current research such as Bootstrap (Haas et al., 1994) and

---

[3] The organization of technologies, methodologies, and organizational influences that are utilized together to produce a given outcome (in our case a software product).

Cleanroom (Dyer, 1992; Mills et al., 1987). Only through the inclusion of these other dimensions can we begin to compare apples with apples.

To produce a better product, one must produce a product that has at least one new, different, or improved feature or characteristic. I cannot envisage otherwise because to produce a different product, it is necessary to do at least one thing differently. Doing things differently defines a new process. If the result of doing things differently (i.e., a different process) would consistently yield a better, higher quality product, then the new process is a better process, so we have managed to improve the process. We define a process that has thus been improved to be of a higher quality than its predecessor.

This does not mean, however, that work of primarily product focus is not of value. In fact, because process quality cannot be assessed without measurement of product quality, one must start with product quality. Valuable work has been done on many different aspects of the software product artifact. This work, among other things, focuses on the following:

- Ways to clarify the features a product must possess to be deemed of quality;
- Ways of providing a measurement basis for assessment of product quality features; and
- Identification and measurement of the influence of product characteristics that impact each product quality feature.

By its nature, however, this type of work is largely a posteriori, because if anything can be said about a product with certainty, then that product must exist. A software product can therefore be subjected to such analysis only after it has been produced. This is in line with the traditional manufacturing view of software and the idea of output quality control (Taylor, 1911). According to this view, artifact quality is determined for the purpose of acceptance or rejection of that product after it has been built.

If, however, the aim is to ensure that a quality product is built in the first place, then focus must shift to how quality products are built. This necessitates the study of the link between product quality and the process by which such a product can be built. This stance is essentially at the core of the second category of work in software quality: the quest for establishing a firm and quantitative relationship between product quality and the software process. One requirement for this is the importance of a search for a predictive model for software product quality.

The Link Between Product and Process

To establish a link between the quality of the product and the process that is utilized to build that product, research must be done in areas covered in the following sections.

Determination of Product Quality Attributes

A large body of work has concentrated on the issue of determining what quality attributes are of importance (e.g., Fenton, 1991; Gillies, 1992). This is significant and fundamentally difficult research to conduct. The difficulty lies in the fact that quality is highly subjective and, as such, determination of a static set of universally accepted quality attributes is problematic, if not impossible. Despite this, attempts have been made to arrive at a universally acceptable set of quality attributes through accommodated consensus. The ISO 9126 standard is the outcome of one such attempt.

Measurement of Product Quality Attributes

Once a set of quality attributes is agreed on, it will be necessary to measure these attributes according to a scale that allows differentiation of various products of differing quality against these yardsticks. A large portion of research in software metrics (e.g., Fenton, 1991; Fenton & Pfleeger, 1996; McCabe, 1976) is targeted to this end.

This work has enjoyed a high profile but little practical adoption by industry (Henderson-Sellers, 1996; Pfleeger et al., 1997). One reason for such lack of adoption might relate to the "advocative" nature of many of such proposed measures. Very few quality metrics are built on a sound scientific basis and in observance of measurement theory (Fenton, 1991; Henderson-Sellers, 1996; Pfleeger et al., 1997). This severely limits the utility and generality of a measure (Fenton, 1991). It is no surprise, therefore, that debate frequently rages on the effectiveness, appropriateness, and applicability of many metrics (e.g., see Fury & Kitchenham, 1997).

In a recent status report on software measurement, Pfleeger et al. (1997) still felt the need to devote much of the article to the issue of the need for a scientific (as opposed to advocative) basis for proposing of metrics.

Determination of Process Components

Questions that are central to this particular domain include the following: Which elements must be present in a software process? How are they identified? How do they impact the process?

Work in this area also continues at several levels. It has generally been recognized that there are only a small number of principal activities that are necessary in the development of a software product. At the highest level they might be presented as discover, invent, and validate. The aims of these activities may be accomplished via a selection from a range of tasks (basic units of work). Tasks, in turn, may be accomplished using a selection from a set of techniques (Graham et al., 1997). This framework allows identification and classification of activities, tasks, and techniques and aids in the gradual but orderly introduction of new ones. As mentioned earlier, one such scheme with which I have been closely associated is the OPEN framework (Graham et al., 1997; Henderson-Sellers et al., 1998).

Determination of Process Quality Attributes

This research aims at the determination of general quality attributes that effective software processes must possess. This work is at a much higher level of abstraction than the associated research that endeavors to establish specific quality attributes of components of the process (discussed later). This work concentrates only on attributes such as granularity, generality, understandability, and so on, of processes and must be distinguished from research into determination of process component quality, which looks into issues such as quality characteristics of the validation stage of the process, or the characteristics of a design model.

Determination of Process Component Quality Attributes

Once various process components are identified, it is possible to investigate the attributes required of those components for the process to be of high quality. This research, as mentioned earlier, deals with a lower level of granularity and quality characteristics of process components such as analysis models, design models, testing, coding style, and so on.

Measurement of Process Component Quality Attributes

Having determined the quality attributes of software process components, it is useful to establish a measurement for each one. It is only through establishment of a quantifiable scale that we can say anything meaningful and universally applicable about the relationship between product and process components.

Establishment of a Causal Relationship Between Process Component Quality Measures and Those of the Product

This is the "holy grail" of researchers in this stream of investigation. The aim is to establish firm and validated relationships between product and process attributes. This can only be done if there is an adequately quantifiable measurement associated with both dimensions of product and process.

Process Focus

This stream of research is based on the assumption that process quality does indeed underpin the quality of the product. As such it is assumed that any process improvement by necessity will be a useful activity that will enhance the quality of the artifact being developed. Researchers in this area therefore have focused on the software process as a whole. Attempts have been made to develop and validate frameworks for the determination of the level of capability and maturity of processes leading to frameworks such as the Capability Maturity Model (CMM; Paulk et al., 1993) and Software Process Improvement and Capability Determination (SPICE; El-Emam, 1997), or the degree to which they conform to specific standards such as ISO 9000. Proponents of this approach argue that it is through the assessment of capability that process shortcomings can be identified and action plans developed to breach those gaps, thus improving the process.

Arguments based on the requirements of the scientific approach and measurement theory show that although potentially useful, these approaches have a number of limitations. Alternative (complementary) approaches to frameworks, such as the CMM, that are based on a constructive approach and are at a much lower level of granularity, are emerging.

Recent Developments

Irrespective of the approach taken, the question of software quality determination must start from the product perspective. As mentioned previously, the actual aim of all of this is to be able to determine the quality of the software product; determining software process quality is in many ways a means to that end.

As discussed earlier, determining product quality is not an easy task. In the past, attempts have been made to determine a number of quality attributes and then utilize these to assess the quality of the product. Although this approach is fundamentally reasonable, Dromey (1996) criticized it on several grounds, the most important of which are the issues of combinatorial explosion of attributes and subattributes and their nonorthogonality. These issues were also mentioned by Gillies (1992), among others.

An important development in the study of software from the product perspective has been the work of Dromey (1995) in which a possible solution to the problem of combinatorial explosion and nonorthogonality of software quality attributes is presented.

The fundamental axiom on which this approach is built states that "a product's tangible internal characteristics or properties determine its external quality attributes" (Dromey, 1996, p. 33). Based on this assumption, it is important to realize that high-level quality attributes cannot be built into a product directly. Rather, a consistent, complete, and compatible set of product properties must be selected and incorporated into the software, resulting in manifestations of these high-level attributes, such as reliability. This is—not accidentally—also a cornerstone on which the work presented in this book is based.

Dromey's model is therefore a general model for relating (through their properties) components that compose a software product to the high-level attributes for the software product that determines its quality. This is illustrated in Figure 1.2.

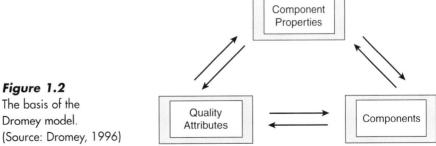

Figure 1.2
The basis of the
Dromey model.
(Source: Dromey, 1996)

The advantage of this model is that it places only a single level (of quality-carrying properties) between the high-level product quality attributes and the components that compose the product. The model is currently proposed in considerable detail, but it remains to be validated.

What is important in all of this from our perspective is that recognition, prevention, identification, and ultimately removal of defects from software products are useful things to do. Specific techniques, in fact all techniques we use, should be conscious of the importance of this. In other words, in all steps of software development we must be vigilant to either prevent defects or, if they are already extant, to remove them effectively. We can thus look at the entire discipline of software engineering from a defect management perspective.

Approaches to Defect Management

It has already been established that defects affect all external dimensions of software quality. Correctness (lack of defects), therefore, is an essential feature of high-quality software (Sommerville, 1995) in that it is a logical assumption that lack of defects in a software product is a desirable property. Therefore, effort expended to prevent the introduction of defects or one that assists in their removal if introduced is a worthwhile process activity provided that the efficacy, effectiveness, and efficiency (Checkland, 1981) of the activity are acceptable.

There are logically only two primary approaches to the development of low-defect software:

- Preventing the introduction of defects into the software when being constructed (defect prevention), and
- Removal of defects introduced during construction through employment of a defect detection and removal activity (defect removal).

In a balanced approach to defect management, both approaches are of central importance.

However, the definitions and terminology in this area need clarification. Defect management has been traditionally referred to as *testing*, at least by the majority of early writers. For example, Hetzel's (1988) title for the chapter of his book on testing is "Testing Through Reviews," implying that activities that examine the source code for defect identification (e.g., reviews) can be considered testing. This is not the case, however, as testing is actually the activity of running the software for failure detection. Myers's (1979) work also uses a similar classification by including inspections under the title of testing. More recent writers (e.g., Ghezzi et al., 1992; Musa & Ackerman, 1989; Sommerville,

1995; Wallace & Fujii, 1989) have adopted the term *validation* (often in conjunction with the term *verification*) to refer to those activities that attempt to identify and remove defects whether through identification of failure during execution or through identification of defects in the source code. In this respect, validation refers to both testing and to activities such as inspection or walk-throughs.

Another source of confusion is the relationship between defect management and the stages of the life cycle. The confusion probably stems from the tradition of using the waterfall process model, which contained explicit testing phases within the last two stages of the life cycle, implying that testing was an activity to be practiced only in relation to the execution of the software code product (e.g., unit testing, system testing, etc.). The growth of this misconception led to the application of subsequent validation methods such as inspection originally only to code; hence *code inspection* (Fagan, 1976). Despite some earlier recommendations (Ackerman et al., 1984), only more recently, in keeping with the principle of early defect detection (Boehm, 1984), is validation applied to other stages of the process (Strauss & Ebenau, 1995) in a consistent manner.

Even when taken in its broader context and applied to all the elements of the life cycle, defect detection is not the only approach to defect management. Another important approach is defect prevention. By this we mean the utilization of methods (e.g., program derivation; Dromey, 1989) that attempt to minimize the introduction of defects into the software in the first place.

Based on the preceding considerations, Appendix A presents a diagram that reflects the current state of defect management.

Conclusion

Defect management may be seen as the very essence of software engineering. For this to be so, we must view software engineering as a process of preventing defects from appearing in the product we are building and the removal of those defects that, despite our best efforts, have crept into our artifacts. Given this perspective, defect management techniques can be either corrective or preventive with respect to a given phase of the software process. The purpose of this defect management is ultimately to improve the quality of the product to be built. As such, this chapter introduced the concept of quality and how its attributes with respect to a software product might be recognized. Once such attributes are recognized, it is possible to aim for defect management that, through managing defects of specific types, aims to reduce the likelihood of system failure from the perspective of that quality attribute.

As this is a book on defect management of object-oriented software, we also delved into the essence of object orientation and how the object paradigm might influence the way we go about the business of defect management.

In the later chapters of this book, we build on the work presented here to provide discussions as well as techniques relevant to the management of defects in every phase of the software process. Both preventive and corrective techniques are discussed.

Chapter 2

DEFECTS AND DEFECT MANAGEMENT IN AN OBJECT-ORIENTED ENVIRONMENT

There is well-publicized evidence that adopting the object-oriented paradigm would present opportunities and advantages with respect to many activities of the software process. Less publicized are the areas in which the object-oriented paradigm actually creates challenges and difficulties, or at least does not improve the situation in a discernable fashion. There is nevertheless a belief that taking the good with the bad, the object-oriented way of doing things represents a net gain when considered over the full life cycle of a project. The popularity and success of the object-oriented approach is built on this very perception. True or false,[1] defect management is one area where new challenges are faced by developers and software engineers. In this chapter we take a somewhat detailed look at why object orientation might present such challenges and what it will be like to manage defects in an object-oriented environment. To do the former, we study the principles that form the essence of the object-oriented paradigm and how they might handicap us in managing defects. This part of the treatment is therefore a product-oriented treatment. To do the latter, we look at the environment and the individual tasks and activities that are specific to or integrally associated with developing object-oriented systems and how they might impact the job of defect management. This part of the treatment therefore takes a process-oriented approach.

[1]The author's personal opinion on this matter is in favor of object orientation.

Why Does Object Orientation Present Challenges in Defect Management?

Voas (1997) found that in general, object-oriented systems score lower in testability in comparison to procedurally written systems. There are a number of potential reasons for such low testability characteristics. Some can be traced to the structural essence of how object-oriented systems are composed and developed. Many of the product-oriented difficulties with managing defects of an object-oriented system can be traced to the concepts of abstraction, encapsulation, inheritance, polymorphism, genericity, and message passing. We discuss some of these issues in the sections that follow.

Abstraction

Abstraction is that essential property in object orientation that allows the selection of a logical and coherent conceptual boundary so that an object is identifiable by its essential characteristics; that is, those characteristics that define what it is and what it does without concern for how it is accomplished.

In other words, a well-formed object in an object-oriented system is viewed as an abstraction: a set of properties and features that fit together coherently and in a cohesive manner to define an identifiable entity. In a well-defined and well-formed object-oriented model, these abstractions collaborate by providing services to each other to simulate the interactions of their real-world or design-world counterparts. All other characteristics, and particularly the details of how these services are made available, are hidden away and abstracted from the viewer (Booch, 1994). This is of potentially great benefit to the modeler, the designer, and the user, but it is often a hindrance to the tester. The reason for this impediment may be obvious to many who have had the responsibility for testing an object or an object-oriented system.

The difficulty stems from the general reduction in what is called *observability* in object-oriented systems (Voas & Kassab, 1999). Observability, or internal state visibility, is the ability to examine the internal state of an object at any one time; that is, the values associated with all of an object's attributes and all the local variables of the routines concerned, at any one time and irrespective of accessibility level defined for them. Abstraction, in essence, masks from access much of the information that is needed to observe the internal state of an object, so it reduces observability dramatically.

Although work-arounds have been developed to counter this problem, none resolve the problem without introducing further difficulties. We discuss two of these work-arounds here.

Use of Inspector Routines

These are publicly accessible routines, written to examine the value of each relevant attribute of an object that would otherwise not be accessible due to abstraction. This could be a helpful solution, but it suffers from a number of problems. Aside from the cumbersome nature of creating such classes, a class may not have been designed with all the necessary inspector methods implemented. Additionally, even if these methods are there, they may themselves be defective, making the job of testing much more difficult.

A variation of this approach that might be useful is to design each class as part of a state design pattern (Gamma et al., 1995). The utility of this design pattern is to capture and report the internal state of the associated object without breaking encapsulation.

Use of an Encapsulation-Breaking Mechanism

Friend functions in C++ (Stroustroup, 1992) belong to this category. Friend functions can be defined to cut across the encapsulation wall of an object. They can thus access the internal state of an object, but they have inherent side effects that make their use inadvisable in an object-oriented system.

Another area in which abstraction provides a challenge to the tester is in the proliferation of interfaces between the various segments of the system. A class that features a number of interfaces defines each object. These features are the accessible routines and sometimes attributes. Functional cohesion dictates that a routine must perform one well-defined task. As this principle of cohesion is applied, routines of a class tend to become smaller and more coherent, which is good. However as composite, noncoherent routines are decomposed into more coherent smaller ones, their numbers proliferate. This creates a problem for the tester because each interface must be tested not only in terms of the validity of its footprint and parameters, but also in combination with each other and with respect to likely client software and with possible reuse in mind. This combinatorial explosion can significantly increase the testing effort required.

Aside from the concept of abstraction, there is also the issue of testing of abstract classes. An *abstract class* is a class in which at least one feature is not implemented. Although doing so renders the class uninstantiable, it also affords us an opportunity to add the missing functionality later. This is often done through inheritance, but it can also be achieved through use of other mechanisms. Because we cannot instantiate the class directly, we cannot test the class directly. This poses a problem.

Encapsulation

There are two further issues that relate not so much to abstraction, in terms of presentation of the essence of an object and masking of other concerns, but to *encapsulation,* or the fact that an object is defined as a collection of interrelated concerns wrapped into a logical unit (see Figure 2.1). In object orientation, the application of the concept of encapsulation is not restricted to the composition of classes and objects, but includes higher levels of encapsulation, for example, forming packages and subsystems.

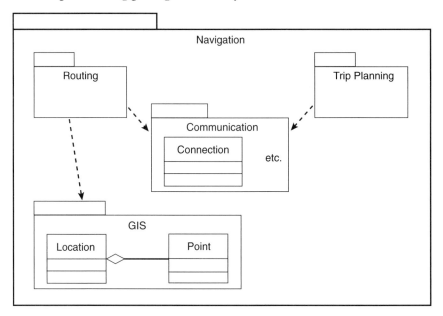

Figure 2.1
Encapsulation and hierarchy in UML structural diagrams.

All of this has the implication that the routine no longer can be considered the logical unit for testing. That honor now must go to the class. This does not mean that we do not test the routines of a class, but that unit testing in object orientation must be done in the context of a class.

The second issue relates to integration testing. How does one test whether the encapsulations at levels higher than the class level are communicating with each other in the expected fashion? The integration testing process component of a well-defined object-oriented process is therefore substantially different from those for a traditional non-object-oriented process. We talk more about this issue when we consider the process issues of object-oriented defect management.

Genericity

One of the principal benefits of object orientation is facilitation of software reuse; that is, writing software through utilization of components that have been created and used previously in other circumstances or applications. To facilitate this, it is most useful to write components (e.g., classes) that work with a variety of types under a variety of situations. This concept is called *genericity*. Not all programming languages provide facilities for genericity at the moment, but it is likely that its implementation and use will increase in the future. Eiffel (Meyer, 1992) is one of the few object-oriented languages that implements this concept in a very useful fashion.

The rules for using generic features and classes in Eiffel are quite straightforward. We simply declare the type to be of some generic identifier (usually T, G, or ITEM) and then use that same identifier as a placeholder or name for whenever a given type is to be referred to. As such, generic classes are not classes in the strictest sense; they are templates for classes that hold at least one unspecified type. Only when all the unspecified types are pinned down does a class emerge. This means that one can write a generic class but cannot create an object of that generic class. For that to happen, one has to first specify all the generic type placeholders using valid extant types, thus creating a true class. Only then can one create (instantiate) an object.

For example:

```
Class ORDERED_ PAIR [G1, G2]
creation,......
```

It is now possible to create in Eiffel an ordered pair of INTEGERs by doing the following:

```
my_pair : ORDERED_PAIR[INTEGER,INTEGER]
!!my_pair.make
```

Similarly, we can now use this class AGAIN, by saying:

```
your_pair : ORDERED_PAIR[CHARACTER,CHARACTER]
!!your_pair.make
```

Using genericity, it is then possible to provide a wide range of libraries of very useful reusable classes such as container (object structure) and GUI classes.

Genericity creates many opportunities, and given support for it in one's development environment, it is quite easy to use. However, testing objects created out of instantiation of generic classes can be tricky. An example demonstrates this assertion.

Imagine a simple generic class that implements an ordered pair as written here:[2]

```
class ORDERED_PAIR[G1,G2] inherit
     ANY
              redefine
               out
               end;
creation   make
feature
     first:G1;                       -- First Item
     second:G2;                      -- Second Item
make   is                           -- Initialization
     do
     -- Nothing here
     end;   --make
set_first(an_item:G1) is            --   an_item as first item.
     do
       first :=an_item;
     end;   -- set first
set_second(an_item:G2) is      -- an_item as second item.
     do
        second :=an_item;
     end;   -- set second
```

---

[2]There is certainly a better way to write this class to avoid the very problem we are trying to demonstrate here. Adopted with modifications from Gore, J., "Object Structures: Building object-oriented software components with Eiffel," Addison-Wesley, 1996.

```
out:STRING is        -- (first,second) with void item    --
replaced with - NOT SET-- .
  do
        Result :=clone("(");
        if first /=Void then
        Result.append_string(first.out);
        else  Result.append_string("-- NOT SET --");
        end; --end of if
        Result.append_string(",");
        if second /=Void then
        Result.append_string(second.out);
        else  Result.append_string("-- NOT SET --");
        end; --end of if
  Result.append_string(")");

  end;   --out


  end   --class ORDERED_PAIR
```

We can now instantiate this generic class template and obtain a pair of strings, for example, an entry in a simple dictionary:

```
a_word : ORDERED_PAIR[STRING,STRING]
!!a_word.make
a_word.set_first(House)
a_word.set_second(Haus)
```

Now if you examine the elements of this ordered pair, you find no surprises; so far, so good.

Now what if one used this generic class to create an ordered pair but set only the first element and not the second?

```
a_word : ORDERED_PAIR[STRING,STRING]
!!a_word.make
a_word.set_first(Water)
```

Examining the contents, we get (Water, -NOT SET-), which is exactly as expected. Even setting neither element would yield (-NOT SET-, -NOT SET-); again, no surprise.

47

One might be tempted to stop testing here; but let us see what happens when we change our usage to a different type. For example, use this generic ordered pair to implement a set of discrete coordinates:

```
a_coordinate : ORDERED_PAIR[INTEGER,INTEGER]
!!a_coordinate.make
a_coordinate.set_first(25)
a_coordinate.set_second(30)
```

The output is (25,30) which is our expectation. Now let's try to set only the first element of the ordered pair representing a set of coordinates:

```
a_coordinate : ORDERED_PAIR[INTEGER,INTEGER]
!!a_coordinate.make
a_coordinate.set_first(25)
```

Examining this code now we get (25,0) and not (25, -NOT SET-). This is certainly incorrect and undesirable. This happens because of the way Eiffel assigns default values to certain types. However, what is important here is realizing how easy it would be to miss this defect even after thorough testing.

Inheritance

Inheritance has been recognized as one of the central features of object orientation. Although it is not necessary to have inheritance in place to have an object-oriented system, most such systems do incorporate inheritance as a feature. An interesting by-product of the concept of classification, inheritance can bring many advantages, the most frequently cited of which is facilitating reuse. However, inheritance can provide significant challenges and pitfalls when it comes to defect management of object-oriented systems. Let us briefly discuss those essential elements of the concept of inheritance that have implications with respect to testing and defect management first.

Subtyping Versus Subclassing

A class should be the means to implement a particular type. A subclass therefore is best to implement a corresponding subtype. In other words, to achieve type extensibility (Meyer, 1992), the essence of flexible reuse, our class hierarchy should mirror our type hierarchy. This is usually called the subtyping form of inheritance or extension. Other forms of inheritance, however, do not follow this mirror image principle between subtyping and subclassing, including specialization and restriction. Although extension itself is not free from problems in testing, a fact that we reflect on in the next section, specialization and restriction do provide particular testing challenges because they do not support a subtyping hierarchy.

To better understand these issues, this example discusses the three kinds of inheritance enumerated here: Imagine a banking system with accounting that is automated using an object-oriented system. In such a system we might identify several types. One principle type would be the type ACCOUNT. An account is identified by those characteristics that are common to all accounts (e.g., account holder name, account number, etc.). In such a system, a CREDIT_ACCOUNT is a particular type of ACCOUNT. A CREDIT_ACCOUNT has all the characteristics of an account plus some specific characteristics that make it a CREDIT_ACCOUNT, such as *initial_loan_amount*. This makes a CREDIT_ACCOUNT a type of ACCOUNT, in that a CREDIT_ACCOUNT can do everything an ACCOUNT can do and more, so CREDIT_ACCOUNT extends ACCOUNT. It is a subtype of it. In a situation like this we still have one of each method involved, and one implemented version will suffice.

Now consider the case of the programmer who is burning the midnight oil. Her task is to write a class, SIMPLE_INTEREST_ACCOUNT. She looks into the class library and identifies a class called COMPOUND_INTEREST_ACCOUNT. Inheriting from COMPOUND_INTEREST_ACCOUNT, she alters the *calculate_Interest( )* method to cater for the simple situation. This is called overriding a method. She now has a new class that is a subclass of COMPOUND_INTEREST_ACCOUNT but is not its subtype! SIMPLE_INTEREST_ACCOUNT cannot do everything COMPOUND_INTEREST_ACCOUNT can do. It does not extend it, it specializes it. In this case, the specialized method and the original method that was overridden have to be both considered separately for testing in all potential situations.

Additionally, a client object might now erroneously use the subclass SIMPLE_INTEREST_ACCOUNT in lieu of the superclass COMPOUND_INTEREST_ACCOUNT, assuming that it is a subtype and therefore can stand in for it, an action that routinely and correctly can be taken when we are dealing with extension. This produces a defect of functionality that is very hard to identify until late in the process.

Restriction occurs when a feature of a type is blocked to produce another type. Needless to say, the new type is not a subtype of the old one. Yet, it is possible to use object-oriented class inheritance to produce such subclassing. For example, we have a case of restriction when we take a class such as SIMPLE_INTEREST_ACCOUNT and suppress the interest-calculating

features of it altogether to produce the new type NO_INTEREST_
ACCOUNT. This new type does not have interest-calculating features and
thus cannot act as a subtype of SIMPLE_INTEREST_ACCOUNT although
it is a subclass of it. Again, this creates a problem in testing because we do not
know whether to test the suppressed features (as they are still part of the
inheritance structure and implementation) or to ignore them (as they are not
part of the type being implemented)! Under such circumstances, testers will
tend to look at the contract for the restricted type and then only test according to that contract, leaving behind all the potential side effects of the suppressed features. Of course the problem of erroneous substitution by a client
object discussed earlier would also be a concern with restriction.

Many designers recommend the use of subtyping (extension) as the only
inheritance mechanism in an object-oriented design (Henderson-Sellers et al.,
1998). Strict adherence to such a principle may be too restrictive, but an effort
must be made to use extension as much as possible and to use other types
of inheritance only when absolutely necessary. These occasions are indeed
quite rare.

Deeply Nested Hierarchies

Even extension, the subtyping form of inheritance, may present challenges
during testing. One major source of such problems is deeply nested class hierarchies. In an inheritance hierarchy where extension is the form of inheritance, the general tendency would be for only the leaf nodes (those with no
subtypes) to be classes that can be instantiated. The rest would be abstract
classes and as such cannot be instantiated. This, however, does not mean that
all the features of all of these abstract classes are deferred; far from it. Therein
lies the problem. If a class cannot be instantiated, it cannot be tested directly.
Testing a class indirectly must be done carefully so that the class is tested with
respect to all possible permutations of the hierarchy down to each individual
leaf level that can be instantiated. In a deep hierarchy that is also wide, this
creates a combinatorial issue.

There are concerns even in the case of a deep but narrow hierarchy. As the
complete contract of a leaf class is really the union of the contracts of all the
parent types, many of them with some implemented operations, it is possible
to miss testing some of them. High-quality "flattening" tools—those that assist
in producing a unified contract by collapsing the contracts involved in a hierarchy—can be helpful, but the problem is also one of logic and of testing, not
of visualization alone.

Mixing of Inheritance Styles

Many designers mix different forms of inheritance in one class hierarchy. Although, like many of the previous issues discussed, this is ultimately a design issue, it does impact the way we can effectively test a system. In other words, it can contribute to defects in the system and therefore it is within the scope of our interest, albeit more from a preventive aspect rather than a corrective one.

Imagine the following situation. In a particular class hierarchy we have the root Class A, as an abstract class. Class B inherits from A and extends it, being a subtype of it. In Class B we have a number of deferred features and at least one implemented feature. Class C then specializes Class B by overriding at least one of the implemented features. Class D then inherits from Class C and extends it as a subtype. See Figure 2.2.

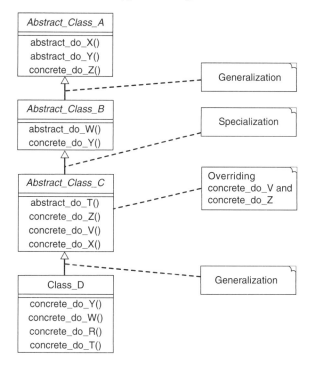

Figure 2.2
An inheritance hierarchy.

The issue here is now that Class D is a subtype of C and can be substituted for it, C, which may be instantiated (or not), is not a subtype of B, making D also not a subtype of B. Class B is a subtype of A, but nothing below it is, even though there might be several further levels.

How would one adequately test such a hierarchy?

Testing Multiple Implementation of a Single Contract

One of the great temptations, and therefore one of the greatest pitfalls in object-oriented testing, is to test a server object only against its public interface or contract. Many might ask if you would ever want to do otherwise. The answer is emphatically positive, despite the fact that eventually virtually all such problems can be identified through testing against the contract alone. This is a matter of efficiency and effectiveness, not mathematical equivalence.

Imagine the following situation: We have a general contract and the corresponding deferred class for a LIST object structure that specifies the general features expected of a list such as element entry, deletion, pointing to an item, and so on. We have elected to implement this LIST once using an ARRAY as its internal storage mechanism and once again a SINGLY_LINKED_LIST. Now as far as a LIST structure is concerned, it never overflows (or gets full), so such probability may not have been anticipated in its specification. This action is not entirely wrong, as the mathematical specification of a LIST does not specify a capacity. However, we know that both structures of ARRAY and SINGLY_LINKED_LIST used here internally do reach a capacity. To be more precise, an ARRAY has a definite bound that can be reached and a SINGLY_LINKED_LIST could exhaust the available memory. Both these conditions have to be tested if our implementations are to work properly.

Even if there is a provision for checking whether capacity has been reached, there is still no guarantee that things will work fine unless we test each version, not according to the contract, but according to the class implementation. For example, another related problem to the preceding case is the situation when a dynamic object structure such as SINGLY_LINKED_LIST, as part of its precondition test for available memory to make a new node, receives a favorable response. However, between that time and the time the memory is to actually be used, a competing process grabs the last available piece of memory. This does not happen with an ARRAY but can with a SINGLY_LINKED_LIST.

The moral of the story is to test the nonpublic features of every implementation and not just the contract.

Multiple Inheritance

It is possible for a class to directly inherit from more than one superclass. This is called *multiple inheritance*. By virtue of multiple ancestries, multiple inheritance introduces a further level of complexity to the issue of inheritance. Needless to say, all other issues discussed in relation to singular inheritance remain in force. Multiple inheritance itself can be of two principal types: simple multiple inheritance and meshed inheritance, also known as repeated inheritance. Simple multiple inheritance is the situation where a class inherits directly from more than one superclass, none of which have a common ancestry (see Figure 2.3).

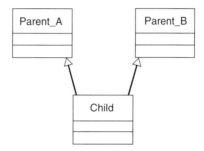

Figure 2.3
Simple multiple inheritance.

Meshed or repeated inheritance is the alternate case, where at least two of the superclasses have a common ancestry (see Figure 2.4).

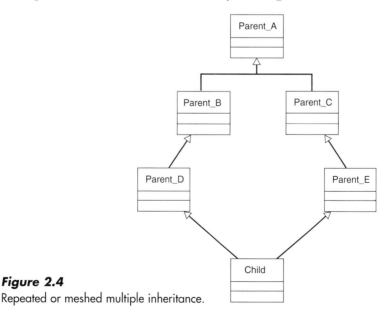

Figure 2.4
Repeated or meshed multiple inheritance.

The most obvious issue with testing in a multiple inheritance situation is that a subclass may inherit a feature with the same name from more than one parent. The child class could use one or the other, but testing with respect to one might not be adequate when the other is used.

A variant of this situation is when a client calls a feature in the child object that is implemented in terms of another feature that is present in more than one parent or in the ancestry of more than one parent.

Meshed or repeated inheritance creates many defect opportunities relating to the possibility that an instance of a subclass, and therefore its methods, can possess more than one symbolic address. The object may interact with other objects, including a shadow or alias of itself, with many strange and unexpected consequences, including method run-time clashes.

Polymorphism

Polymorphism, the concept that an object can be of many forms, is a powerful, important, and useful mechanism available in most object-oriented programming environments. In this context, polymorphism is considered the ability to substitute a type for another or, in other words, bind a reference to multiple instances of different types. Polymorphism is often closely linked to the concept of dynamic binding.

Dynamic binding allows the binding of an object to be deferred to as late as run time, thus permitting the use of different object types, depending on the context. This allows homogeneous objects (conceptually similar ones) to share a common message protocol. It is thus possible to call methods of the same name and footprint but locally different context and implementation in different objects based on the type of the object to which they are bound at run time.

For example, assume that a LIST object contains the records of the employees of a small company. There are four different types of employees in this company:

1. Directors, who are compensated through profit sharing.
   They receive 1% of the annual net profit of the company.

2. Managers, who receive a base salary and a bonus.

3. Staff, who are on a fixed salary.

4. Sales representatives, who are compensated on a
   commission-only basis.

In many object-oriented programming environments it would be possible to declare the list to be of EMPLOYEE type, which has four subtypes corresponding to the four groups of employees. Then you could populate the list in any desired order at run time, with records of individual employees. The list would not know at compile time what subtype will be stored in each of its nodes. For that matter, these nodes would not even exist at that time.

We further assume that each subtype of the type EMPLOYEE implements the deferred function *report_salary(person)* of its parent type to reflect how salary is calculated for that person.

Now, sending a message to a given node after it has been populated with a given employee record to report on that employee's salary first requires determination of which type of employee is stored in that node. Then the correct *report_salary(person)* method is invoked to do so.

This type of capability brings with it not only advantages, but also several disadvantages, particularly when it comes to defect management. Obviously from a psychological standpoint, complex polymorphic relationships could hinder the understandability of the code, at the same time assisting it from another perspective. However, the story does not end here.

When polymorphism and dynamic binding are utilized as design mechanisms in conjunction with an inheritance hierarchy, it can reduce the cognitive "surface area" that one needs to deal with, thus assisting in understandability. For this to be the case, the hierarchy we are dealing with should implement an extension inheritance; that is, strict or nearly strict subtyping. This would increase the chance that the polymorphic features potentially used thus would be homologous, used to perform the same conceptual action, but implemented locally. This might not be the case if we were to deal with heterogeneous hierarchies that incorporate classes that may not be conceptually closely related but are structurally related.

Given a heterogeneous hierarchy, it becomes evident that accidental or inadvertent binding of a message to the incorrect method creates significant problems. In a way, from a defect management perspective, this may be less of a problem than incorrect binding in a homogeneous structure, as in the former a defect resulting from such binding is often very evident. In homogeneous systems when various methods belonging to a polymorphic structure are closely related both conceptually and operationally, testing might not easily reveal a binding to an incorrect method. As an extreme example, a binding to the incorrect method *translate(item)* in a heterogeneous environment, where *x.translate(item)* refers to a movement of an object on the Cartesian grid and *y.translate(item)* means changing from one language to another, could be easily discovered. In a homogeneous environment of, for example, calculating various levels of income, *x.report_salary(person)* and *y.report_salary(person)* both calculate the income of an employee. Even the incorrect binding could return a sum in a currency type that might be entirely within expectations, possibly even identical to what the correct binding might have produced!

The logistics of testing polymorphic code is also noteworthy. One of the biggest problems of testing in a polymorphic situation is that all possible bindings might not be tested under all possible conditions, which is a necessity if confidence in both the correctness of the binding and the actual operational accuracy is desired. For example, take the case of the employee list again. It is entirely possible to test a number of nodes of this list, maybe even all of them, and not encounter a binding to a particular implementation of *report_salary(person)*, say for a sales representative. If we are sufficiently unlucky, that particular implementation we have missed may be faulty. This problem can be minimized or managed when we are aware of the underlying inheritance structure of the system giving rise to the polymorphic situation in the first place. Unfortunately this is not always the case and sometimes this testing has to be done to a contract or to a specification (black box).

Systemic Issues

The issues discussed up to this point have been largely concerned with individual server classes or class hierarchies of server classes. Whenever there has been discussion of the client–server relationship, it has been from the perspective of the server and server responsibilities. In the following sections, we discuss those issues relating to defect management of object-oriented systems that deal at the systemic level. By this we mean that they relate to the client–server exchange and interobject operation.

Object-oriented systems are noteworthy in that they implement a distributed, collaborative control structure. In the structured paradigm, control and system state are amorphous. In the object-oriented paradigm, state information is localized to the individual object. Message passing between objects invokes operations that alter these states by causing transition from one to another. At any one time, therefore, each participating object in a given object-oriented system must be in a valid state if the entire system state is to be valid. This creates a new set of challenges that impact defect management of these systems. One important issue is that of local object state and local valid transition. The other is system-wide message sequencing.

Local Object State and Valid Local Transitions

All objects on instantiation, or soon after, must be in a valid state described by that object's attribute value set. To remain useful, an object must remain valid through its lifetime. This means that at no time should an object be subject to change in such a way that violates its essence (definition). However, given the collaborative nature of object technology, it is possible for such an end result to ensue.

Imagine the following situation: In a banking system an ACCOUNT class was written to prevent overdrafts. There was an attempt to put a precondition on the *withdraw(sum)* operation that checks for available funds before a withdrawal is made. Unfortunately an error caused the precondition to indicate that at the time of withdrawal *balance* should be tested to be greater than or equal to zero (as opposed to greater than the *sum* that is to be withdrawn). Unfortunately, but not inappropriately, in the implementation of the *deposit(sum)* operation in the same class implementation we have the condition that (as overdrafts are not allowed) a sum deposited is always added to an existing positive balance or to a zero balance to take care of the account opening situation. Given the following scenario, in an account object, say *my_account*, starting with a sum of $1,000, *my_account.withdraw(100)* would work without a problem. However *my_account.deposit(500)* would leave a balance of $500 as opposed to the correct balance of $100 if, in the interim, the client object has successfully issued a message *my_account. withdraw(1300)*, which would pass the precondition because at the time *balance* = $900, which is greater than zero. The essence of the object has been violated. This latter withdrawal (of $1,300) should not have been allowed, as its application has made the object invalid.

Issues of this nature are sometimes very difficult to test for and debug. Fortunately, some object-oriented programming languages have mechanisms to minimize or eradicate such issues. For example, the contrived problem just discussed can be easily caught by the invariant mechanism of the Eiffel language (Meyer, 1992), which can enforce a condition that at all times, *balance* must be greater than or equal to zero. This did not work as a precondition to the *withdraw( )* operation, but it would as an invariant of the entire object.

System-Wide Message Sequence

There are potentially many mutually participating objects in an object-oriented system, each offering a number of services, and many other objects may call on these services. This creates a many-to-many combinatorial explosion of object call sequence. However, only a few (sometimes only one) such sequences are the valid ones that implement the functionality required at that time; all others are invalid. This goes well beyond the single object and the issue of class invariant and encompasses the state of the entire system. A good testing strategy must be able to effectively and systematically separate the valid from invalid object sequences.

Managing Defects

The first part of this chapter concentrated on the challenges that might be encountered when developing software using the object-oriented approach. In other words, we covered some of the potential problem areas. In the next section, we concentrate on the process of managing these defects; that is, on presenting the context in which some solutions to these problems may be provided.

As mentioned in Chapter 1, our philosophy revolves around the fact that defect management might be practiced from two complementary perspectives: defect prevention and defect detection. In addition we take a process approach to our treatment. This means that we trace the impact of defect management throughout the software process and also that we describe each defect management technique from a process perspective, describing each in terms of its planning activities, inputs, outputs, conduct, measures, feedback, and other process description details.

Opportunities for Defect Management

It is important to realize that virtually every step in the software process is an occasion to introduce a defect that ultimately manifests itself in the product being constructed. The reverse side of the same coin is the implication that every step of the software process should be considered an opportunity for defect management. This is the basis of my presentation in this book. We consider opportunities to prevent defects and opportunities to detect and therefore remove defects that have already been introduced.

Another important realization is that no defect management technique by itself is a purely preventive or corrective one. A defect management technique may be viewed as preventive from one perspective and corrective from another. For example, engaging in design inspection might give us the potential to identify and correct many defects that, if unresolved, would lead to defects in code. From the perspective of the design activity, this is corrective, whereas from the perspective of implementation or Verification and Validation (V&V), it is preventive. Utilization of formal models is another example. In our discussions we have taken a perspective centered on the defect contents of the product under consideration. Given such perspective, a discussion of program derivation or use of assertions in design would be considered preventive, whereas a formal design inspection would be termed corrective. Similarly, team programming might be considered preventive, but code inspection or code unit testing would be considered corrective.

The presentation in the next seven chapters is organized as follows. We first discuss, in Chapter 3, techniques that contribute to production of high-quality requirements. These techniques assist in preventing the inclusion of defects of omission and commission into our specification document. This early preventive treatment has the potential to save us much corrective defect management later in the process. This is followed, in Chapter 4, by the presentation of corrective techniques that attempt to identify and remove defects already extant in the requirements document. Chapter 5 deals with preventive techniques that concern design. Chapter 6 deals with design defect identification techniques such as design inspections. Program code defect identification is discussed in Chapter 7, and Chapter 8 covers the testing of classes through presenting corrective techniques such as code inspection or unit testing. Chapter 9 deals with integration and defect management at the system level.

Defect Management Levels

Defect management can be viewed from the perspective of the process and also from the viewpoint of the level at which it is applied. One way to do so is to study the overall software process and the correspondence of the various activities in which we engage to develop software. One interesting way of showing such correspondence is the V model of the software process (Sommerville, 1995). The V model, shown in Figure 2.5, makes explicit the correspondence between the various activities of the software process in a pairwise fashion, linking those activities that evaluate the product (on the right) to those activities that create it. Alternatively therefore, one can look at the V model as a layered correspondence between pairs of software process activities that may contain defect management techniques that may be deemed preventive (on the left) and those that may contain techniques that may be considered corrective (on the right). For example, the role of unit testing is to identify defects left over or introduced during detailed design.

Similarly, component integration testing aims to identify the defects left over or introduced during system design.

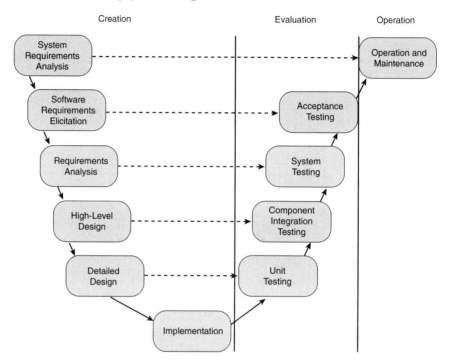

Figure 2.5
The V model.

This means that detailed or object design corresponds to the defect content of the software unit that is evaluated through unit testing. Architectural design corresponds to the quality of components and modules that is evaluated through techniques such as component integration testing. To determine if the requirements as elicited were analyzed correctly, one can engage in system-level integration testing, whereas to determine if the elicitation activity itself is sound, one compares the system to the expectations of the client. This is sometimes called *client acceptance*.

Later in each chapter, we talk about each process component and deal with each level within that context. For example, Chapter 3, which deals with the preventive techniques relating to the production of better requirements, introduces the usecase technique. Therein we discuss the implications of the usecase technique as it applies to that relevant level, that is, the system level.

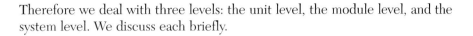

Therefore we deal with three levels: the unit level, the module level, and the system level. We discuss each briefly.

The Unit Level

One critical paradigm shift brought forth by object orientation is the change in how we view a program unit. In traditional, non-object-oriented software, the routine (a function or a procedure) is considered to be the program unit. A collection of routines, working with a separate collection of variables, constitutes the program. In object orientation, the principle of encapsulation provides higher cohesion by packaging the state and behavioral information of a given type together. This makes the class, not the routine, the natural unit of software code. Many authors and researchers have supported this notion (Binder, 1996; Meyer, 1992; Murphy et al., 1994).

Classes may be base classes—instantiable, concrete, or standalone—or dependent classes, which need other classes either as parent classes in an inheritance situation or as components in an aggregation situation. Both categories may be subject to defect management considerations, but as the astute reader may have surmised, the techniques used would be quite different between the self-containment of a base class and the interdependence created via an inheritance or aggregation situation. These may be called base class and dependent class defect management.

Base Class

A *base class* is a class that contains all its own attributes and routines. In other words, it is not derived through inheritance. A base class represents a template for generation of standalone objects. To do so, a base class must contain all the information necessary to define such a template. At a minimum this means the following:

- Class headers and footprints,
- Attributes,
- Routines, and
- Class invariants (implied or explicit).

All these elements need to be evaluated in a properly designed defect management strategy. It becomes evident therefore that the defect management of individual routines is considered an integral part of defect management at the class level. This change of view of what defines a cohesive unit of software is one of the major differences between object-oriented and non-object-oriented defect management approaches.

Dependent (Derived) Class

A *dependent* or *derived class* is one that is not a base class. In other words, a dependent class requires ancestor classes for its construction. From a defect management perspective, the interaction between the dependent class's definition and content and its dependency on other classes creates a number of complications. One can demonstrate that logically a dependent class can be reconstructed from its ancestry plus the content of the class itself. There are, of course, some rules. The reconstruction of a class based on its content and what it inherits from its ancestors is called *class flattening* (Meyer, 1992). A flattened class is therefore a derived class that is being considered as a base class as if all its inherited features are local to it.

Module Level

Objects must further interact with each other to accomplish a certain task. Thus, groups of objects must be evaluated together to ensure our programming objectives are being achieved. Modules, composed of a collection of classes needed to achieve the preceding objective, form the basis for defect management at the integration level.

System Level

Integration is the realization of the design of the system and its evaluation is conducted with respect to the design of the systems and the artifacts describing the design. System testing is, on the other hand, the evaluation of the degree and limits of the design and how the complete collection of all software units and modules combined after integration would satisfy the stated or implied requirements. As such, system-level defect management is done with respect not to design (although it may be informed by it), but to specification. Artifacts such as usecases therefore are utilized.

Conclusion

In this chapter a fault model for the object-oriented paradigm of software development was presented. This fault model concentrated on specific issues, whether based on products or processes, that pertained principally to the object paradigm or resulted from its application. In doing so, however, we made no representations in terms of the absence or impossibility of other forms of faults that can arise independently of the paradigm utilized. As such the model, as presented, is partial and focused.

The fault model describes the many potentials for production of defective software that might emerge as a consequence of utilizing the object-oriented approach and also discusses the difficulties that might be encountered in managing and reducing the ultimate defect content of object-oriented code. The rest of this book is largely concerned with techniques and advice to achieve this very same aim, using a two-pronged approach. We recognize that defect management may be preventive or corrective. We also appreciate the fact that what is deemed preventive from one perspective or during one phase of the software process might be deemed corrective in another. Such preventive or corrective techniques are then introduced, starting with Chapter 3, in terms of the various levels at which defect management might be applied.

Chapter 3

DEVELOPING LOW
DEFECT REQUIREMENTS

One of the most significant sets of activities within the software process is the requirements process component, sometimes called the *requirements engineering process component*. This process component entails the identification of the sources and bases for the understanding, the elicitation, and subsequently the analysis, reconciliation, documentation, and evaluation of the users' requirements and views of the system to be built. This is not a trivial task, nor is it free from opportunities for mistakes to be made and defects to be introduced. It is therefore critical that a disciplined approach aimed toward reduction of such occasions be adopted.

The work of many researchers would be testimony to the fact that although opportunities for making mistakes present themselves throughout the software process, problems arising from mistakes made during the requirements phase are the most prevalent (Boehm, 1984; Lauesen & Younessi, 1998). Additionally, in his seminal work *Software Engineering Economics*, Boehm (1984) demonstrated that the cost of correcting a mistake made during the requirements phase, if left undiscovered, escalates by orders of magnitude as we move further into the project. All this indicates that getting it right during the requirements phase is critically important. This chapter presents the essence of the requirements phase and discusses a number of techniques and approaches that can be useful in preventing or at least curbing the occurrence of mistakes of both omission and commission during the requirements phase.

Chapter 4 discusses some corrective techniques that deal with the output of this process.

The Requirements Process Component

The requirements process component entails all those activities that relate to the identification and documentation of users' needs. In itself, the requirements process component has several elements or subcomponents. The RUP (Jacobson et al., 1999) describes this process component by the requirements workflow. To this we add the business modeling workflow elements, as the requirements cannot be correctly elicited, understood, and documented outside the context that is provided by the business model. The workflow diagrams of these two workflows are depicted in Figure 3.1.

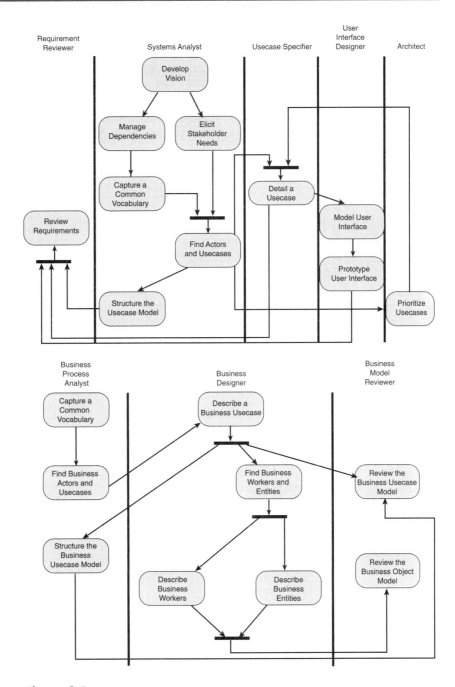

Figure 3.1
RUP workflow diagrams: requirements and business modeling.

The OPEN framework (Graham et al., 1997), shown in Figure 3.2, describes the requirements process component as one of the keystone process components of the software cycle and describes it in terms of the requirements elicitation and analysis and model refinement activities of their contract-driven life-cycle model. To this we must also add some of the considerations that form the evolutionary development portion of the build activity.

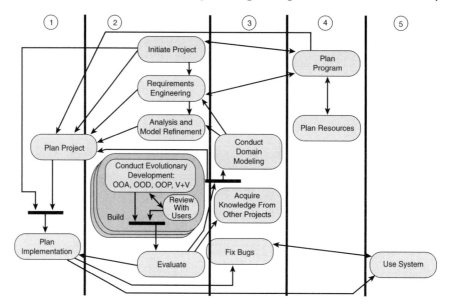

Figure 3.2
The OPEN framework. 1 = short-term planning; 2 = project conduct; 3 = long-term logistics; 4 = long-term planning; 5 = system utilization.

In essence, however, the requirements process component entails the following:

1. Comprehension of the essence and the context of the problem situation or issue at hand.
2. Elicitation of user requirements.
3. Analysis of user requirements.
4. Reconciliation of requirements.
5. Documentation of user requirements.
6. Evaluation and verification of user requirements.

There are a number of artifacts and deliverables that are generated as part of this activity that together assist in capturing, deducing, and documenting individual requirements. Among these one can mention usecases, dictionaries (to capture a common vocabulary), usecase diagrams, rich pictures and context diagrams, module or high-level class diagrams, and high-level sequence, state, and activity diagrams. It is noteworthy that all these artifacts are working tools utilized to capture or help deduce requirements. A properly written requirements document that enumerates each and every requirement is usually the formal output of this process, for which all these other documents and diagrams are support artifacts.

Of these six elements, the last one takes a largely corrective perspective and is the focus of our attention in the next chapter. In this chapter, we deal with preventive techniques that concern the remaining five elements.

Comprehension of the Essence and Context of the Problem Situation or Issue at Hand

The involvement of a software engineer implies that there must be a problem to be solved or at least the perception of a problem to be identified and resolved. Otherwise we wouldn't need to effect a change. Identifying the essence of the problem or the issue at hand quickly, accurately, and adequately within the context in which it appears is therefore the critical task here.

This is easier said than done. The trouble is that problems, issues, and concerns are cognitive artifacts; that is, they are—or at least their manifestations are—in the minds of the various stakeholders involved. Problem situations also appear within a given perceived context. A given context, however, is a matter of perception by a particular observer. This makes the issue rather problematic, as the perception of the problem or issue or its context might not be uniformly conceived among all stakeholders. For example, what might be a critical shortcoming in the current way of doing things to the chief accountant might not be such a big deal to the chief executive, or to the chief engineer. No two people ever see the same thing the same way; this is particularly true of conceptual artifacts such as problems, their contexts, or their solutions. This means that simply asking for a statement of the problem or interviewing one or two like-minded stakeholders and accepting at face value what has been stated is grossly insufficient. A consensus among all stakeholders must be strived for. Failing to do so raises the potential for misalignment of what the requirements engineer has perceived to be required and the intentions of at least some stakeholders. Such misalignment could, and often does, cause defects of commission and omission in the requirements document.

To arrive at consensus, we must first capture and depict the problem situation to promote exposition, debate, and exchange. Through such instruments stakeholders may reach consensus by agreement or through accommodation. This in turn requires clear, unambiguous, and precise language. A common and precise vocabulary is the first step toward achieving this aim. Additionally, identification of the stakeholders in the problem situation and how they perceive the problem and its solution are all essential elements that assist in ensuring adequate understanding of the problem and its context.

Construct a Common Dictionary

The construction of a common process dictionary should start at the very beginning of the process and should include a clear and precise definition of every term used in the discussions culminating in the definition of the problem situation. The composition of such dictionary must continue throughout the process.

A common dictionary must contain each term to be described, any aliases, a description, the structural or compositional relationship between this term and any other in the dictionary, and a cross-reference to where the term is utilized. Table 3.1 shows a sample template for the construction of such a dictionary. Of course many software engineering process support systems would have automated support for the composition of a process dictionary.

Table 3.1. A Process Element Dictionary

Term
Aliases
Description
Structural Relationships
Compositional Relationships
Transformational Relationships
Temporal Relationships

Table 3.1. A Process Element Dictionary (Continued)

Cross-reference
Other
Example

Identify Stakeholders

Given the multiplicity of situational view as just discussed, it is critical that relevant stakeholders to the problem situation be identified and categorized. The more comprehensive such activity is, the lower the chances of missing requirements due to missing the stakeholders whose interest such requirements would have been. At the same time, such identifications set the foundation for subsequent informed debate, hopefully on a level playing field.

Experience with systems methodologies (Checkland & Scholes, 1990; Mumford, 1985; Younessi and Smith, 1995) has shown that an important classification of the roles that various stakeholders play within each system may be presented as follows:

1. Client(s): Those for whom the system has been established. These can be the beneficiaries or victims.
2. Actor(s): The participants who actually run or operate the system.
3. Owner(s): The authority or entity, represented by a person or a group of people, that has the power to abolish the system.

For example, in a typical management information system such as a health insurance system, clients could include the following groups:

- Members of the public and policyholders (e.g., patients lodging insurance claims, or a member of the public making an enquiry regarding membership conditions and policies).
- End users who interact with the system (e.g., health insurance claims-processing staff).
- The accounting division of the health insurance company.
- The government (e.g., the Health Department or the Census Bureau).

Actors could include the following groups:

- End users that interact with the system (e.g., health insurance claims-processing staff).
- System administrator staff.
- System maintenance staff.

Owners could include the following groups:

- The board of directors of the insurance company.
- The government (Department of Health, the insurance ombudsman).

From these lists, it is evident that a particular group of stakeholders may play a role as members of more than one category (e.g., end users who interact with the system). These stakeholder categories and their subgroupings must be identified and their requirements sought with respect to each potential system implementation.

To do so, we must identify each category and at least one, but preferably two, levels of subgrouping for each category. Once this is done, we then proceed to identify individuals or organizations that represent such stakeholder grouping. We then select adequate numbers of willing members from each grouping to represent that particular group. By *willing* we mean those who are sufficiently interested in the system to have a true stake in it and are therefore willing to work to see it succeed.

Obtain a Focus

The identification and categorization of the various stakeholders has a major side benefit: It helps us identify the system boundary according to each stakeholder. A process of reconciliation, accommodation, and consensus reaching would then yield the system boundary that is in agreement by all. Here are some guidelines:

- Identify the way in which each stakeholder perceives the system.
- Identify the way each stakeholder proposes to use (interact with) the system.
- Identify and define the expectation of each stakeholder with respect to a user interface of interest to them.
- Use metaphors to help delineate the system for and with each stakeholder.

- Reconcile and reach consensus as to the extent and context of the system and therefore a common system boundary through a process of debate involving the concerned stakeholder representatives.

Identify High-Level Usecases

The highest level usecases and their corresponding usecase diagrams are nothing more than the description of the system boundary and context and how it interacts with the elements now accepted by all stakeholders to be outside it.

Construct high-level usecases either in narrative form or, preferably, in the form of a list of events that together describe the utility of the system and its interactions with the outside world. You might have to write several of these, because the greater the number of usecases included, the lower the chance of a missed requirement. It is important to include not only normal case usecases but also a wide range of non-normal and abnormal usecases. Draw the corresponding sequence diagrams for these usecases.

Utilize the usecases created earlier and their corresponding diagrams and other support mechanisms such as rich pictures (to be discussed shortly) to encourage debate and discussion so that consensus is reached as to the overall context of the system.

Draw Support Diagrams

It is often useful, for example, during a consensus-building session, to use a drawing that captures the essence of a situation, condition, or requirement or some other aspect of the system without necessarily being formal about the syntax of the diagrams. We can draw little flowcharts, diagrams of how a screen may look, a truth table to capture some logical condition, and so forth. We could draw a cartoon depicting (sometimes with appropriate exaggerations) the situation, some interaction or set of interactions, and so on. These cartoons can be stylized or not, structured or otherwise. A uniformly stylized, structured cartoon of a situation is sometimes called a *rich picture,* an example of which is a system architecture diagram.

Combine and Reconcile to Arrive at Consensus

Once various stakeholder views and opinions are made known, they have to be reconciled to achieve consensus. Many techniques exist to this end. The principal aim is not to satisfy every requirement of every stakeholder, an impossible task, but to reach consensus. Generally such consensus may be achieved by:

1. First identifying universal commonality, those things that everyone agrees about, and including them in our model view.

2. Going through a process of consensus building, attempting to bring together essentially harmonious but presently divergent views. These are those views that are shared by at least two stakeholders or stakeholder categories.

3. Reaching accommodation about those views and requirements that are unique to one stakeholder or category of stakeholder.

Of the extant techniques, one could name the following as examples: The Win–Win Spiral System (Boehm & Egyed, 1998, Lewis & Sprich, 1991); Ramesh and Bui's (1998) technique; Group Systems Group Support Systems (Weatherall, 1998); and Wilson's (1989) technique.

Elicitation of User Requirements

Now that we have consensus on the nature and context of the problem situation, it is time to elicit the individual requirements of the users. The same consensus-reaching mechanisms may be used for each individual user requirement elicited. In other words, there has to be agreement about whether a requirement stated by a particular stakeholder is to be actually implemented. According to Nuseibeh and Eastbrook (2000), requirements elicitation is the process of discovering the primary purpose of the software, which defines the measure of its success. The question then becomes how to improve our requirements elicitation process, utilizing our current resources, without expanding our timeline.

To be able to produce a product in such a way that we can define its measure of success, we first have to define what it means to succeed, in other words the criteria for success. Later, we have to produce a measure for each such criterion. However, success criteria for a software system would be nothing other than the specification of the quality goals for the system. Doing so would not only allow us to have a target to move toward, but also would form the basis of evaluating whether we have actually managed to hit that target at the end of the process. In other words, setting of a success criteria a priori would form the basis for eventual acceptance procedures to be performed at handover time.

Specify Quality and Acceptance Goals

Without a target, we have no way of knowing if we have had a hit. Specifying the quality of the software by specifying a priori what we expect the software to be and do is crucial. This would give us a target to aim for and also form the basis for the customer's accepting of the software.

We discuss system acceptance in a later chapter. Techniques of system acceptance do, however, rely heavily on the specifications of the quality and goals of the system. This stage of the process is when these goals should be determined. A technique for arriving at these follows.

The technique recommended is based on the identification of the quality attributes expected of the software and then whether such attributes can be demonstrated in the finished product. This section deals with the first half of this set of activities determining quality attributes.

Recognizing that quality is a multifaceted perception held by a variety of stakeholders who might have differing or indeed conflicting opinions and objectives, as mentioned before, the approach assists in identification of these objectives and their reconciliation. It thus assures that they collectively cover the requirements stated. It can also assist in determining requirements that otherwise may remain tacit.

Stage 1: Construct a Quality Matrix

1. Identify and name as many relevant systems as possible, where each name is a cognitive handle that allows the identification and communication of a particular coherent and purposeful set of activities. A relevant system name is usually presented in the form of "A system to be/do/achieve *X*." Example definitions include the following:

   - A system to generate birth certificates
   - A system to generate reusable components
   - A system to provide a uniform computing platform across government agencies

   All these examples may actually refer to the same application software!

2. The first dimension of the matrix (rows) identifies and names, with respect to each relevant system, the stakeholder classes belonging to each of the three role categories of client, actor, and owner. Use the following heuristics for such determination:

- Clients are the beneficiaries or victims of the result of the activity being conducted by the system named.
- Actors are those who operate the system.
- Owners are those with the power to abolish the system.

3. Discuss and reach agreement with all stakeholders concerned on the first level (e.g., reliability) and second level (e.g., accuracy) product quality attribute classes that are to form the second dimension of the matrix (columns). In selecting such attributes, we recommend a set that is compatible with the IEEE standards for software product quality or those promulgated by ISO standard 9126. These attributes include those of functionality, reliability, usability, and maintainability. Each of these attributes may be decomposed into lower (second) level attributes. For example, reliability may be decomposed into subattributes of self-containment, accuracy, completeness, integrity, and consistency. Do not eliminate an attribute class unless there is solid reason to do so—and on which there is unanimous agreement.

4. Iterate between Steps 1, 2, and 3 until all stakeholder classes and their respective product quality attribute classes are determined.

5. Physically construct the matrix on paper or CASE tool.

Stage 2: Complete the Matrix

1. Within each intersection of the matrix (cell), identify, negotiate, and agree, with that particular stakeholder, a number of specific goals that, in his or her view, the software needs to satisfy to possess the particular quality attribute in question.

2. For each such purpose, identify and agree on a particular set of premises that need to be in place for each aim or purpose to be achieved (preconditions). Relate each of these aims or purposes to a set of requirements in the requirements specification. If some aims or purposes previously identified cannot be related to specific extant requirements, then a requirements elicitation technique may need to be (re-)invoked.

3. Identify a broad number of criteria that, although not violating the premises identified in Step 2, might assess the capability of the product in satisfying each requirement identified earlier.

4. Negotiate and agree on a subset of the criteria in Step 3 with at least one criterion per stated requirement.

5. Select or devise, and agree on, a measurement or other means (e.g., formal proof) that can show conformance of each criterion in Step 4.

6. Select and agree on a meaningful and measurable level of success for each criterion, consistent and compatible with the measurement devised or selected in Step 5.

Stage 3: Test for Coverage

1. Cross-check to see whether all requirements from the specification have been represented by criteria selected as a result of multiple application of Step 2 of Stage 2.

2. If not, revisit the situation and ask why.

Stage 4: Document

1. Document all the agreements in the appropriate language. This might require involvement of legal professionals.

2. Submit the document to configuration management.

3. Arrange for the document to be signed by the interested parties.

Stage 5: Update

1. Revise and update by going through at least Stages 2, 3, and 4 every time there is an official change to the requirements specification.

Elicitation Techniques

According to Davis (1982), there are four basic approaches to requirements elicitation:

- The asking strategy,
- The deriving strategy,
- The analyzing strategy, and
- The prototyping strategy.

Each of these strategies could be implemented using various techniques. I briefly introduce each, but it should be noted that at all times a mix of strategies and techniques is used for effective requirements elicitation.

The Asking Strategy

This is when the system developer would elicit requirements by asking the customer or its representatives (domain experts). Some techniques belonging to this category include interviewing, questionnaires, group meetings, nominal group technique, and joint sessions (Henderson-Sellers et al., 1998).

The Deriving Strategy

The deriving strategy is the technique of using existing system examples and procedures to extract (derive) the requirements of the system to be built. Some techniques include observation and temporary assignment, inspecting documents, inspecting software, and research in the field.

The Analyzing Strategy

This strategy studies the aims and objectives of the organization or a unit and determines how these may be achieved in terms of inputs, outputs, operations, decisions, and interactions with other units. In other words, given an objective for a system, we analyze what such a system should be and what it should do. Two techniques that are noteworthy are critical success factors and systems dynamics (Abdel-Hamid & Madnick, 1989).

The Prototyping Strategy

This is a strategy in which we involve the users to react to a mock-up (a limited functionality system or part thereof) created to reflect the developers' current understanding of what the system should look like and do. Prototyping tools or software appropriate for rapid development are usually used.

It is essential to resist the temptation to use the prototypes created for this purpose as part of the delivered system. Prototyping is a way of finding out what the problem is, not what the solution would be.

As mentioned before, these strategies are not to be used in isolation. Usually a mix of techniques spanning across a number of strategies would be used. Requirements elicitation methodologies such as the coherence method (Viller & Sommerville, 1998), viewpoint analysis (Easterbrook, 1991), SSM

(Checkland & Scholes, 1990), and SBM (Younessi & Smith, 1995) use a mix of such strategies to develop a cogent and coherent requirements elicitation approach.

Analysis of User Requirements

Once a requirement is identified it must be analyzed for feasibility, consistency, and clarity. This is an activity that has its corrective counterpart. When analyzing user requirements—this phase—we ensure that we are producing a desirable or useful set of requirements that can then be documented. When examining the user requirements document—the topic of Chapter 4—our aim is to ensure that the said document possesses certain characteristics. In this section we are concerned with the process and how to capture good requirements. Later, we will be concerned with validating and verifying if the output artifact of this process possesses the characteristics desired of it.

Feasibility Analysis

A requirement must be feasible; that is, it must be implementable given currently available technology. For example, a completely error-free, multilanguage, multispeaker speech-recognition system might be a desirable interface for many systems, but at the time of the writing of this book, it is outside the realm of technical feasibility.

Feasibility is not restricted to consideration of technical possibility; economic efficacy is another important consideration. A technology that comes at a cost may be prohibitive for implementation in one system and completely within budget for another.

Consistency Analysis

Requirements of a system must be compatible with each other. First and foremost, requirements must be noncontradictory. This means that no two requirements must in whole or part require services that cannot be both present and fulfilled in the system. For example, a requirement that demands the furnace to be turned down by 200 degrees when certain conditions occur would be incompatible with another requirement that demands that the furnace be turned up under those same conditions. This is a case of full incompatibility because these are contrary requirements.

Systemic inconsistency occurs when a requirement does not contradict another but is logically not inline with the conception of the rest of the system as a whole; for example, a requirement that demands monthly interest payments to be made to the borrower.

Clarity Analysis

Requirements must be clear. They must convey, unambiguously, to all potential readers what is to be accomplished. A good way to do this is to state each requirement in terms of the vocabulary available from the system project dictionary (discussed earlier), indicate clearly the criterion or criteria for success (fulfillment) of that requirement, and use only quantifiable and verifiable measures to do so. For example, contrast the three statements of a requirement as described here:

- The tolerance calculation module must be highly reliable.
- The defect density of the tolerance calculation module must not exceed X.
- The tolerance calculation module must not produce more than two incorrect results when subjected to the test suite provided in T.

The first is neither quantifiable nor verifiable. The second is quantifiable but not verifiable, or at least practically so. The third is both quantifiable and verifiable.

Reconciliation of Requirements

Many incompatibilities stem from multiplicity of views and demands from the system made by different stakeholders. The source of such incompatible or infeasible demands on the system might be one of the following:

- Lack of understanding of what is to be or can be accomplished from a domain or business perspective.
- Lack of understanding of what is to be or can be accomplished from a technical perspective.
- Hidden agenda and personal interest, preference, or taste.

It becomes essential to reconcile these differences. One way to assist in the process is to enhance understanding and promote debate through the use of a

prototype. Conflict resolution techniques discussed in the previous section can often be also used gainfully.

Documentation of User Requirements

Once a requirement is determined, it must be documented. A requirements specification is the output product of concern here. Such documents come in a variety of forms: those that narrate each and every requirement, those that provide models from which requirements may be deduced, those that provide a mix of both, and those that provide both.

Requirements Narration

Requirements narration is precisely that: simply narrating in text our understanding of the requirements. A document containing a narration of the important aspects of the system required by the client will be the result of such an approach. This is usually called a *requirements definition document.*

Although possibly sufficient for very small and simple systems, this approach soon becomes insufficient for capturing the requirements of a large and complex system. Problems and limitations of the simple narrative approach include ambiguity, volume, incompleteness, inconsistency, and tedium. We can enhance such a document easily and solve, at least partially, some of these problems.

Logical Organization

This can improve the readability, and reduce tedium, ambiguity, and volume. Some inconsistencies may also be identified and removed. One way to logically organize the requirements is to recognize that there are several types of requirements, each dealing with a specific quality aspect of the system, including:

- Functional requirements,
- Usability requirements,
- Reliability requirements, and
- Maintainability requirements.

Often times (and mistakenly) only the functional requirements are spelled out. Another way is to recognize that not all requirements must be delivered. We could in fact rate requirements as absolute, desirable, and nice to have. We could attach a numerical value to each or use a wider or indeed narrower ordinal scale.

Another way is to use a logical hierarchy to keep the requirements that relate to each other logically together (e.g., all account-related requirements together, and within that, all interest-rate-related requirements together again). A hierarchical mnemonic system might be helpful here (e.g., R8.4.12F1, R8.4.12U2, etc.). Needless to say, it is possible to use all these logical organization schemes together.

Taking a Modeling Approach

The problem situation to be understood can be looked at from a systems perspective. This means that we can look at the problem in terms of its boundaries, interactions, transformations, and other systems properties in an attempt to describe it as a system. This system description, which would be a model of the system required, would then be used to convey the requirements. Models do not state requirements explicitly. They convey them through depicting the desired system. The user must deduce actual requirements through the use of these models. I describe some approaches in the following sections.

State Behavior Definition

This approach attempts to focus on the purpose of the interaction rather than the mechanics of accomplishing a given task: the why, not the what or how, at least directly to construct a model of it. State behavior definitions dovetail neatly into other systems-theory-oriented techniques for analysis such as textual analysis.

Constructing a state behavior definition starts with capturing some specific information about each interaction. An *interaction* is one end-to-end use of the system for some specific purpose. Later we see that an interaction could be a high-level usecase, an expanded usecase, or an internal interaction. The specific information needed falls into the following categories:

Purpose: Why do we do this?

Roles:

   Client: Who is the beneficiary or victim of this interaction?

   Actor: Who acts to make the situation be realized?

   Owner: Who can stop the process?

States and behaviors:

Obtain: What information would each role player obtain or provide?

Retain: What information does the system need to retain?

Transform: What transformations take place?

Generate: What information or work products are generated?

Environment:

Site/Organization: Bank, branch, and so on.

Structure: What structural interdependencies exist?

Context/Interaction: History, politics, cultural norms of issue.

Then we use these items of information to develop a one- or two-paragraph definition or description of that specific interaction. We often use a template to do this for uniformity. The following is a sample template:

A(n) *Owner* owned system operated by *Actors* belonging to a *Structure* composed of *Sites/Organizational Units* that provides *Clients* with *Generate* so *Purpose*. This is done by the *Role Players (Clients, Actors, Owners)* obtaining *Obtain* and the system retaining *Retain*, so *Transform*. This takes place in the context of *Context/Interaction*.

Usecases

Usecases are an important component of many software requirements capture methods, particularly those following the object-oriented paradigm. For example, the RUP incorporates them as an essential part. In fact the RUP is *usecase driven*. Usecases define the interaction between the user and one end-to-end transaction with the system of interest.

Before we go much further, we must make a distinction between usecases and usecase diagrams. Although conceptually related, usecases are a technique for understanding the problem domain and an integral part of many object-oriented processes including RUP. Usecase diagramming is a diagramming technique of some modeling languages, including UML. These diagrams, in the absence of their corresponding usecases, are of relatively low information and modeling value. Usecase diagrams, if drawn correctly, can enhance the usability of usecases greatly.

A usecase is an essentially narrative document. It describes the sequence of abstracted events of an abstracted actor (user) using the system to complete a task. Usecases are thus concerned with use of the system and not with the processing that takes place. Usecases may be high-level (dealing with a major utility of the system) or expanded (dealing with an individual task or even subtask).

Constructing Usecases

This is where opinions differ. There are essentially three approaches:

- Identify the actors (users of the system) first and then for each, identify the interaction the actor has with the system to achieve goals. Each such iteration will yield a high-level usecase.
- Identify the major deliverables of the system, and then the actors and interactions required to produce each.
- Start the structure modeling process to help uncover the usecases.

This example is an expanded usecase:

```
Usecase:          Check credit, is OK
Actor:            Salesperson
Initiating Actor:Salesperson
Description:
                  Salesperson checks the customer creditworthi-
                  ness (See Check with CAS). Then (s)he checks
                  the credit limit of the customer (See Check
                  Credit Limit).

Usecase:          Check credit, not OK
Actor:            Salesperson
Initiating Actor:Salesperson
Description:
                  Salesperson checks the customer creditworthi-
                  ness (See Check with CAS). Then (s)he sus-
                  pends the order (See Suspend Order).


                  Alternate Style

Usecase:          Check credit, is OK
Actor:            Salesperson
Initiating Actor:Salesperson
Description:
                  1. Check customer creditworthiness.
                       1.1   See check with CAS
                  2. [OK] then check credit limit
                       2.1   See check credit limit
```

84

```
Usecase:         Check credit, not OK
Actor:           Salesperson
Initiating Actor:Salesperson
Description:
                 1. Check customer creditworthiness.
                     1.1   See check with CAS
                 2. [Not OK] then suspend the order
                     2.1   See suspend order
```

Usecases, and particularly expanded usecases, can be grouped into three categories:

- Normal course (normal use),
- Non-normal course, and
- Abnormal course.

For example, you can use an ATM to withdraw cash from a checking account (normal), withdrawal limit exceeded (non-normal), and line drops (abnormal, if not allowed for).

It is one of the important capabilities, and in my opinion, the primary strength of usecases that they allow segregation of individual interactions (instances of use). This makes for clarity because through such an approach, operations (matters of action) and conditions (matters of logical determination) are separated and can be treated individually. Unfortunately, this advantage afforded by usecases is often ignored or not utilized. Thus often we see usecases that attempt to cover multiple cases at the same time through the use of conditionals (if and case statements), thus confounding the situation. See the following example:

```
Usecase:         Check credit
Actor:           Salesperson
Initiating Actor:Salesperson
Description:     1. Check customer creditworthiness.
                     1.1   See check with CAS
                 2. If OK, then check credit limit
                     2.1   See check credit limit
                 3. If not OK, See suspend order
```

Clearly these are two distinct situations, two distinct logical conditions, that occur at different times and under different conditions. In short, they are not the same usecase.

Graphical Models

Some models are created using graphical languages, which utilize certain icons to depict various elements required for the model to be constructed and a set of rules to combine them to make more complex but still meaningful diagrams, eventually yielding a model of the system.

There are many types of such diagrams, but three types are paramount: structure diagrams, transformational diagrams, and causal or dynamic diagrams. These are naturally the corresponding graphical depictions for structure models, transformational models, and causal models.

There are many different conventions for each type. The de facto standard for model depiction in object orientation is UML.

UML Diagrams

UML is described adequately elsewhere (Rumbaugh et al., 1999) and I do not duplicate this effort here. What is worthy of mention in this context is that UML is constructed on the basis of a metamodel or a grammar. One can thus determine syntactical correctness of models constructed manually or automatically using a syntax checker. Such a facility (or activity) would assist in removing a variety of defects of commission of syntactic type from the work product with little effort.

Formal Methods

The most effective (but not necessarily the most efficient) form of defect management is preventing defects from occurring. To achieve this, precision and rigor are required. Traditionally we have sought recourse in the formality of mathematics to this end, what is popularly termed *formal methods*. Defect prevention in this context therefore is composed of three tightly interrelated approaches, namely those of formal specification, formal derivation, and correctness proving.

Formal Specification

Formal specification is the use of mathematics to construct models of systems. These models serve as specifications of system behavior that, due to the use of mathematics, are unambiguous and tractable. Formal specification has traditionally not been accounted as part of V + V, or in our terminology, defect management. However, it can, from the perspective of defect prevention, be viewed as a vital activity in correctness assurance. A precise statement of requirements can be as follows:

- A firm, workable, and reliable basis for formal design;
- A vehicle for removal of specification ambiguity (particularly syntactic ambiguity),
- A firm basis for comparison of the final product and what the customer wanted (the specification), and
- A firm basis for testing or inspection.

There are several approaches to formal specification. Of these, functional approaches and model-based approaches are the most commonly utilized. Despite an earlier interest in functional approaches, model-based approaches have tended to be more widely used in the recent past. The Vienna Development Method (VDM; Bjorner, 1979) and Z (Spivey, 1992) are the non-object-oriented precursors of techniques such as object-oriented VDM (Minkowitz & Henderson, 1987) and Object Z (Duke & Rose, 1998), examples of which we have already seen (see Figure 3.3).

The concept of formal specification, program proving, and program derivation have for a variety of reasons not been widely utilized by practitioners. Some of the reasons usually stated are enumerated here:

- There is no concrete evidence that they are cost-effective in realistic industrial settings.
- There is a very steep and high learning curve and achieving proficiency in effective use of formal methods is difficult.
- There is no real guarantee of correctness even if formal methods are applied.

On the other hand, others (Ghezzi et al., 1992; Hinchley & Bowen, 1995; Luqi & Goguen, 1997) have provided justification and support for the use of formal approaches to software construction and defect management. There are also emerging quantitative indications that cast a shadow of doubt over the industrial utility of formal approaches (Pfleeger, 1997). In fact, truly successful, fully formal development processes, measured in terms of wide commercial acceptance, are nonexistent. The cleanroom approach (Mills et al., 1987),

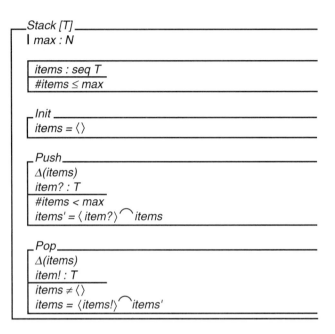

Figure 3.3
An example of part of a formal specification in Object Z.

which uses formal methods as one of the several components of the process it advocates, is the closest we have to a commercially successful application of formal approaches. The growth of formal methods continues to be slow.

The Requirements Document

Requirements are captured for several reasons, including these:

- To ensure that our understanding of what is to be done coincides with that of the customer,
- To provide a basis for the writing of contracts,
- To be able to convey to our design and implementation colleagues precisely what needs to be developed, and
- To provide a basis for evaluating whether we have completed the project successfully.

Start Constructing a Requirements Traceability Table

A requirements traceability table (RTT) is a useful tool that captures each requirement as it is discovered and relates it progressively to all decisions made to fulfill that requirement. As such, construction of this document should be started as soon as the first requirement is confirmed. The document then continues to grow and mature throughout the process, through and beyond acceptance procedures. This traceability helps a great deal in the software engineering process and goes a long way to ensure that each and every requirement is attended to.

Each row in the table deals with a given requirement. If this requirement is operational (functional), there are one or several usecases related to it that operationalize it. If, on the other hand, the requirement is a structural (nonfunctional) one, then we must seek fulfillment of it via operationalization through a usecase or, more probably, through topological, architectural, and design considerations. These decisions may not have been made (they usually would not have been made) by the end of the requirements phase and therefore would be added later.

An example RTT is depicted in Table 3.2.

Table 3.2. Example RTT

1. Requirement ID

2. Synopsis

3. Reason

4. Success Measure/Criterion

5. Stakeholder/Owner

6. Req. Validated by (reference°)

7. Usecases

8. Arch. Feature

9. Sequence Diagram(s)

10. Design Feature

11. Model

12. Design Validated by (reference)

13. Module/Class(es)

14. Test Cases

15. Implementation Validated by (reference)

Table 3.2. Example RTT (Continued)

16. Included in Prod. Version

17. User Accepted by (reference)

*Note. (Reference) indicates the need for inclusion of a reference to the document or documents that provide evidence for such validation.

Once we have valid entries in Rows 1 through 5 for all requirements, we can deem the requirement elicitation process completed. The next phase would be that of the requirements documentation. Once the requirements document is produced it can be subject to a number of techniques (described in the next chapters) that together would endeavor to validate each; that is, to fill out Row 6 of the RTT. Beyond that, the design process takes over.

It should be mentioned that certain design and architectural decisions may have already been made and their impact already depicted in the RTT during this early phase of the project. Remember that software engineering is essentially iterative and opportunistic leaps from analysis to design to coding and back to design or analysis would neither be uncommon nor undesirable, as long as order, coverage, traceability, and control are maintained. Therefore, it is possible that a number of usecases, architectural features, topologies, or even sequence diagrams have already been produced.

The aim at the end of the requirements elicitation phase is to not have any "holes" left behind in Rows 1 through 5. If some entries are made beyond Row 5, that is acceptable if they have been made in accordance with the preceding provision.

The Requirements Document Set

To ensure that our understanding of what is to be done coincides with that of the customers, we need an easy-to-understand, easy-to-read, not necessarily very precise document in their language.

To be able to set a basis for contracting or for evaluating whether we have completed the project successfully, or to convey to our design and implementation colleagues precisely what needs to be developed, we need a very precisely worded document in the language of the developers, but still understandable to "expert" customers or their nominee consultants.

It is very difficult to write one document to satisfy both requirements for other than very simple projects. We need two different documents that say exactly the same thing in two different styles and levels of precision. The first is usually called a requirements definition, and the second is a requirements specification. Tables 3.3 and 3.4 contain suggested templates for these two types of documents.

Table 3.3. Suggested Contents for a Requirements Definition Document

---

1. Table of contents and list of figures and tables
2. Preambles, caveats, conditions
3. Executive summary
4. Synopsis of system
5. Current situation and environment (which the system is to improve)
6. Operating environment and conditions (e.g., specialized hardware, security, support)
7. Outline of process to be followed
8. System description (an informal narrative of what the system is to do)
9. High-level system models
10. Functional requirements listing (including a statement of measure of success)
11. Nonfunctional requirements listing (including a statement of measure of success)
12. Other requirements, constraints, or conditions (including a statement of measure of success)
13. Postamble or concluding remarks
14. Appendices

    14.1 Listing of usecases, state behavior definitions, and similar artifacts

    14.2 All other diagrams and supporting materials

    14.3 Glossary of terms and definitions

    14.4 Index

    14.5 References

Table 3.4. Suggested Contents for a Requirements Specification Document

---

1. Table of contents and list of figures and tables
2. Preambles, caveats, conditions
3. Description and definition of special notation used, values of constants, and so on
4. Executive summary
5. Synopsis of system

Table 3.4. Suggested Contents for a Requirements Specification Document (Continued)

6. Current situation and environment (which the system is to improve)

7. Operating environment and conditions (e.g., specialized hardware, security, support)

8. Outline of process to be followed

9. High-level architecture and system description

10. Expanded system models

11. Precise functional requirements specification (including precise statement of measure of success)

12. Precise nonfunctional requirements specification (including precise statement of measure of success)

13. Precise specification of other requirements, constraints, or conditions (including precise statement of measure of success)

14. Postamble or concluding remarks

15. Appendices

    15.1   Listing of usecases, state behavior definitions, and similar artifacts

    15.2   All other diagrams and supporting materials

    15.3   Glossary of terms and definitions

    15.4   Requirements traceability table

    15.5   Index

    15.6   References

Conclusion

Prevention is better than cure. The majority of system defects stem from the requirements stage. Dealing with defects early in the process is economically more advantageous than letting them percolate to the subsequent stages. Based on these principles, it makes good sense to employ techniques of requirements specification that minimize the chances of introduction of defects in the first place: preventive approaches.

Chapter 4

IDENTIFYING AND REMOVING REQUIREMENTS DEFECTS

In Chapter 3 we discussed a number of preventive approaches and techniques that assist in the development of requirements and requirements documents with lower defect content. These techniques, as their name suggests, prevent the introduction of defects of commission or omission in the work product while it is being constructed. This chapter instead concentrates on corrective techniques. These are techniques that—given an extant requirements document—might be used to identify and allow removal of defects already in the work product, introduced as a consequence of an imperfect requirements elicitation and documentation process.

To accomplish this task, we must first recognize that it is not a process but an artifact, the output of the requirements process that is to be examined. This is a critical issue. This artifact, which we call a specification, can potentially be composed of a number of subsidiary artifacts that may or may not exist in every instance of a specification. Among these are the following:

1. A system description. Sometimes called the *synopsis* or *requirements statement*, this is some narrative text that describes the system and what is required of it. Being informal and usually informally developed, it may contain many defects of omission or commission. It is important that such an artifact is used as a secondary resource.

2. A requirements list. This is a listing of individual requirements, sometimes organized hierarchically or grouped into categories based on criticality or urgency or a similar attribute. Each and every one of these requirements must be featured in the Requirements Traceability Table (RTT). In fact, the aim of this chapter is to provide techniques to assist in correctly filling out Row 6 in the RTT. It is essential therefore that each requirement passes a certain number of examinations.

3. Usecases. Usecases provide the functional view and to a much lesser extent some of the nonfunctional views of the specification. They must relate to the individual requirements of the system as specified on the one hand, and the specification models generated on the other. They must therefore be examined carefully for content and form.

4. Specification models (graphical). Graphical specification models (e.g., UML diagrams) convey the structure, the transformations, and the causal relationships of the required system. Thus they must relate to the functional and nonfunctional requirements as indicated by all other artifacts listed herein, particularly the requirements list. All models should therefore be examined for certain internal and external characteristics.

5. Specification models (formal). Similarly, if formal specifications exist, they must be validated.

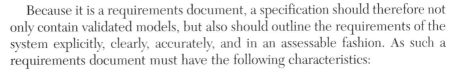

Because it is a requirements document, a specification should therefore not only contain validated models, but also should outline the requirements of the system explicitly, clearly, accurately, and in an assessable fashion. As such a requirements document must have the following characteristics:

1. Correct. This means that a specification should be devoid of defects of commission as much as possible.

2. Complete. By complete we mean that a specification must be devoid of errors of omission, missing requirements, incomplete statement of requirements, requirements that only state what is needed with respect to only one or a nonexhaustive set of possibilities in a given situation, and so on.

3. Concise. A requirements specification must contain all the necessary information needed but not more. Any extra information provides potential for misunderstanding, duplication, or wasted effort and other possible diversions.

4. Consistent. A requirements document must state a closed and coherent set of facts. There must be no logical contradictions in the description of the system or its requirements.

5. Clear. Ambiguity is the bane of all requirements engineers. A requirements specification must clearly state each requirement so that there is only one way to interpret that requirement. Sometimes the language of mathematics or other means of formalizing natural language (e.g., pseudocode) is used to this end. The use of a process dictionary (see Chapter 3) also goes a long way. Another aspect of clarity is measurability. Requirements often become much more clear when a genuine attempt is made to make them measurable. To be measurable, an entity has to be both quantifiable and verifiable. For a detailed explanation, see Chapter 3.

To ensure our requirements document possesses these attributes, we must examine it with respect to these criteria. To do so we must do the following:

- Examine the conformance of the specification document to stated or implied standards and templates and determine whether it contains all the necessary components, then
- Examine and validate each subsidiary artifact (e.g., each model), and
- Verify the coherence between the subsidiary artifacts.

Examining Conformance to Standards

This may be done independently or in conjunction or as part of a formalized inspection process (discussed later). Either way, this activity entails examining the specification document present with the standard or template it is supposed to follow. This template or standard might be an industry accepted standard (e.g., IEEE); specified by a particular process (e.g., RUP); recommended by other researchers, authors, or practitioners (e.g., the template provided in Chapter 3); or developed in-house.

Examine the presence of each section as required by the template or standard. If missing, investigate why. There can be a variety of reasons including these:

- The section was inadvertently omitted. In that case, add the section.
- The section is actually there but it is included as part of another section, as an appendix, or with some similar deviation from the format. Identify why such a decision has been made and if no compelling reason exists, recast the document to conform to standards.
- The section is intentionally omitted. In this case, investigate why this decision was made and if unreasonable, add the section. If reasonable, see if this decision is an isolated or special situation or likely to recur. If the latter, revise your process to allow for inclusion or exclusion of this section as the situation dictates.

Model Validation

Model validation involves examining the model artifacts created as part of the requirements definition or specification process and ascertaining whether they adequately and accurately convey a picture of the system that is required. The reader may remember that specification models do not spell out what the requirements are; they convey them. It is left to the reader of the model to discern the individual requirement or set of requirements that has led to a particular feature or aspect detailed in the model. Nevertheless, it becomes critical, once a model is created, for it to be validated.

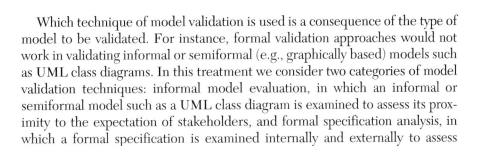

Which technique of model validation is used is a consequence of the type of model to be validated. For instance, formal validation approaches would not work in validating informal or semiformal (e.g., graphically based) models such as UML class diagrams. In this treatment we consider two categories of model validation techniques: informal model evaluation, in which an informal or semiformal model such as a UML class diagram is examined to assess its proximity to the expectation of stakeholders, and formal specification analysis, in which a formal specification is examined internally and externally to assess mathematical validity of the expressions composing it.

Informal Model Evaluation

As stated before, informal model evaluation concerns itself with whether an informal model such as UML class diagram has been drawn correctly and in accordance with the syntax of the modeling language, whether the model contains all the information it is expected to convey, and whether that information is accurate.

Such determinations relate to and are dependent on the type of the model (e.g., is it a class diagram, a sequence diagram, a state diagram). I therefore present a number of techniques, each appropriate for evaluating a particular model type or set of types. It must be noted that informal does not necessarily mean ineffective. In fact, the technique you are about to read about is one of the most effective in all of software engineering.

Class, Responsibility, Collaborator (CRC) Approach

Originally introduced by Beck and Cunningham (1989), the Class, Responsibility, Collaborator (CRC) approach allows the software engineer to anthropomorphize the object–class universe and its interactions. The CRC technique is based on the construction of cards to represent cohesive object-oriented model elements, usually classes but also possibly other, higher level modules such as packages. Each card then becomes the responsibility of a person who would act out its responsibilities and interact with the collaborators of the card to achieve a task according to the requirements. The CRC technique is used either after usecases have been developed or while this is happening. It has essentially three uses:

- To identify model elements such as classes, methods, and associations;
- To validate or complete usecases; and
- To highlight model flaws.

The process of production of CRC cards is most aligned with the first use. A CRC card is a 4 x 6 or a 5 x 7 index card on which there are three main compartments (see Figure 4.1): class name, responsibility, and collaboration.

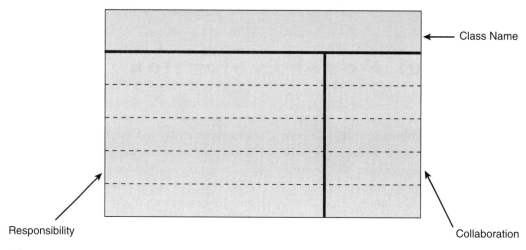

Class Name

Responsibility

Collaboration

Figure 4.1
CRC card.

Figure 4.2 shows an example of how a CRC card might look early in the process.

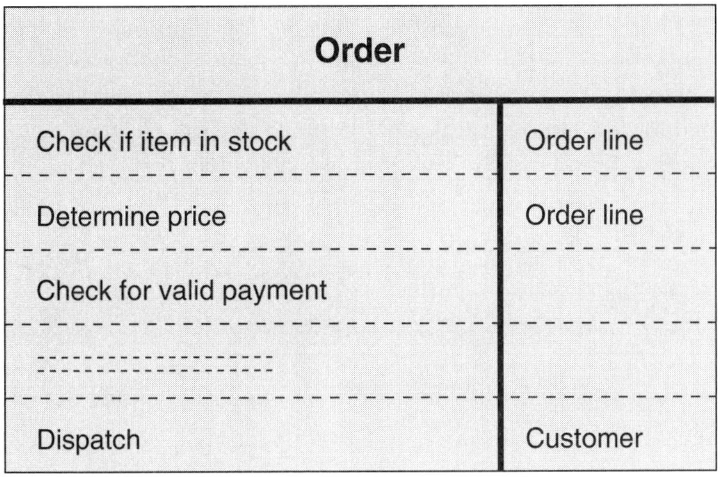

Order	
Check if item in stock	Order line
Determine price	Order line
Check for valid payment	
- - - - - - - - - - -	
Dispatch	Customer

Figure 4.2
Example CRC card.

On the back of the card there are usually up to four compartments, as shown in Figure 4.3.

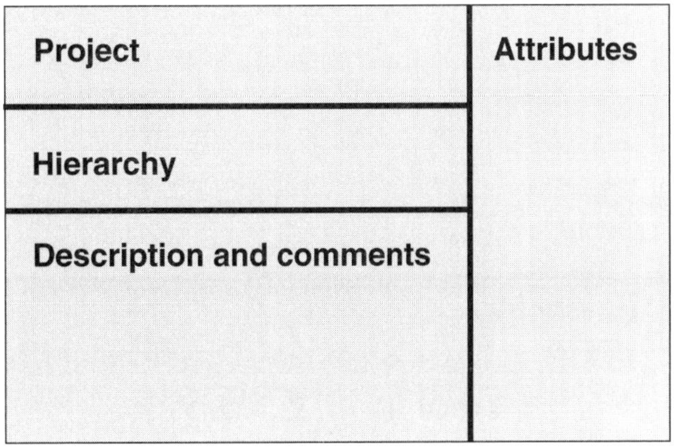

Project	Attributes
Hierarchy	
Description and comments	

Figure 4.3
Reverse side of a
CRC card.

In the Project compartment we record the name of the project or segment of the project to which this card belongs. This is for housekeeping purposes and to manage reuse at the card level later.

The Hierarchy compartment reflects the relationship of this card with any ancestor or descendant card (in an inheritance sense). For example, if the present card (`Order`) inherits from a class called `Agreement` and is itself the parent of `Cash-order` and `Credit-order`, then we record this on the back of the card in the Hierarchy compartment like this:

```
Hierarchy:

↑   Agreement
↓   Cash-order, Credit-order
```

The Attributes compartment contains the attribute set of the class the card represents.

For example:

```
Attributes:

order_Number:
date: Date
order_line:
amount: Currency
etc.
```

The attributes may or may not show types.

In the fourth compartment, Description and Comments, we can record any notes or information of interest including special business rules, for example, $amount \leq max\_amount$.

Creating CRC Cards

Creation of CRC cards usually takes the following steps:

1. Identify a potential class.
2. Create a card for that class by first selecting a name and putting that name on the card.

3. Identify the various responsibilities for which you feel this class must exist.

4. Identify other potential sources and sinks of information and ultimately other classes that might be needed before this class can discharge each of its responsibilities.

5. Identify the specific pieces of information needed to identify this class, or those that the class needs to hold. Write them as attributes on the back of the card.

6. If this potential class is in a hierarchy, depict the hierarchy.

7. Include some notes and comments if needed and identify the project.

8. Produce a similar card for any new potential class that was discovered.

Once you have a handful of interrelated CRC cards that collectively describe the system or at least some of its functionality, you are ready to play the CRC game. The game is played in two different forms, depending on whether the intent is to validate the model or to refine it. To refine the model, you have to have your CRC cards and one person to play the role of each class (see Table 4.1). To validate you have to have a table and a set of chairs, a reasonably complete set of cards, a reasonably comprehensive set of usecases, one person to play each class, and a small bean bag, ball, or similar object (see Table 4.2).

Table 4.1   CRC Model Refinement

1. Sit around the table and give each person a card he or she is to play the role of.

2. Start at a logical place with some class. Debate if it is needed or if it needs to change.

3. Start a thread that can be initiated by invoking one of the responsibilities of that class.

4. Identify the target class. Is it one of your collaborators? If yes, pass control to that class; if not, include the collaborator identified or create a new class card if none is available.

5. Keep playing until every responsibility on every card has been either discharged or debated and discarded. Proceed similarly for every attribute.

6. Do not be afraid to combine classes, split them as necessary, or indeed discard them if no longer useful.

7. Add responsibilities as and when needed or delete them if not required.

Table 4.2   CRC Model Validation

1. Give each person the card he or she is to play the role of. Also nominate a person to play each external actor.
2. Start with your top-ranking usecase. Identify the actor who initiates things and give him or her the bean bag.
3. The actor starts a thread that can be initiated by passing the bag to the correct class according to the usecase.
4. The class checks if it can accept the bag. If yes, it does so; if not, we raise an alarm and debate and rectify the model. The class now looks to its collaborators to pass the bag.
5. Keep playing until the usecase is complete.
6. Update the model if necessary.
7. Go to the next usecase.

Once the model is validated against all usecases, we might want to capture the information thus obtained in a diagram. We do this by positioning the cards on a board and considering each as a class. We then draw association, aggregation, and inheritance relationships between them as defined by the collaborations.

We can also consider each card as a class and thus instantiable into individual objects. In fact, when we were playing the CRC game, each person was an object (at least at any one time) and collaborated as an object. Thus we can identify the number of instances of each card required for the scenarios concerned and produce these by photocopying the card to the number of copies required. Now we can, through the use of our usecases, validate our cards and draw a collaboration diagram. The collaboration diagram should validate the ones developed through separate dynamic modeling. In other words, by developing these collaboration diagrams through the use of card instances, our system sequence diagrams must be implied, thus examining the dynamic behavior of the system.

Formal Model Validation

Formal model validation does not prove correctness and must not be confused with that. Formal model validation is examining a formal specification, say in

Object Z, to ensure as much as possible that it correctly reflects the requirements of a system to be developed. It cannot prove the correctness of such a document, as specifications are inherently an open system. By this we mean that although we may demonstrate that what has been specified is concise and free of defects of commission, we have no control over what has not been specified, or what has been omitted.

Formal correctness proving, on the other hand, attempts to prove the correctness of a program (source code) against its formal specification (say in Object Z). This is a potentially closed system and therefore proof of completeness, as well as other characteristics such as correctness and conciseness, is possible. Even then, completeness can only be assessed against the degree to which the specification is complete.

The situation for formal model validation, however, is not hopeless. It is still possible to check internal consistency and logic of the formal specification. For example, in a formal specification we have identified two Boolean variables X and Y and three conditions (A, B, and C), each having been specified as the outcome of a combination of values for the two variables:

X	Y	Condition
0	0	A
0	1	B
1	0	C

What about when $X = 1$ and $Y = 1$? This is a logical question that must be asked and answered. Formal model validation can identify and flag such omissions.

Similarly, in a formal specification, the operational schema to push an element onto a stack is written as:

$$
\begin{array}{l}
\underline{Push} \\
\Delta(items) \\
items? : T \\
\hline
\#items < max \\
items' = items \frown \langle item? \rangle
\end{array}
$$

A subsequent model validation identified that this statement should have been written as:

$$
\begin{array}{l}
\underline{Push} \\
\Delta(items) \\
item? : T \\
\hline
\#items < max \\
items' = \langle item? \rangle \frown items
\end{array}
$$

The astute reader would note that several defects have been identified and removed:

1. The input variable was called *(Items?)* in one instance and *(item?)* in another.

2. The sequence *items* and the cardinality of that sequence had been written as *(Items)* rather than *(items)*.

3. Probably most important, the statement *items' = items^(item?)* implies that the element to be inserted is concatenated at the end of the sequence of items, not at its head as required in a stack. The statement *items' = (item?)^items* corrects this error.

A detailed listing and description of the syntax of Object Z is provided in Appendix B.

Requirements Document Inspection

An inspection is a formalized technique of determining defect contents of a product through a direct examination conducted by concerned experts, aided in the process by a number of artifacts such as checklists, forms, and process guides. As many readers might already be aware, inspections are unique neither to software engineering nor to the process of requirements specification. In software engineering, we use inspections to evaluate requirements documents, design documents, code, user documentation, and many other artifacts.

The requirements document inspection process specifies a number of roles and role players, specific tasks to be accomplished, and specific artifacts to be used or produced. Although at a sufficiently high level of abstraction, the inspection process for all artifacts would be identical, each software artifact having its own special characteristics, thus requiring a specific set of process specifications unique to the inspection of that process.

Appendix C specifies the general process of inspection and contains the necessary documents, forms, and information for the inspection of an object-oriented requirements document.

Conclusion

In this chapter we discussed the important activities that can lead to defect detection in the requirements document. Conducting such activities is both important and necessary as no amount of vigilance, attention, and precision—in practice—can prevent the occurrence of defects of omission and commission during the requirements engineering phase. A verification and validation phase heavily reliant on examining the various artifacts developed by the requirements elicitation and capture phase must be utilized.

The next chapter goes forward to discuss a number of preventive approaches to object-oriented design.

Chapter 5

PREVENTING DESIGN DEFECTS

Chapter 3 dealt with preventive techniques in requirements engineering. This discussion continued in Chapter 4 to cover corrective techniques that might apply to the specification of the product and the document that contains it. This chapter begins a discussion of techniques that might be useful in preventing design defects. To do so, we first must identify what this step of the process entails and what products it might produce. Thus we begin with a discussion of software design, its elements, limitations, products, and qualities that both the design process and the design product should possess. Only after having done so will we be on firm footing to discuss, initially in this chapter, the preventive techniques and then later in Chapter 6, corrective techniques that pertain to the design process and its artifacts.

We have already discussed the steps leading to the production of a system specification. Therefore, having determined what is required of us to build, we now must get on with the business of providing a solution; that is, actually delivering a tangible product. This is the process of design.

However, to achieve our stated aim, the process of design should be an efficient process of providing a solution that leads to a quality product. In the first part of this chapter we lay down the foundation to do this by providing means of approaching the design process in a manner that would allow us to achieve this aim.

Software Design

At the outset, we must make an important and explicit distinction. In software engineering parlance, the word *design* often refers to two distinct elements: One is a product, the other a process.

The Design Process is an interrelated set of methods, technologies, and contextual elements utilized to provide a solution to a specified problem.

The Design Artifact is the model produced as the work product of the design process. This model represents the solution proposed. It stands to reason, however, to assert that for our software solution to be of quality and be produced efficiently, both the design process and the design product have to have a number of characteristics including the following:

- The design product has to represent a quality solution. This means that the solution we are proposing, of which our design artifact would be a model, must have the potential of building a product that possesses attributes such as functionality, usability, reliability, and maintainability. These attributes, you might remember, were among those identified as desirable in a high-quality system.

- The design process has to be efficient. This means that it has to utilize resources such as methods, staff, and technology in the best possible way to deliver the design artifact. In other words, the design process must not be wasteful of resources.

To sum up, therefore, we need to design for functionality, reliability, usability, maintainability, and process efficiency. These are the principles of good design.

We should also mention that usecases and models created based on usecases concentrate mainly—although not solely—on functionality. Therefore in most object-oriented approaches, usecases are how we capture the required functionality of a system. But what about the remaining nonfunctional requirements? This is where architecture comes in. Architecture is the primary vehicle by which we ensure meeting of nonfunctional requirements such as maintainability, efficiency, and reliability. A good design should therefore take both usecases and other means of capturing functionality and produce a design that "folds in" the nonfunctional requirements through the use of architecture.

Design for Functionality

First and foremost, to achieve proper functionality, we need to ensure that our design is traceable to the functional requirements.

Traceability

Every functional requirement must have some design element that caters to it. Remember that one of the most significant issues hampering software development, and one of the major risks to the software process, is misimplementation of requirements. For example, gold plating, one of the major risks according to Boehm (1991), is a direct consequence of inadequacy of traceability of design to original requirements.

To be certain that functionality is being delivered, we must ensure that in addition to operational issues, our requirements specification also contains adequate information regarding issues such as portability, efficiency, security, and availability.

Traceability involves being able to map a particular portion of the design to a particular requirement. To achieve this, it becomes important to have a design that can be viewed in terms of specific and largely separately identifiable units, segments, or components. To assist with traceability, it is therefore clear that the design should have the property of modularity.

It should be possible to distinguish parts in the design and identify that each part is for a particular purpose, which is the fulfillment of a requirement. It should also be possible to concentrate on what each module does to satisfy a requirement without getting lost in the details of how it does it. We should also be able to hide design details when they are not needed or bring them to the fore when they are. In other words, a design should have the property of abstraction.

A well-organized document should not only be organized in sections, but it should also have good headings for each section. The same is true of good design. It should be formed not only of modules, but each module should represent an abstraction of the contents.

Additionally, it would be useful to have abstraction at multiple levels. In other words, the design should have several levels of detail, from the general to the specific. A good design must possess multiple levels of granularity. Later on, we cover how these desirable properties may be instilled in a design.

Design for Reliability

To ensure that our designs lead to a product that is reliable, we must ensure availability, fault tolerance, and robustness. To do so, our designs must have the properties of accuracy, consistency, recoverability, and redundancy.

Accuracy means that each design element can be interpretable in only one way that is in line with the requirements. In other words, every state that the system is required to achieve is reachable through a known set of transitions, and additionally, no other (invalid) states are entered.

Consistency means that there is no attempt to satisfy a requirement or portion of a requirement in multiple fashions that are contradictory or incompatible. Inconsistency can force the system into an invalid state.

Recoverability means that in the event that the system should go into an invalid state (e.g., due to lack of sufficient accuracy), there would be a means of forcing the system into a meaningful valid state.

Redundancy means that in case of failure of some critical function, the design would provide alternate ways to ensure delivery of the required functionality.

It is very difficult to produce accurate designs. Deviations from the letter or the intent of the requirements are always possible. To achieve accuracy, a number of techniques are used.

Use of Modularity

It is generally easier to demonstrate the accuracy of a small portion of design (a module) than the entire thing. Similarly, it is generally easier to arrive at an accurate design if we divide and conquer. If we have a design depicted in terms of a number of smaller modules, one can be virtually assured of the accuracy of the whole design if the following two conditions exist:

- The way the modules are interrelated is accurate. *the communication between modules is accurate*
- Each module is internally accurate. *each module internally aren rat*

It is much easier in most situations to satisfy these two conditions than it is to ensure the accuracy of a large, monolithic design.

Use of Abstraction

It is also generally easier to show accuracy of a module by first showing the accuracy of its interface to the rest of the world (i.e., that it has the potential to deliver what it should) and then that each such potential is correctly realized. In other words, the module has the right interfaces and each behaves as expected.

Granular, Multileveled Approach

Remember that when we were talking about modularity, we asserted that a modular design would be accurate if its modules are interrelated accurately and each module is internally accurate.

To demonstrate the internal accuracy of a module, however, it is possible to approach it utilizing the same principles. This means that to ensure the internal accuracy of a module we can segment it at a lower level into a set of smaller submodules that we ensure are interrelated accurately to represent the higher level module. Each smaller submodule can then be either accurately designed at that level or subdivided into still smaller modules. It is usually more successful to approach a problem at multiple levels of detail.

Formal Derivation

In earlier chapters, we discussed the notion of formal specification: presenting the specification of a system formally using mathematical expressions that precisely specify an aspect of the system.

We can use mathematical transformations to change this formally produced set of requirements into an equivalent design model. Given the inherent exactness of mathematics, to the extent that we have correctly applied appropriate transformations, the design model accurately reflects the stated formal requirement. One advantage of such formally derived models is that we can mathematically "prove" their accuracy. In addition to their roles in assisting in achievement of accuracy, modularity, abstraction, granularity, and formality, all can also have a positive impact on design consistency.

Dividing the system into modules would add visibility and can help ensure that each service is provided by one module only. This is the essence of consistency. If only one module is responsible for the provision of each service, then by definition there is consistency.

Abstraction can assist in the examinability of the design for many design flaws including lack of consistency. For example, it is usually easier in a design with good abstraction to identify if two or several modules (or even one) have inconsistent operations intended to do the same thing than it is in a design with full visibility.

Granularity allows for examination of consistency at multiple levels, making it easier to pinpoint any inconsistencies. We will be looking for a needle in a progressively shrinking haystack.

Formality gives us the ability to "prove" consistency. Therefore, for consistency to be a feature of our design, the design has to be in the form of multiple levels of precisely defined abstract modules, each containing operations that are logically and functionally related, appear once, and are themselves precisely defined.

Recoverability is actually an attribute of the system to be built, not that of the design solution leading to it. However, in this context, by recoverability we mean that property of the design that leads to a system that possesses this property.

Such a design must anticipate the potential deviations that might lead to invalid states or drastic failures (often called *exceptions*) and design around them.

Sometimes it is not enough to simply trust the design to be accurate and not fail or that if it did, it would recover. Sometimes we need uninterrupted operation without failure. For example, the software system that controls the public telephone system must not fail. It has to be in operation, with a high degree of availability, 24 hours a day, 7 days a week, year round.

Under these circumstances, a design has to provide more than one way to deliver the required feature. Usually this is done by replicating or duplicating (or indeed perhaps multiplicating) portions of the design so that in case of failure of the primary system, the other(s) would take over.

Design for Usability

Usability goes beyond the "look and feel" of a product and encompasses other issues related to the interface between the product and its users. Some of these are learnability, rememberability, efficiency in use, and user appeal.

There are two aspects to designing for usability:

- How to design a usable interface, and
- How interface design decisions impact the underlying design of the system.

How to Design a Usable Interface

This is a very broad subject and much of the discipline of human–computer interaction (HCI) is devoted to this issue. The choice of appropriate combinations of text, graphics, sound and motion, choice of color, placement, selection of appropriate metaphors, and so on, are all very important considerations that would eventually yield a user interface. Important as they are, we do not deal with this issue here. Interested readers may refer to other books on this topic (e.g., Preece et al., 1995).

How Interface Design Decisions Impact the Underlying Design of the System

Applying the concept of modularity to the overall situation, we can immediately deduce that the user interface can be perceived as a distinct subsystem.

This separation of concerns assists with the flexibility of the system, as we can now change the user interface—if need be—without having to change the underlying system. This is the principle of segregation or separation of concerns.

Also, if we segregate the user interface, we can then design it in parallel using the same principles we employ for the underlying system (plus those specific to HCI).

Important Note

segregation is having multiple interfaces for each client instead of one common interface for all clients

It is sometimes asserted that interface design decisions impact the overall system efficiency, and this is absolutely true. A complicated graphical interface imposes greater demand on the computing resources available than a simple command-line interface. However, in a well-designed system in which the user interface subsystem is segregated from the underlying system, the potential for such impact should be more manageable. The overhead should be localized in the interface subsystem and, if need be, redesigned. The advantage of such segregation is therefore that problems with and changes to the user interface do not impact the rest of the system and can be separately attended to.

It can be seen easily that segregation is a direct consequence of modularity and abstraction. Therefore the level of modularity, abstraction, and therefore segregation of the interface subsystem is critical in achieving this aim. This is a concept to which we return later in this chapter.

Design for Maintainability

Much of the cost of ownership of a system is tied to how well it can be improved, how it reacts to changed requirements, or how it is repaired while in operation. The ability for a system to be improved while in operation is called *perfective maintenance*. The ability for a system to react to changed requirements in operation is called *adaptive maintenance*, and the ability for a system to be repaired after installation and commissioning is called *corrective maintenance*.

The fact that a significant portion of the cost of ownership of software is in maintenance means that the systems we design must be easily maintainable and, as such, the underlying design should cater for maintainability. The basic tenets of maintainability are localization and side-effect management. *Localization* is the ability to quickly identify the area in the design that has to change for the maintenance to take place. *Side-effect management* is the ability to limit undesirable or unanticipated change in system behavior in one place when an intentional change is made elsewhere.

Obviously, modularity, abstraction, and granularity help in localization because it is easier to find a problem in a small module than it is in a large one or a design that is not modular.

But this is not all. Perhaps more subtly, but equally important, it is much easier to identify a problem when we can associate that problem with a specific service or feature of the design. If the design is modular and abstract we can identify much more quickly that part of the design that is responsible for the service and therefore needs attention.

If you knew the context of the maintenance required, it would be much easier to find and change a specific module than the area or areas in need of change in a monolithic design.

It can also be argued that modularity, abstraction, and segregation assist in side-effect management because the smaller and more modular the unit, the greater the chances of it accurately implementing a service without undesirable side effects. Also, the more singular the purpose and functionality of a module, the less likelihood of its design being used in a nonconventional fashion that would confound the search for the source of the required change.

One of the side effects of connecting a stereo system to a television is that one can control the volume and other sound characteristics of the television program via the stereo system. This is fine until:

1. Something goes wrong and you have no TV sound. Where would you look? In the sound reception mechanism of the TV? In the sound production mechanism of the TV? In the sound reception mechanism of the stereo system? In the sound production mechanism of the stereo system? In the interface between the stereo system and the TV?

2. One asks someone who is not from that household and does not know about this TV–stereo link to turn down the TV volume. Which appliance would he or she go to? Which knob would he or she turn? Which remote controller would he or she grab first?

Design for Process Efficiency

Religious and philosophical connotations aside, anything is possible given infinite resources. In the real world, however, resources are limited. Software design, like any other constructive activity, thus becomes an exercise in compromise and maximization of process efficiency (doing more with what you have). To not have to compromise too much, we can employ two fundamentals to help with process efficiency. We thus design for reuse, to design and develop an artifact once and use it in similar situations many times, and parallel development as parallel activities shorten the overall project time and better engage available resources.

Reuse can only take place effectively when the item to be reused does something very specific; it is sufficiently well defined, particularly in terms of its interfaces; and it is flexible to fit similar but slightly different situations.

Modularity and abstraction assist with the to-be-reused item being specific to the task at hand. Formality and abstraction assist with the artifact being well defined. Flexibility is helped by abstraction and genericity.

You might recall from Chapter 2 that genericity is the property of type independence. By type independence we mean the ability of a module to perform similarly, irrespective of the type of input provided it or output required of it as long as the operation or operations in question are meaningful.

On the other hand, parallel development is only possible if there are identifiable, specific, and—most important—largely independent segments of the design that can be given to a specific developer or team to implement. Otherwise the constant need for communication and collaboration across development teams necessitated by the inherent interdependence of the design makes parallel development impossible or at least not worthwhile.

The key word here is *independence*. Independence is achieved when we organize the design into abstract segregated modules that communicate minimally. In other words, make sure that the module serves only one logical purpose, can always serve that purpose, and depends on other modules only when it is necessary to communicate.

Basic Elements of Good Design

A quick survey of how the quality requirements of a design might be satisfied results in the following list of the basic elements of good design:

- Modularity, *– cohesion, coherence, coupling*
- Abstraction, } Segregation
- Minimality of interaction,
- Multiplicity of levels of granularity,
- Formality,
- Anticipation of invalid states (exception handling),
- Redundancy (when needed), and
- Genericity.

In this section we study how we might recognize, measure, and achieve these properties in our designs.

Cohesion: A Measure for Modularity

[handwritten: all classes are functionally related]

A module should represent a coherent idea semantically and should be integrated structurally. Therefore, cohesion is a measure of the "togetherness" of a module. The notion of how well a module represents a single idea or concept externally or conceptually, known as *semantic cohesion*, is a largely subjective notion and there is no acceptable metric for it yet.

Syntactic cohesion or structural cohesion deals with the construct of the module, or how a module has been put together. It is an internal property of the module. One can define as many stages of cohesion in a system as there are levels of abstractions and modules. We can talk of the following:

- Component cohesion, or cohesion at the level of class or abstract data type. *[handwritten: a single class/object cohesion]*
- Module cohesion, or cohesion at a level where several components are grouped together in a module or several modules into a higher level module. *[handwritten: some classes or modules put together]*
- System cohesion, or cohesion at the top module level that encompasses the entire system. *[handwritten: all modules put together]*

In terms of cohesion within a module, Constantine and Yourdon (1979) defined seven levels of cohesion. We enumerate these from bad to good; that is, from least desirable to most desirable.

Coincidental Cohesion

Coincidental cohesion occurs when there is no pertinent relationship between the parts, except that they have all been "packaged" together.

For example, imagine the module shown in Figure 5.1, called Package 12, which contains three submodules: One is related to Fourier transform, a mathematical algorithm; another, Phone Directory, stores a list of names and phone numbers; and Error Handling is a module that deals with management of program errors. Although it is unlikely that such a grouping would be practiced, it is possible. This is coincidental cohesion, the grouping of elements in a module for no apparent reason other than coincidence.

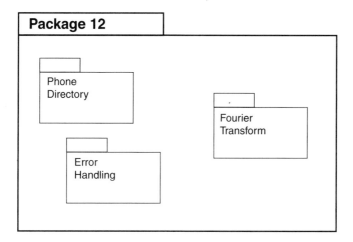

Figure 5.1
Coincidental cohesion.

Logical Cohesion

Logical cohesion occurs when the various components or modules put together perform logically similar tasks.

The module shown in Figure 5.2, called Input Module, contains all modules dealing with obtaining and managing input to various programs in our application. The logical concept of input is the element providing the cohesion.

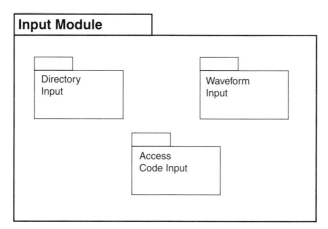

Figure 5.2
Logical cohesion.

Temporal Cohesion

Temporal cohesion occurs when the components are related to each other by time of activation or deactivation.

In the example shown in Figure 5.3, the submodules File System Check, Transaction Initiation, and Process Initiation all relate to the start-up of the system. In other words the element that binds these submodules together is the time at which they are used.

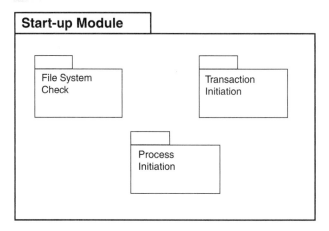

Figure 5.3
Temporal cohesion.

Procedural Cohesion

Procedural cohesion occurs when the module contains one or several components that together perform a specific procedure. Figure 5.4 shows an example of procedural cohesion.

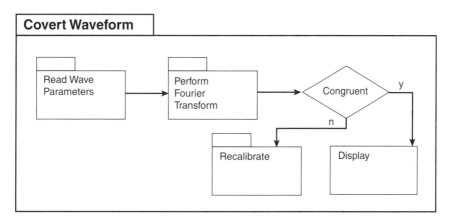

Figure 5.4
Procedural cohesion.

Communicational Cohesion

Communicational cohesion occurs when the elements of a module rely on the same input or output data. To print records or to display them in a window, the module requires the same input data (see Figure 5.5).

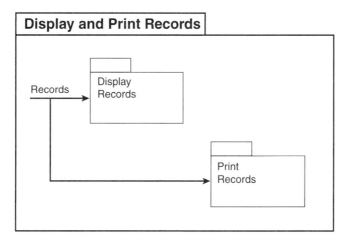

Figure 5.5
Communicational cohesion.

Sequential Cohesion

Sequential cohesion occurs when the output of one element is the input of another. Figure 5.6 shows an example of sequential cohesion.

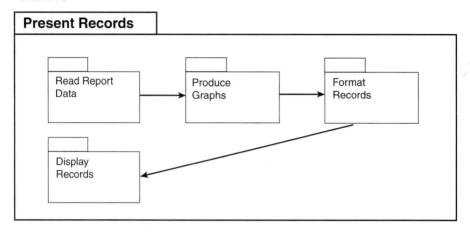

Figure 5.6
Sequential cohesion.

Functional Cohesion

Functional cohesion occurs when the module performs a single, well-defined operation. Figure 5.7 provides an example of functional cohesion.

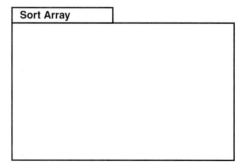

Figure 5.7
Functional cohesion.

Macro and Buxton (1987) introduced a still higher level cohesion called abstract cohesion or object cohesion.

Object Cohesion

Object cohesion occurs when the module is encapsulated in such a way that the state of the module is described by the set of attribute values describing the module, which may be read, used, or modified by the integrated operations *within* the module to provide a specific service expected of the module externally. Figure 5.8 provides an example of object cohesion.

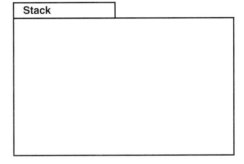

Figure 5.8
Object cohesion.

Coherence: Another Measure of Modularity

As proposed by Durnota and Mingins (1993), a module is defined as coherent if the methods work together to carry out a single, identifiable purpose. They define the coresponse set of two methods as the common set of methods called by each of the two methods concerned. This is done in a pairwise fashion for the entire set of operations in the module and extended down recursively. The basis of this metric is that the larger the coresponse set compared to the total number of distinct methods called from the two methods, the greater the degree of coherence.

Achieving Modularity

It stands to reason that to achieve modularity, one must strive for high cohesion. We must lump attributes (state information) and operations pertaining to one named phenomenon or concept (an object or module) together. In short, we must strive for the module to be encapsulated. This means that the state of the module is described by the set of attribute values abstracting the module. These attributes should only be read, used, or modified by the integrated operations within the module to provide a specific service expected of the module externally.

For example, a complex number is a numerical type of the form $x + jy$ where x and y are real numbers and j is $\sqrt{-1}$. We can encapsulate the characteristics of this type into a module. In such a module, the state of the object is defined by the values of x and y, which can be changed via operations that are a part of the object definition itself. Externally, we expect a number of operations from a complex number such as being able to add, subtract, multiply, and divide them; converting them to a vector (magnitude and angle) form, and so on (see Figure 5.9). These operations are part of the module and accessible to users.

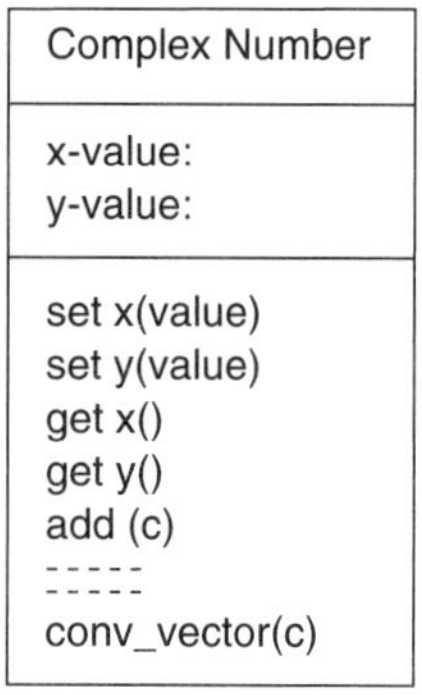

Complex Number
x-value: y-value:
set x(value)   set y(value)   get x()   get y()   add (c)   -----   -----   conv_vector(c)

Figure 5.9
Encapsulated object.

Coupling: A Measure for Minimality of Interaction and for Segregation

Modules should have minimal interdependency and should be segregated structurally. Therefore coupling is a measure of interconnectedness between modules. Semantic coupling represents the notion of how independently modules implement a single objective or concept externally. There is no acceptable metric for it yet. Syntactic coupling or structural coupling deals with the construct of the modules, and how tightly they are connected together.

Similar to cohesion, one can define as many stages of coupling in a system as there are levels of abstractions and modules. We can therefore talk of the following:

- Intermodule coupling, or coupling at a level where components are grouped together in a module or modules into a higher level module.

- System coupling, or coupling at the top module level that encompasses the entire system.

From the perspective of measuring coupling, we can speak of the following:

- Binary coupling, or coupling between two modules.
- Multinary coupling or network coupling, which is coupling between several modules.

Constantine and Yourdon (1979) defined seven levels of coupling. We enumerate these from bad to good; that is, from least desirable to most desirable.

Content Coupling

Content coupling occurs when one module actually changes the contents of another module. In the example shown in Figure 5.10, the third line in Module A jumps to Module B and changes it.

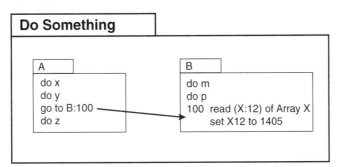

Figure 5.10
Content coupling.

Common Coupling

When two or more modules use and modify the same common data source, we have common coupling.

In the example illustrated in Figure 5.11, Module A writes w into a file, called File X. Module B in turn reads this value from File X and uses it. Thus the relationship established between Modules A and B is via a common data source.

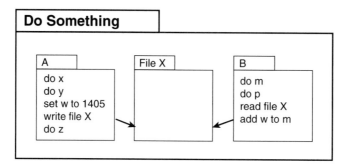

Figure 5.11
Common coupling.

Control Coupling

When one component passes a parameter to control the behavior of another module or several other modules, we have control coupling. Figure 5.12 shows an example of control coupling.

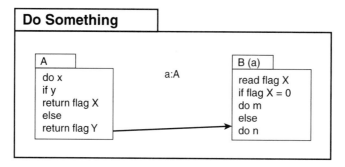

Figure 5.12
Control coupling.

Stamp Coupling

Stamp coupling occurs when a module passes an entire data structure to another module. In the example shown in Figure 5.13, the array is passed to B.

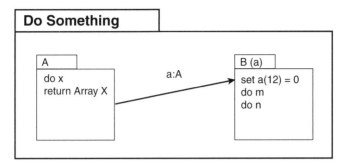

Figure 5.13
Stamp coupling.

Data Coupling

Data coupling occurs when only data but not the data structure is passed. Figure 5.14 shows an example of data coupling.

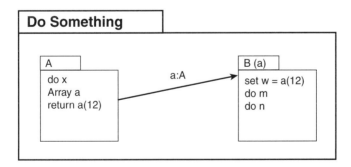

Figure 5.14
Data coupling.

No Coupling

Unfortunately, when there is no coupling, there is no communication and therefore no system.

Achieving Segregation

We can achieve segregation through low coupling. This can be best done by passing a message containing data to one interface (operation) of the called object.

Achieving Abstraction

concentrate on module interfaces - what a module does for us

To achieve abstraction, we must concentrate on the bare essentials; that is, on what the outside world expects of this module and not how the module should deliver on this expectation. Concentrate on how the outside world recognizes or describes this module. Define a necessary and sufficient set of interfaces. The example in Figure 5.15 shows a stack.

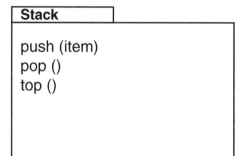

```
Stack

push (item)
pop ()
top ()
```

Figure 5.15
An abstraction at the class level.

Achieving Multiple Levels of Granularity

Any well-defined module—if need be—should be readily decomposable into lower levels of granularity. Each operation can be deemed as a set of interacting states and simpler operations between possibly simpler lower level modules.

Achieving Formality

This can be done in several ways and to several extents. Here we discuss formal derivation and contract specification and its extension, design by contract.

Formal Derivation

As discussed before, formal derivation is the precise conversion of a set of formal requirements into a design using the language of mathematics. Several paradigms and styles exist, which are discussed in detail in a later chapter. Among these we have introduced functionally based and model-based approaches.

Despite an earlier start in favor of the functional approaches, model-based approaches have recently attained greater popularity. Of these we learn about the Z and Object Z modeling languages.

Contract Specification

As seen before, contract specification combines some advantages of precise mathematical specification with the flexibility of semiformal modeling approaches (e.g., through usecases). This is achieved through identification of modules (e.g., classes) through conventional means, followed by a somewhat formal specification, not of the entire structure of the module, but of the three principal areas vital to any abstraction:

- Preconditions for every module operation (interface),
- Postconditions for every module operation (interface), and
- Invariants for every module.

Preconditions

Sometimes called entry conditions, generally preconditions are those conditions that must be logically or operationally satisfied before an operation can begin. In the context of a module, such as a class definition, it is possible to precisely define these requirements in a mathematical or even executable language. Programming languages that allow such definitions (e.g., Eiffel) would then permit a higher degree of formality to be examined automatically through execution of these preconditions.

Precise and complete specification of the preconditions of all operations of an abstraction (a module) provides great protection against illegal or inadvertent invocation of a service.

Postconditions

Sometimes called exit conditions, postconditions are those conditions that are satisfied on complete execution of an operation in a module. Should we succeed in precisely specifying all the postconditions of all operations of a module (often a very difficult task) and then automatically check for satisfaction of these on the execution of the module, we can—among many other benefits—safeguard against entry into many invalid states generated as the result of the execution of operations.

Some languages (e.g., Eiffel) allow for postconditions to be specified in an executable form.

Class or Module Invariants

Class invariants are those conditions in a module that must remain the same at all times, before, during, and after the execution of each and every operation or set of operations. A violation of a class invariant indicates some serious issue of validity and reliability with respect to that module, its parents (in an inheritance sense), or its use.

Again, it is possible to spell out these requirements using a precise language such as mathematical formulation or programming code. Some programming languages such as Eiffel permit such facility.

Design by Contract

Design by contract is an extension of ideas of contract specification first formulated by Meyer (1992), the creator of the Eiffel programming language.

Design by contract uses all the ideas of modularity, abstraction, minimality of communication, and formality. It specifies a module as an abstract encapsulation in which the concepts of pre- and postconditions and class invariants are used.

To this, the design by contract framework adds the concept of the contract between modules. A software design contract between modules is an analog of a contract between real-life legal parties. In a legal contract, the understanding is that if Party A satisfies Condition B set by Party B, then Party B shall deliver what Party A requires of it.

For example, if Party A pays $20,000 by 5:00 P.M. today, then Party B shall transfer the ownership of a particular car to Party A. Now if Party A meets or exceeds the requirement to pay $20,000 today, then Party B has to give up the car. Note, however, that Party A must always meet but can exceed the requirements. For example, he or she can pay $22,000 or pay the required amount by 2:00 P.M. instead of 5:00 P.M.

Should Party A pay the required amount on time, then Party B is obliged to deliver the car. However as the contract stands there is no obligation on the part of Party B to deliver it at any particular time. So Party B could easily take the money and deliver the car at his or her leisure without breaking the contract.

Should Party A meet the requirements, Party B must deliver the car, but is at liberty to deliver more than just the car.

According to software design by contract, exactly the same rules apply to contracts between software modules. A software module might call one of the services (operations) of another module and as long as it satisfies or exceeds the preconditions of that operation, we can be assured in a correct design that the called module would deliver the required service, meeting or exceeding all its postconditions and invariants.

Achieving Anticipation of Invalid States (Exception Handling)

Work with inputs and input states, pre- and postconditions, and invariants if available.

Achieving Redundancy

When necessary, duplicate and multiplicate identical modules or modules delivering the same service. These approaches are actually solutions to a particular category of design problem usually presented as a specific architectural style, which we discuss in depth later on in our discussion.

Achieving Genericity

Genericity is a very useful concept that is easily understood and, provided the language facilities are available to support it, easily implemented, or at least so the myth goes. In reality, the first assertion is actually true, and the second only partly so. The basic idea behind genericity is to make modules as independent as possible of the type, particularly inputs into it and also, when appropriate, outputs from it. This, when implemented correctly, would greatly contribute to flexible use and reuse of a module.

When there is language support for it, a generic module is generally specified through the replacement of each independent type by a generic label. At use time (e.g., instantiation), each of these generic labels must be bound to a specific actual type.

The concept of genericity was discussed in Chapter 1.

Architecture

The elements and principles enumerated in the previous section can be brought together into a coherent association called an *architecture*. This is an attempt to provide a strong foundation for our continued ability to develop a quality product. A proven architecture, when used in an appropriate situation, would assist us in a number of ways:

- A proven architecture embodies a large number of design decisions that would no longer be made individually, thus saving time, effort, and resources.

- A proven architecture embodies proven knowledge, tested successfully in a variety of similar situations, and is therefore at least as likely to work in actuality as the one of our own invention.

- A proven architecture assists in organizing and harmonizing the rest of the design. It helps in setting the scene.

Architectural Topology

A system can be laid out in a particular configuration. If the designers of the system have utilized good design principles, such configuration would be appropriate not only to the problem environment, but also to the design decisions made to deliver a solution to the problem. Therefore architectural topology (how a design is laid out) is important.

In computerized system solutions, two categories of topology become important: physical topology and logical topology. Here, we discuss these two issues, particularly the latter, which has a much greater impact on software design.

Physical topology deals with how the physical elements of a system have been laid out. This can often impact issues such as performance, reliability, or even functionality. Software design decisions have to be made in a way that is harmonious with the type of physical topology adopted and vice versa.

Issues of physical topology are adequately detailed in textbooks of data communications and networking. For our purposes we need only consider one particular distinction: A system topology can be a single node—standalone—machine, or a multinode—networked—configuration. We see later that distributed logical topologies are only effective in the context of a networked physical topology.

Logical topology deals with the logical interrelationship of design elements as opposed to physical equipment layout. Logically, a topology can be centralized or distributed. When distributed, it can be distributed based on data, process, or both.

Communication and flow of information can be on a peer-to-peer or client–server basis. Logically, the structure of all software systems may be described in terms of three concepts or elements:

- The facility, module, or object that performs the required service;
- The facility, module, or object that requests a service to be performed; and
- An effective means for communication of the two preceding elements.

Centralized Topology

Simply put, in a centralized topology these three elements are colocated, or more accurately, are not explicitly separated logically or physically.

Distribution: Distributed Topology

Principles of good design such as modularity and abstraction, particularly combined with an implementation in a networked environment, often lead to or suggest a logical topology other than centralization.

We can logically abstract into modules specific services that can be supplied, and into other modules those that might request these. These collaborating modules would then communicate via an appropriate mechanism of communication usually (but not necessarily) based on a multinode physical topology such as a bus, ring, or internetwork. Such multinode physical topology is colloquially called a network. When these communicating modules are placed noncentrally (usually on more than one physical node), we have distribution. Such a system is called a distributed system.

It is possible to distribute a system based on location of the data elements. For example, a detective might use a desktop machine to check the criminal records of a person. If the databases containing these records are not on that desktop machine, and the system has to communicate over a network with other computers that host these types of databases (e.g., at the FBI, Interpol, Scotland Yard, etc.), then we have a data-distributed system.

Another example is a remote banking system in which the automated teller machine (ATM) might have to consult several databases at various banks (physically and logically elsewhere) to check a cardholder's account details, depending on where the account is held.

Data distribution may go beyond this multiple database configuration and we may have a distributed database situation. In a distributed database situation, a single logically coherent database may be physically placed on several machines in several distributed locations. Distributed databases are gaining in popularity and they might become the dominant data storage strategy in the future.

It is also possible to distribute the processing performed in a system. For example, in an online stock brokerage system, the share trading operations might be on one node (the customers') and the system administration processes might be available only on a specific node and location at the company headquarters that is not accessible to the clients.

Process distribution can also go beyond this level so that, for example, there would be process distribution even within a single unit of work. For example, share trading can be deemed as a single activity or unit of work. However, for the online stock brokerage system it is possible to have the presentation processes (GUI, etc.) on one category of machine and the share transacting processes on another.

As the astute reader might have already surmised, pure data or pure process distribution is limiting and logically difficult to achieve. Distributed systems usually are distributed based on both data and process. A popular form of such distribution is object distribution, in which individual objects or small collections might be on any machine, yet provide the required functionality as if present locally.

Irrespective of type of distribution, the interaction between modules might take the two distinct forms of client–server or peer-to-peer interaction, which are discussed shortly.

The arrangement or protocol by which the module requesting a service from another module does this via sending it a message is called the client–server arrangement (sometimes also called a client–server architecture). In such an arrangement the module sending the request is called the client and the module serving the request is called the server (see Figure 5.16).

Client–server arrangements can be made at various levels of abstraction. For example, one can conceive of an entire system that is a client to another system, a subsystem might be a client to another subsystem, and a module might act as a client to another module. In fact, the object-oriented paradigm can be viewed as the implementation of the client–server arrangement at the individual object level.

In most client–server arrangements, the request message sent to the server is usually transported physically via a network. It is, however, possible to conceive of a client–server arrangement in which all the modules are on the same node or machine. For example, a centrally located object-oriented system is centralized, but it has a client–server organization.

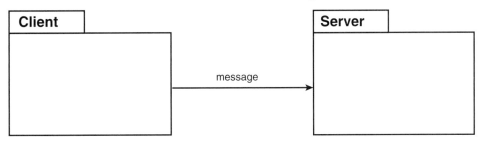

Figure 5.16
A client–server arrangement.

This arrangement is actually a generalization of the client–server situation in which each module can act both as a client and a server. In a situation like that, we call the modules peers of each other. Figure 5.17 shows an example of this.

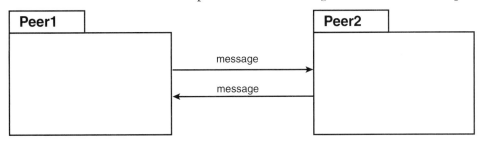

Figure 5.17
A peer-to-peer arrangement.

Implementing Distribution

The way distribution is implemented is (by definition and circularly) an implementation issue. However, decisions leading to implementation of distribution have design implications. For example, in a distributed system, the client is usually unaware of the location of the server module. Under such circumstances how does the client know where to send a message to get some service performed? Similarly, in a distributed system, the server and the client may have vastly different architectures and have been written in different programming languages. Again how would communication be possible under such conditions?

To solve these problems and others similar to them, a design layer and a corresponding set of products called middleware have been introduced. Products such as CORBA and Java RMI are among these.

These products permit the designer or implementer to isolate these access issues, and they allow for access to remote objects transparently. This usually is achieved by allowing the designer to design the application object without concern for remote access. All communication is modeled as sending messages as if to local objects. It is the task of the middleware layer products (e.g., CORBA) to do the rest. You learn more about these later in this book and much more in books dedicated to distributed software system design and implementation.

Architectural Design Styles

Bridge designers or architects do not design their bridges or buildings from scratch every time. There are a number of interrelated design concepts and ideas that work well under certain conditions or are appropriate in solving a particular type of problem. For example, a particular arrangement of pylons and spans leads to a particular bridge design called cantilever. There are many cantilever bridges worldwide, and although all are different, they all have the same basic design style in terms of the arrangements of their basic design elements.

Similarly, in software design, a particular scheme of relating subsystems or modules with each other to deliver a solution is called an architectural style. We next discuss some of the most important of these styles. There are many styles of architectural design available. Some are specific to a particular application area or a particular type of design problem. Although usually called design styles, these are best referred to as a particular solution pattern or a framework, depending on the level of abstraction, extent, and detail provided. Some, however, are more general and can be truly called design styles. Of these we cover the following, postponing the discussion of the former category to later:

- Layered,
- Partitioned,
- Encapsulated,
- Repository, and
- Pipes and filters.

Layered Style

Applying the design principles of modularity, abstraction, and provision of multiple levels of granularity can lead to a particular arrangement called a *layered style*. In a purely layered style, the system is decomposed into several hierarchical modules, each called a layer. These layers are then arranged in such a way that each is only a server for the layer or layers above it and a client to the level or levels below it. As such, a layer can request services from the layer or layers below and utilize these to provide more complex, higher level services in turn for a higher level client layer to it.

communications through the messages but only to the neizhboring layers, as oppose to encapsulated style communication is possible between any modules

A layered system may be of a stack style, in which each layer constitutes only one module, or more generally of a tree style, in which a layer may have more than one subordinate layer (see Figure 5.18).

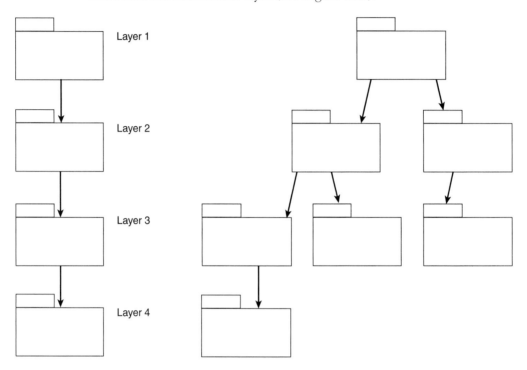

Figure 5.18
Layered architecture.

tree
style
stack
style

Layered style can be open or closed. An open layered style is one in which each layer can depend on more than just the immediate layer below it. A closed layered style is one in which each layer can only access the level immediately below it and no further. Both styles are frequently used, but the closed style is winning preference as it displays a greater number of good design principles (see Figure 5.19).

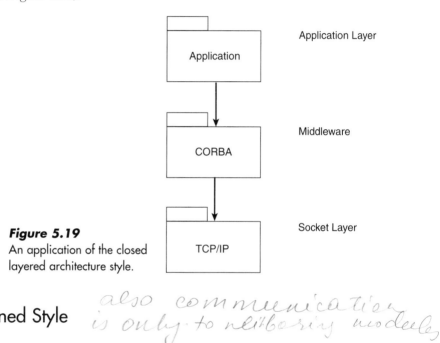

Figure 5.19
An application of the closed layered architecture style.

Partitioned Style

also communication is only to neiboring modules

We saw that the layered style utilized the client–server arrangement. Using a peer-to-peer arrangement and decomposing the system in such a way that its primary decompositions (submodules) are at the same level instead can lead to another style called a partitioned style.

In a partition style the system is decomposed into a set of subsystems. These subsystems, which are at peer level with one another, each become responsible for a different category or class of service.

Partitioning is widely used in the design of most modern operating systems where the system is decomposed along the various major areas of responsibility of an operating system, as shown in Figure 5.20.

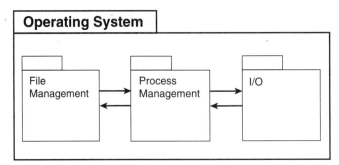

Figure 5.20
An example of the partitioned architecture style.

Encapsulated Style

The encapsulated style is in fact the implementation of the object-oriented paradigm as a design style. In an encapsulated style, abstracted modules communicate via messages in a client–server arrangement. Modules can contain many classes and the organization of classes within these modules or indeed the organization of modules within subsystems may be based on a layered or partition style, but it is usually a mix of both. This style lends itself well to distribution.

Repository Style

The repository style is one in which otherwise relatively independent modules or subsystems communicate by accessing and modifying a central backbone (usually a database or knowledge base) called a *repository*. The repository style architecture is widely used for management information systems or other similar systems that heavily rely on databases. It is an appropriate architecture for situations in which largely independent subsystems rely on a complex and large data structure. One advantage of the repository system is that control flow, and particularly concurrent data access, can be controlled relatively easily through the existence of the central repository. Control flow may be central or distributed.

The architecture of a modern compiler, shown in Figure 5.21, is a good example of a repository system.

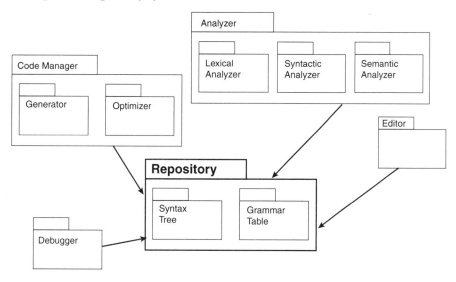

Figure 5.21
An example of the repository style.

Pipes and Filters Style

An established and interesting style, this architecture type uses the metaphor of pipes and filters. In this style, processing units are called filters through which data is piped. The output or outputs of one filter become the input of another. A well-designed filter should be designed to perform one very specific service, knowing only the format and content of its input data but nothing of the construct of any other filter. The UNIX shell is an example of this style.

This style should be distinguished from a layered style. In this style the filters are often at the same level of abstraction, whereas in a layered style each layer is at a different level.

Table 5.1 enumerates the advantages and disadvantages of each style just discussed.

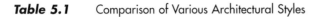

Table 5.1   Comparison of Various Architectural Styles

Advantages	Disadvantages
The layered style	
Low coupling	Difficult to design (layers not obvious)
Incremental testing	System performance
Relatively easy reuse	Hard to add functionality
The partitioned style	
Easy to design	Hard to design good partitions
Easy to test (staged testing)	System performance
Relatively easy to reuse	Partition proliferation
	Possibility of deadlocks
The encapsulated style	
Low coupling	Difficult to implement
High cohesion	Complex set-oriented operations on data
Independent testing	
Easy to design	
Very easy to reuse	
Easy to maintain	
System performance	
The repository style	
Set level data manipulation	Relatively high coupling
Easy to design	Difficult to test
Easy to add functionality	Difficult to reuse
Easy to test	Performance bottlenecks
Relatively easy to maintain	
The pipes and filters style	
Easy to maintain	Appropriate only for stream type operations
	Limited user interaction

140

Table 5.1   Comparison of Various Architectural Styles (Continued)

Advantages	Disadvantages
Easy to reuse	
Easy to modify (reconfigure)	Performance bottlenecks
Easy to test	Difficult to change data representation

Styles of Control

architectural styles

The preceding styles basically discussed the structural aspects of module relationships. Styles of control flow discuss patterns or sequencing or exchange of events between modules in a system. There are basically two styles, each with some variations: procedure-driven and event-driven. The procedure-driven style has two major variants: single-thread and multithread. The event-driven style also has two variants: broadcast model and interrupt-driven. We deal with each in turn.

Procedure-Driven Style

The procedure-driven style is the one in which control starts at the beginning of a main routine and is transmitted to other routines or objects as procedures are performed and decisions are made, sometimes involving a user. On completion, control returns to exactly where we left off in the calling routine. Thus, in a procedure-driven system, control remains with the program that executes to a decision point where external input is needed and then waits until that input arrives. The stack of calls and variables defines the system state. Once a routine calls another, the control returns to the calling routine on completion.

This model is simple and it becomes very straightforward to check control of flow through the system and its response to data input stimuli.

The major disadvantages are that using this model makes it very difficult to implement the message-passing paradigm, particularly between objects. The designer has to predict and "flatten" the complex, usually user-decision-dependent, and often inherently concurrent interaction between objects into a strictly predictable sequence of procedures and subprocedure calls, returns, and decision points.

Handle Exceptions

The second issue is particularly problematic because the designer has to convert each event into a procedure call and then predict and code the order in which these calls might be made. This is very limiting, if not impossible, with highly interactive systems.

Related to this issue is the problem of exception handling. Exceptions are best handled when their consequence can be localized. With a procedure-driven system, such localization is very difficult, as there is essentially one (sometimes a few) thread of control for the entire system. The extent of this problem might be helped by lots of checking of code but cannot be entirely overcome.

For example, Object A calls Object B, which in turn calls Object C to perform a service and return to B a value that it needs to complete a service for A. While reacting to the environment, a serious exception occurs in Object C, causing it to terminate. Object B, which is still alive and waiting, now has to be informed so it can potentially handle the situation. How would B be informed if C has been terminated? Additionally, even if B is somehow informed of C's demise, how will it handle the situation so that A is not adversely compromised? We (i.e., the designer) must "predict" and write program code to handle the situation.

Multi- versus Single Thread of Procedural Control

Procedural control may be single threaded or otherwise. In concurrent systems several independent or largely independent tasks might need to be operational at the same time. Under those conditions, each task has to have its own thread of procedural control. However, it is possible that one task may need input or interaction from another to continue. This intertask communication must be handled with care. Some programming languages (e.g., Ada) have inbuilt mechanisms called concurrency control managers or thread managers for this purpose. With many other programming languages, intertask communication is handled via the operating system. Either way this is a sensitive issue, as we need to be careful about many potential pitfalls, including deadlocks.

Event-Driven Style

This is the control model that rectifies many of the limitations of the procedurally driven style.

In the event-driven style system functionality, usually through objects, is attached to events. As an external relevant event occurs and is recognized by the system, the objects that are "interested" in that event are notified. They in turn react to the arrival of the event. Thus in an event-driven model we need a mechanism for each object (procedure) to register interest in a particular event and a monitor or system to receive and interpret events and to notify interested objects of that event's arrival.

There are several models of event-driven style of control. Of these we consider the two most important models.

The Broadcast Model

In this model, the objects register their interest in a particular event with a dispatcher system (usually a main loop that waits for events). Once that event occurs, the dispatcher system broadcasts the arrival of the event to those objects that have registered interest in the event.

An alternative is for the dispatcher to broadcast the arrival of all events to all objects and let those interested decide if they want to react to the event. In this style, objects do not need to preregister.

The advantages of the event-driven style are obvious. The biggest disadvantage is that the object originating an event (e.g., a user or another system object) has no way of knowing when or even if the event will cause a reaction. This is because any number of objects might be interested in that event (including zero). If no object is interested, the event will go unhandled; if more than one is interested, then there is potential for conflict. There is nothing wrong with more than one object being interested in an event, but it is the job of the designer to control as much of the potential conflict that might arise as possible. Sometimes these conflicts are logical and easily handled, but sometimes they are quite unpredictable.

Interrupt-Driven Model

In this style, used almost exclusively for hard real-time systems where timing and order are critical, a number of interrupts and their priorities are known to a central register. Once one occurs, control is transferred (sometimes via a hardware switch, sometimes through software) to the object with the responsibility of beginning to handle that particular interrupt.

Solving Specific Architectural Problems

General architectural styles for software design can be used exclusively or in combination to arrive at a particular solution. In most cases, a combination must be used as each segment of the problem lends itself to a particular architectural style. For example, we might have a system that is composed of three partitions. The first partition might have been designed as three closed layers, each of which might have a different architecture. The second partition might be a system of pipes and filters and the third a repository style architecture with encapsulated, event-driven clients around it.

However, there arise in software design specific, recurring problems that have recognized elegant solutions that have worked well in almost all similar situations before and therefore are likely to work well for the present, if they represent the same problem. It is impossible to present all possible specific design architecture patterns, but we cover a number of the more general ones. For more, the reader is referred to the design architecture and patterns literature.

[handwritten margin note: some known problems and well-developed solutions;]

Parallelism for Fault Tolerance

The basic idea behind this architecture is that system failure is a consequence of component failure. Thus by identifying the critical components of a system and taking steps to reduce the likelihood of failure in performing the task assigned to that component, we can reduce the chance of system failure. The traditional solution to this problem is to employ redundant components, like a second latch on a trap door in case the first fails, or a reserve parachute.

The same approach is taken in many fields of engineering. Mission-critical equipment, such as satellites, has a "hot stand-by" control mechanism to the primary control. Employment of an identical multiple redundant system (i.e., exactly duplicating or multiplicating the same design component) might be the answer to many problems of this nature. This might work with installing a duplicate metal shaft, an extra cable or plastic latch, or sometimes even a second identical electronic circuit, but it rarely works effectively in the case of software.

[handwritten margin note: redundancy in a mechanical system solves the problem but not in software]

The reason is that physical components usually fail for different reasons, at different times, at different places, and sometimes with different consequences. For example, if a metal shaft of a turbine breaks as a result of metal fatigue, it is unlikely that the backup shaft would also break at the same time, in the same location, and as a consequence of metal fatigue, because most physical systems fail as a result of wear or load.

With logical systems, this is rarely if ever the case. Software does not wear in the traditional sense. It sometimes behaves similarly to excess load as with physical systems, but the main cause of failure in software is logical, not physical. This means that if two components are identical, they will have the same logical defect in them. If a set of circumstances would cause the first to fail, it would most probably cause the second to fail in exactly the same way. Therefore parallelism using identical components is of limited use with software.

[handwritten note at bottom: parallelism of identical software components is (no) good!]

Even in many physical systems, the backup redundant system is not identical to the primary system. The manual override on many electronics systems is a good example. These are two systems with the same functionality but vastly different designs, so the likelihood of identical failure is reduced.

This is the approach usually taken with parallelism in software and is at the core of what is called the *N-version architecture.* In this approach, *N* different design versions are built—often by different design teams—based on the same specification. The assertion is that given the different design structure and implementation, it is unlikely that the different versions would contain the same defects leading to the same failures. Given this arrangement, usually all *N* versions operate in parallel and the output is sent to an output comparator that employs a comparison algorithm to reject the inconsistent output from the "failed" version, as shown in Figure 5.22.

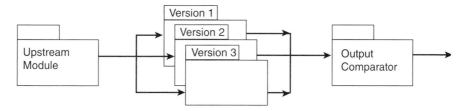

Figure 5.22
The N-Version architectural style.

Unfortunately, however, the assertion that different design teams producing different designs are unlikely to end up with products containing similar logical faults has been vigorously challenged (Brilliant et al., 1990; Knight & Leveson, 1986). Despite this, N-version style remains the favorite solution to the requirement for fault tolerance.

Feedback/Feedforward for Process Control

Process control is a very important and frequently occurring design problem for which computing is utilized. Process control occurs when a system is used to monitor the variables influencing a situation so that some output is kept at a specific point or within a specified range. The thermostat on an air conditioning system is a simple example of such a process control mechanism. Other examples are furnace control mechanisms for refineries or smelters, autopilot systems on aircraft, and cruise control on automobiles.

It turns out that to control the output of the process, one can take two alternate approaches, reactionary or anticipatory. In a reactionary or feedback system, the output of the process is examined using a mechanism called the controller or the comparator (see Figure 5.23). Should changes be necessary to bring or maintain the output in line with the desired range, input variables into the process are manipulated to effect the desired change, hence the terms *reactionary* and *feedback*.

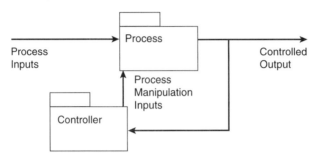

Figure 5.23
Feedback.

The problem with a reactionary or feedback system is that it takes time to react. There are situations in which by the time the output has been fed back and measures have been taken to manipulate the system to bring it back into control, the damage is already done. In such cases, we attempt to control the process by anticipating what change might be needed and making it in time for it to be effective. This is achieved through the feedforward style. In a feedforward loop, the input variables are fed through the controller. Rather than waiting for the output, the controller examines historical data and inputs that are good indicators of what the output behavior might be and anticipates and affects the required manipulation (see Figure 5.24). For example, the current rate of flow of gas or the air–fuel mix ratio might be a good indicator of what the furnace temperature might be in one minute.

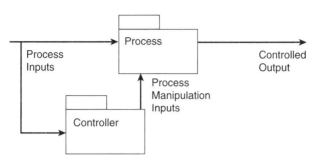

Figure 5.24
Feed forward.

The feedback and feedforward loop arrangements might both be considered specific cases of a partition style of architecture where there is a peer-to-peer separation of functionality (the process) and control (the controller).

Blackboards for Polling

A blackboard is referred to a repository with central control flow. As we said before, in a blackboard, the state of a repository is used to trigger the peripheral subsystems or modules. This makes blackboards an appropriate structure where there are alternatives in the peripheral modules to be activated based on the state of the repository (the blackboard). As the state of the blackboard changes, the appropriate peripheral modules respond, at times updating the repository and hence potentially changing its state. This change may then trigger another peripheral module and cause it to respond, and so on.

For example, in a game-playing system based on artificial intelligence, decisions about what move algorithm to invoke are usually made based on the state of the game board (stored as a blackboard).

MVC Partitioning for User-Interface Independence

MVC stands for model/view/controller. The MVC architecture is a specific utilization of the partitioned style employed to separate the various components of a system, as shown in Figure 5.25. The three partitions are as follows:

state of the system

- Model, which maintains domain knowledge;
- View, which handles the interface of the system to the outside world; and
- Controller, which handles the sequence interaction between the system and the user.

Alternatively, one might consider the model as a repository with the view and controller subsystems as peripheral modules.

The separation of the view and controller from the model allows the interface, which is based on the view and controller, to change independently of the model. In other words, one can alter the user interface without changing the underlying application logic, thus allowing for multiple interfaces. This change does not need to be total. The interface (i.e., the view and controller) is subject to minor changes and fluidity much more than is the underlying model. We look more at the MVC architecture when we consider design patterns.

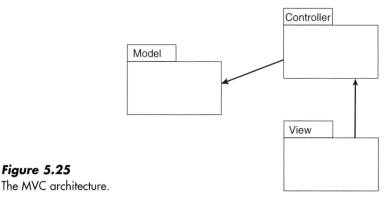

Figure 5.25
The MVC architecture.

Basic Steps for Architectural Design

There is no prescribed process for software system architecture design. In fact, design of anything is a process that is very difficult to understand and model, as it involves both procedural application of known facts and human ingenuity. Neither is design an isolated stage of the software process. It seems that the process of software construction involves tiny cycles of, "investigate a bit, analyze a bit, design a bit, code a bit, and test a bit," with wild, opportunistically motivated jumps all over the place. However, there are a number of activities that have to be completed before the design is complete. Nevertheless, most authors, taking an operational approach that takes into account a variety of system quality objectives, have provided heuristics and process prescriptions for the software design stage. Rumbaugh et al. (1990) listed these activities as they are typically applied to large software system projects. They prescribed the following:

- Organize the system into subsystems.
- Identify concurrency inherent in the problem.
- Allocate subsystems to processors and tasks.
- Choose an approach for management of data stores.
- Handle access to global resources.
- Choose the implementation of control in software.
- Handle boundary conditions.
- Set trade-off priorities.

Probably taking a lead from Rumbaugh et al., Bruegge and Dutoit (2000) provided an almost identical list of activities. They suggested the following:

- Identify design goals from the nonfunctional requirements.
- Design an initial subsystem decomposition.
- Map subsystems to processors and components.
- Decide storage.
- Define access control policies.
- Select a control flow mechanism.
- Identify boundary conditions.

Many other authors suggest basically similar steps, although in different order or using different terminology.

There are also those who take a usability approach to design (Preece et al., 1995). These authors usually suggest radically different approaches to design than those conventionally utilized. These approaches would be discussed in a course on HCI.

To arrive at a list of activities that define the design stage, we must have the quality requirements of our system in mind. Looking at system quality requirements for a software product, it therefore seems logical that:

- To achieve a high level of functionality, we need to focus on the functional requirements.
- To achieve high levels of reliability, usability, maintainability, and so forth, we need to focus on the nonfunctional requirements, and architecture is central to this.
- To implement concepts of good design such as modularity, as discussed earlier, we need to decide on an initial overall topology (physical and logical) and architecture.

Based on the overall architectural choices, we decide on subsystem organization, software–hardware mix, and data transport mechanism.

For each major subsystem, we need to evaluate and select appropriate architectural styles. In harmony with the architectural styles selected, we need to decide on strategies for persistent data storage and any and all middleware. Access and flow control policies must also be selected.

Availability of reusable software libraries that might assist with the economical implementation of the system must be considered and appropriate to-be-reused software must be earmarked. We need then to evaluate the design against all design criteria, stated or implied, particularly for overall feasibility, usability, reliability, and economy and make any necessary changes. Thus our list might read something like this:

1. Identify functional design goals from functional requirements.
2. Identify other design goals from nonfunctional requirements.
3. Decide on an overall coarse-grain design topology.
4. Identify subsystems, also those available already as reusable components or legacy systems, and decide on a decomposition.
5. Decide on hardware–software mix.
6. Decide on intersubsystem data transport mechanism.
7. Based on 4, 5, and 6, refine the overall design topology arrived at in Item 3 and assign subsystems to hardware platforms.
8. For each subsystem, evaluate and decide on an architectural style.
9. Based on the foregoing, decide on a strategy for persistent data storage and management.
10. Decide on choice and use of middleware and distribution software.

11. Decide on access control mechanisms and policies.

12. Decide on an appropriate control flow mechanism.

13. In view of all these items, and particularly Item 4, identify and earmark reuse libraries.

14. Evaluate and revise the design based on quality criteria and design goals.

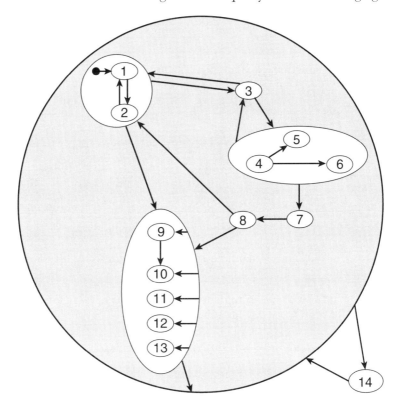

Figure 5.26
A potential depiction of the interinfluences in a typical software architectural design process.

I next describe each activity in turn.

Activities 1 and 2: Identifying Functional and Nonfunctional Design Goals

We must clearly define design goals in terms of the specific project at hand. One major difficulty often encountered is that design goals are stated too generally and without clear definition and success criteria. Therefore, for each quality factor important as a design goal (e.g., reliability; refer to Chapter 4 for a possible list of these and how they might influence the design) identify specific requirements as stated in the requirements document. Relate each to a design decision and define this relationship clearly. Include a measure or set of criteria for success.

As an example, in a missile system it is possible to place the trajectory calculation software (a) on board the missile, or (b) at the control base. Taking the approach suggested in (a) has the advantage of making the missile relatively independent of the launch base. All we need to do is transmit to the missile the coordinates of the target; the trajectory is calculated and adjusted by the missile itself. The disadvantage is that we need to place a sophisticated computer with lots of processing power and memory on board. Taking the approach suggested in (b) requires a lot of communication with the launch base, but will then allow the on-board system to be relatively simple by placing the trajectory calculation subsystem on the ground.

Now, the system requirements document says that the missile is to work in an environment where electromagnetic interference or interception might be a major issue. A generalization of requirement R-32-1 says that "The missile shall calculate and retain a correct trajectory despite electromagnetic interference typical of combat situations." Requirement C-1-1 says that "The overall cost of the system must be minimized." This creates a design challenge.

Leaving the trajectory subsystem on board will satisfy requirement R-32-1 but violate requirement C-1-1. However, the cost of specialized on-board hardware to accommodate the trajectory calculation subsystem is very high, whereas there is spare capacity at no cost at the launch base computer. What do we do?

Further study and referring the matter to the client ultimately results in a decision in favor of R-32-1. An architectural design decision, one of logical and physical topology, is made. We opt for a client–server arrangement with a point-to-point physical topology with the server hardware on board. We are not finished yet. We now need to ascertain—if not done during the requirement phase—what constitutes correct calculation and retention of trajectory and what constitutes a typical combat situation. Only if our design decision can support the system under these conditions is it correct. To do so we need to have knowledge of error margins allowed in the calculations to determine what is correct and what is not. We also need to assess the exact extent of electromagnetic stress or interception technology the client perceives to be at play and its impact on our systems. These considerations, in turn, have further hardware and software design (e.g., exception handling) ramifications.

Activity 3: Decide on an Overall Coarse-Grain Design Topology

A first pass through all important design goals (as per Activities 1 and 2) should give us a basic idea of the physical topology of the system and the technologies and major software and hardware subsystems involved. We need to depict this but be prepared to modify it based on further visibility.

To continue with our example, we now know that we have a ground station computer, a transmitter–receiver system, and an on-board computer. The on-board system is responsible for trajectory and altitude control. We need a subsystem to verify the correctness of communication between the two computers. The ground computer hosts the subsystems to handle abort or reassignment functionality, and so on.

Activity 4: Identify Subsystems, Also Identify Those Available Already as Reusable Components or Legacy Systems, and Decide on a Decomposition

Going down at least one level of granularity, we now need to identify the individual software subsystems. We can do so through the employment of good design principles as discussed earlier.

For example:

Maximize cohesion: Strive to have all components in the same subsystem be functionally related (functional or object cohesion).

Usually classes extracted from the same usecase or a closely related set of usecases yield cohesive subsystems.

Minimize coupling: Strive to have only a very small number of lines of communication or association cross between subsystems.

We can play CRC (at multiple tables). In this variation, each person represents an object and each table represents a subsystem. Strive to keep the interaction on the same table and communication between the tables at a minimum. Modify the overall design topology if need be.

One major influencing factor on process efficiency is reuse. At this stage, it is possible to take into account the possibility of employing reusable components or legacy subsystems. Depending on the balance of requirements, it may be prudent to allow the availability of sufficiently high-quality reusable components to influence the design.

In our missile system, we might decide that we will use a particular, already available, and certified communication subsystem or object library that has been successfully used in a similar system to take care of the receive and transmit verification. A command legacy system that might be used is also available.

Having arrived at a coarse-level topology and the principal subsystems of that topology, it is prudent to present each subsystem as an abstraction at this level of granularity. Among other benefits, this increases the understandability of the design. We can do so by abstracting each subsystem (including the legacy systems that might not be particularly modular; we see how this is done through the use of the façade or the adaptor design patterns) as if it were a single class with a given set of responsibilities (attributes and operations). For example, the communication verification subsystem might be presented as a class with the following operations only:

```
receive_communication (a_source)
transmit_verified (a_destination)
```

Activity 5: Decide on Hardware–Software Mix

An old Japanese proverb says "A person with only a hammer sees the entire world as nails." Similarly, not all design flexibility that can be implemented in software should be implemented. Often there is a decision to be made about whether to solve a particular problem with hardware or with software. We must decide on this at some stage.

For example, error checking may be done via a software program or the use of error-checking hardware circuits. We need to decide what is appropriate for our particular situation.

Activity 6: Decide on Intersubsystem Data Transport Mechanism

It is best to isolate data transport or transport control mechanisms into separate subsystems. This allows for flexibility when, for example, it is determined that one particular mechanism is not appropriate. This is particularly crucial when the system is highly distributed. For example, the communication verification and data transport facility of the missile system is best modeled as a separate subsystem.

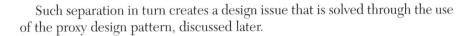

Such separation in turn creates a design issue that is solved through the use of the proxy design pattern, discussed later.

Activity 7: Based on 4, 5, and 6, Refine the Overall Design Topology Arrived at in Item 3 and Assign Subsystems to Hardware Platforms

Before we make any binding decisions regarding hardware platforms, we must review and refine the overall topology and ensure that the topological organization as presented meets our requirements, particularly that it is workable, efficient, and cost-effective. This might result in a number of alterations in our design.

Playing CRC, client presentation, and simulation are among the techniques that might assist at this stage.

Selecting a Hardware Platform

Selecting a hardware platform involves more than merely deciding on the make and model of a particular piece of electronics. It entails considerations such as these:

- Hardware certification and robustness: For example, is it tempested? Can it operate at below 200 degrees Kelvin?
- Hardware architecture: Is it vectorized? Is it fault tolerant at hardware level (redundant)? Is it a multiprocessor?
- Throughput and transaction processing capability, operating capability: For example, does it have multitasking and multiprocessing ability, what is the size in bits of the machine word?
- Availability of specific software on that platform: Particularly of operating systems, database management systems, compilers, and middleware.
- Cost.
- Build or buy.

Once we have decided on these matters, we must assign each software subsystem to a hardware platform.

In UML a hardware platform is depicted as a rectangular prism (a three-dimensional rectangle) with the subsystems it hosts depicted inside it. They are related to each other via arrows that depict communication between them, as shown in Figure 5.27.

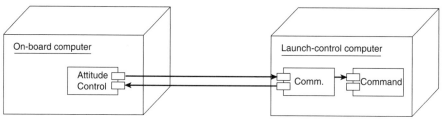

UML Deployment Diagram: Incomplete

Figure 5.27
Allocation to hardware platforms.

Activity 8: For Each Subsystem, Evaluate and Decide on an Architectural Style

It is now possible to consider an internal structure (an internal architecture) for each of our subsystems. If need be, we can continue the architectural decomposition one or more levels further before we are able to decide on what architectural style each module might have. As mentioned previously, certain design problems such as need for redundant operation or process control have established solutions. For the rest we would consider the best style or combination of styles that would fit.

Activity 9: Decide on a Strategy for Persistent Data Storage and Management

Here we need to decide how we are going to store persistent data, data that has to be retained between distinct executions of a system. In other words, data with a lifetime longer than a single execution. Data storage strategies depend on the nature of data. Choices are flat files, indexed files, relational databases, and object-oriented databases. Each has its own distinct advantages and disadvantages that have to be weighed against one another.

Flat files are simple abstractions provided by virtually all programming languages through the operating system. The data format is usually very simple (often only a sequence of bytes) and data manipulation must be handled within

156

the application. This is both an advantage and a disadvantage. The simple structure of the flat file allows for various tailoring of data storage and retrieval to suit a particular application. This can yield high levels of optimization, but given the simple structure of the file abstraction, much of the work of data storage, retrieval, formatting, and presentation must be explicitly done in the application, often in multiple places.

Flat files are therefore suitable in the following situations:

1. There is a stable, specialized, and simple data storage requirement. By stable requirements we mean that it would be unlikely that the content, format, volume, association, or type of data storage or retrieval is altered (e.g., a file containing a look-up temperature conversion table). By specialized we mean specific to one particular operation or application (e.g., historical sensor readings of a particular sensor, or a core dump file). Simple means that the information content of each unit of information stored is small. In other words, the data types are not complex (e.g., a simple number or a simple ordered pair).

2. The information unit granularity is coarse. This means that there are a large number of bytes required to store one unit of information (e.g., a map, an image, or a computer-aided design model).

3. Information density is low. This means that the information value of each unit is binary or near binary (e.g., an access log).

4. There is low requirement for complex set operations. This means that the information is retrieved and used in the same way or nearly the same way as stored. For example if a unit (a record) is written in one operation (*write_record(a_record)*) it is also read in the same way through a complementary operation (*read_record(a_record)*). There is no need to mix or group records or parts of records. The retrieval is at unit level rather than the set of units level.

The simple format of a file abstraction often allows for certain optimizations. The most popular of these is indexing, where special operations and structures are added to the file abstraction to provide an indexed file abstraction. Indexes make retrievals using the indexed variable much faster. An example is a telephone directory, where the file might be indexed on the last name of the owner. Use an indexed file when there is one or a very small number of preferred search variables.

Relational databases are at a much higher level of abstraction than the file. With this come certain advantages and disadvantages. The disadvantages are that direct and specialized manipulation is no longer easy, as there is a further level of abstraction, called the schema, between the user and the storage mechanism. This might constrain certain specialized, simple data storage requirements such as reading and writing of simple records. There is also a general speed and cost penalty that comes with adding layers of abstraction such as a database management system.

The advantage is that the schema introduces a set-at-a-time data manipulation capability. The database system takes over much of the effort in writing, retrieving, grouping, and presenting records.

Use a relational database when the following conditions exist:

1. There is a need for complex, often set-level manipulation of data units.
2. There is a need to accommodate and relate large tables of similar data.
3. More than one application, subsystem, or system needs to utilize the data, often concurrently. A relational database takes care of concurrency issues.

The relational model breaks encapsulation as it segregates data from operations on data.

Object-oriented databases are at a higher level of abstraction from the relational model, as they store objects and their associations together. The advantage here is that each element can now be treated as an object and manipulated as such. In addition, relationships and facilities that were not possible or were extremely difficult to model in the relational model now become possible. For example, we can mention very complex user defined types, inheritance, abstract types, and aggregate types. Use an object-oriented database when the following conditions exist:

1. The design model is object-oriented or object-based.
2. Tabulation is not possible, not permitted, or is at a significant loss of information, particularly abstract associations such as subtyping.
3. There are complex relationships (associations) between objects in the model.
4. The object sets are not very large.

Activity 10: Decide on Choice and Use of Middleware and Distribution Software

The choice of middleware may be dictated by corporate mandate, previous investment, or existing standards. Under these conditions we must conform to such choices. Otherwise, middleware decisions compatible with the rest of the design should be selected.

Activity 11: Decide on Access Control Mechanisms and Policies

Access control means deciding who can use or manipulate what part of the system and under what conditions. The first step in access control is to create a mechanism to identify each user or class of users so that the following statements are true:

1. Only those allowed to interact with the system can do so.
2. Those users who are allowed to interact with the system are known to the system.
3. Each user or group is protected against accidental or malicious access to the environments under their control by others.

This is called *authentication*. User access authentication is traditionally achieved via a "security pass" mechanism. This is a combination of a user name that identifies the user to the system and an item of information or pattern uniquely known or available to the user, such as a password, a retinal pattern, a fingerprint or voice print. The individualized access codes are usually encrypted and retained in an access repository, for example, the UNIX password file.

The access and authentication mechanism lends itself to a repository-based design style where the access data is retained in a repository and the authentication, encryption, and management modules utilize it.

Once users are known to the system, we need to determine which users should have access to various parts of the system. Again, this can be done through a central mechanism based on the repository style of design where a global access table acts as a repository. Every user and every operation of every class registers with this repository. Looking up this table allows us to assess whether a particular user has a particular access capability or not.

Alternatively, we can attach an access control list to each class. Where access is allowed, the list contains an entry for each user with respect to each operation of that class. Similarly, it is possible to have a list of all classes and operations therein attached to each user.

These access control mechanisms work well when access knowledge is known a priori. In situations when access rights are to be dynamically figured at run time, we need a different mechanism. We need to model the access as an independent association between the user and the target service or object. This is the same design problem as with the case of subsystem separation discussed earlier in the case of transport data isolation. The design pattern proxy that was of help there can also be used here.

Activity 12: Decide on an Appropriate Control Flow Mechanism

The choices are as presented before. These are basically procedure-driven or event-driven. For concurrent systems, multithreaded control flow must be considered. Particularly in the case of event-driven systems, it is prudent to segregate and localize the control flow mechanism from the rest of the application. This assists with flexibility and maintainability of the system. In conjunction with the MVC style of architecture, the command design patterns can be gainfully utilized to achieve this segregation in an orderly and flexible fashion. We discuss this later.

Activity 13: In View of All These Items, Particularly Item 4, Identify and Earmark Reuse Libraries

In a mature development environment, reuse is actively practiced. Capability and schedules are planned in full view of the potential for reuse of existing intellectual property. By this we mean more than just reusable code. It also includes analysis patterns, application frameworks, design modules, reusable subsystem-level components, and reuse class and other code libraries. It is prudent to consider reuse throughout the process, but at this stage we must consider specific reuse libraries that are to be used. Issues of compatibility and availability become important.

Similarly, it should be noted that reuse libraries are to be maintained and enhanced; consideration of how this particular project may contribute to the reuse library should be given here. It is sometimes even prudent to rework the design into a more general and less optimal version if doing so yields greater

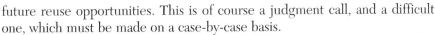

future reuse opportunities. This is of course a judgment call, and a difficult one, which must be made on a case-by-case basis.

Use of abstract types, genericity, and employment of established architectural styles and design patterns goes a long way toward assisting with future reuse.

Activity 14: Evaluate and Revise the Design Based on Quality Criteria and Design Goals

We now must evaluate the design as it stands. This does not mean that we refrain from evaluation throughout the other activities; it just means that an explicit evaluation is called for at this stage.

Design is by nature an iterative activity. It is micrograined. It requires methodical technical knowledge and discipline and artistic, inspired, opportunistic ingenuity to work hand in hand. This means that many aspects, if not every aspect, of design influence many other aspects, if not every other aspect, explicitly or otherwise. The designer must constantly ask these questions:

- How is this decision going to help make this product (this overall design) a better product?
- What are the consequences of making this decision? What, if anything, must change?
- Will the balance of these changes lead to a better situation, that takes us closer to our objectives?
- How can I show that this is the case?

These questions help lead the designer through the design process. They are part of the personal design evaluation process. However, overall evaluations at logical points in the process will also be helpful.

Design Reviews

Design evaluation must be made against specific criteria. These must directly relate to both the quality criteria expected of the product and the specifically stated or implied design goals, which themselves should be a specific interpretation of the product quality expectations. It is best that these design quality criteria are measurable and stated a priori, including a statement of the conditions under which such evaluation would take place. From a client viewpoint, a good design document should be adequately correct, complete, and consistent. From a practical viewpoint, a design also should be cost-effective and comprehensible.

There are several techniques of design evaluation based on the nature of the design itself, including those outlined in the following sections.

Formal Correctness Proof

formal specification

This occurs when there is a design formally derived from a formal specification. Under these circumstances, we can prove the correctness of that derivation against the specification. This activity demonstrates the correctness, consistency, and to a degree the completeness (as much as the specification is complete) of the design, but does not go far in demonstrating implementability, cost-effectiveness, and understandability.

Design Review

This is a process in which the design is put through a peer-review process. Design review processes (often simply called design reviews) are specific software process techniques that are conducted in accordance with a preagreed defined process that has been demonstrated to be effective. Process descriptions and templates for conducting such reviews exist in the literature and are often excellent examples of good process specification. During a design review the reviewers might evaluate the design product, the design process, or both. Both are usually considered.

Design evaluations may be considered corrective defect management techniques, and they are discussed in Chapter 6.

Architectural (System) Design Documentation

As design architecture decisions are made, they should be documented in the form of diagrams, models, notes, mathematical expressions, and so on. Once an overall design architecture is obtained and stabilized it must be coherently documented by bringing all the interim documentation together and ensuring that it represents the current situation. As mentioned before, this document must be correct, consistent, and complete. It should also be concise and comprehensible.

There are many templates available in the literature. One such format is provided in Table 5.2.

Table 5.2   System Design Template

1. Table of contents and list of figures and tables
2. Preambles, caveats, and conditions
3. Description and definition of special notation used, values of constants, and so on
4. Executive summary
5. Synopsis of system
6. Current situation and environment (which the system is to improve)
7. Operating environment and conditions (e.g., specialized hardware, security, support)
8. Outline of process to be followed
9. Current high-level architecture and system description
10. Proposed high-level architecture and system description
11. Expanded system architecture:
    11.1 Overview
    11.2 Identifying functional and nonfunctional design goals
    11.3 Physical and logical topology and major subsystems
    11.4 Subsystems descriptions and subsystem architectural styles
    11.5 Storage mechanisms and data transport
    11.6 Distribution and middleware
    11.7 Access control
    11.8 Flow control
    11.9 Reuse issues
12. Postamble or concluding remarks
13. Appendices
    13.1 Listing of important usecases
    13.2 All other diagrams and supporting materials
    13.3 Glossary of terms and definitions
    13.4 Traceability to the requirements specification document
    13.5 Index
    13.6 References

Object Design

System architecture design depicts a solution in terms of a set of interacting subsystems and modules, but it is insufficient in detail to be implemented. Each subsystem or module now has to go through further design steps before there is enough visibility (information) for the system to be successfully implemented.

This stage of the process, often called module or object design, therefore concentrates on the individual object or class or closely interrelated sets of classes, often within the same module or subsystem. In other words, the role of each subsystem has now to be precisely specified. Module design therefore usually entails the following stages:

1. Composition of an architectural decision or style in terms of collaborating objects.
2. Selection, modification, and utilization of existing reusable artifacts.
3. Modification of existing design to accommodate the intended reuse.
4. Modification of design for future reusability.
5. Class specification.
6. Design model improvement.

Activity 1: Composition of an Architectural Decision or Style in Terms of Collaborating Objects

The architectural styles we have selected and our other system design decisions are simply abstractions. They cannot be implemented. For the gap between our solution as an idea and code that might run on a computing platform to come closer, we need to provide further information by adding detail to our design. Design decisions must be presented in the form of artifacts that have a direct implementation time counterpart. In other words, we need design artifacts that can be directly translated into programming artifacts.

Fortunately, to take this step we do not have to reinvent the wheel every time. In many cases, generalized solutions or patterns for solving specific problems of a given nature have been previously discovered, utilized, validated, and documented. We can reuse these design solution patterns.

Design patterns are individual classes, or more often a small group of associated classes, arranged in a particular configuration to solve a specific category of design problem. These patterns and templates are generalized, so they apply to a relatively large number of situations that have a logical concern in common. For example, whenever there is a need to encapsulate an artifact and give it a simple, well-defined interface, we can use the façade design pattern.

Now the artifact encapsulated might be a legacy system; a specific subsystem (perhaps non-object-oriented) that is to be reused as part of our new system; a utility (e.g., a compiler) that has a sophisticated multimodule construct but needs only to provide a simple interface; a file system or a database facility; and so on. The artifacts are various, but the design problem is the same and has the same design solution.

The fact that design patterns are general is advantageous because they can be applied to a wide variety of design situations. However it should be noted that there is no guarantee that a given pattern is necessarily the optimum solution for a given specific situation. Actually, the mere fact that these patterns are general solutions make them possibly less than optimal for an individual situation. However, they usually are reasonably good solutions that have been demonstrated to be effective. Most have been shown to assist in the reuse process and contribute positively to design efficiency. Their use, of course, is never mandatory.

Generalized solutions are not limited to the level of design patterns (fairly low level and small grained). It is possible to employ a generalized solution at a much higher level, such as the application or subsystem level. These are usually called *frameworks*.

A framework is a complete or partially complete reusable application or subsystem-level solution that can be customized to produce specific applications. Again, the same dichotomy between generality and optimality that existed in the case of design patterns exists here. Frameworks can be of two types:

Utility Frameworks

Utility frameworks are used to solve a specific, well-defined, often problem-domain-independent technical problem, such as distribution or database connectivity. These are sometimes called middleware. Java RMI, Microsoft's DCOM, and various implementations of CORBA are good examples of such frameworks.

Enterprise Application Frameworks

Enterprise application frameworks are domain-specific partial or complete solutions in a particular enterprise or technology environment such as retail, financial management, data and telecommunications, and transport logistics. Before an enterprise application framework can be utilized, we must ascertain its degree of fit into the overall solution. Often modifications are required.

In addition to design patterns and frameworks that are artifacts composed of interassociated classes and objects, there are also other reusable artifacts that might be useful in the design process. Components and class libraries are also important.

Components

Components are specific, often already-compiled individual objects (instances of classes) that are designed and implemented to deliver a very specific service as described by their contracts. They are the software equivalent of the IC chip. They may be put together, possibly with some new objects written to compose an application.

Class Libraries

Class libraries are tools or building blocks to construct an application. They are usually not application oriented (i.e., interrelated to compose an application) but utility oriented (i.e., interrelated, usually hierarchically, to be used across a number of application domains to address a specific type of need). Class libraries are usually passive (i.e., they are just a set of classes interrelated through inheritance without any control flow or message passing between them). They do not do anything, but they can be used to build things that do things. Java foundation libraries, GUI libraries, and so on, are good examples. Readers familiar with design patterns have noticed that these patterns are of a general nature. They solve general design issues but are not specific design solutions. They are an accumulation of design wisdom and experience depicted in terms of interacting general object or class casts and not specific objects or classes.

However, for a specific design to be workable or for a specific architectural style or design decision made in the context of the application domain to become a solution, the collaborating objects must be specific objects that include all the necessary solution-specific domain knowledge and semantics. Use and interconnection of design patterns alone does not suffice in composition of an architectural decision or style in terms of collaborating objects.

Many of these objects and classes would belong to the problem domain and have already been identified as part of the specification model. Others would be solution-time objects and classes identified as being necessary to make the design work (e.g., container and object structure classes). Others would be interface and boundary classes such as classes that allow the composition of the user interface (e.g., a Motif or Windows application programming interface [API]). These classes would need to be interrelated in such a way that not only satisfies the overall design decision and architectural style, but more important, form a precise and implementable (in a programming environment) design solution, solving that portion of the original application problem that it intended to solve. These classes mentioned earlier may all be written as original classes. However, some may come from reuse libraries, some may come already interrelated in the form of an enterprise application or utility framework, and still others may be components. It is the role of the designer to put all of them together (maybe through the use of appropriate design patterns) so the original problem is solved and the solution is in keeping with the earlier architectural and design style decisions; it is robust; it satisfies the principles of good design (e.g., modularity, etc.); and it is workable, elegant, and cost-effective. A design review or playing CRC would help in making such determination.

Activities 2 and 3: Selection, Modification, and Utilization of Existing Reusable Artifacts and Modification of Existing Design to Accommodate the Intended Reuse

In a proper design process, most components of these two activities should have already taken place in that the design team should have an excellent idea of the frameworks, class libraries, or components they would be using in connection with the design. One important factor, however, is the recognition that the selection of reusable components is not and should not be made in isolation and independently with respect to each module's design. For example, unless the application specifically requires otherwise, an entire system should use only one GUI class library, so reuse should be coordinated.

Reusable artifacts are seldom usable right out of the box. There is usually a need for modification of both the reusable artifact and the existing design for them to work together. Simple subtyping and a number of design patterns would assist at this stage. Some examples are the adapter, the bridge, the command, the decorator, the façade, and the strategy patterns (Gamma et al., 1995). In attempting to achieve such fusion, the designer often needs to trade off between keeping the reusable component's API unchanged and keeping the existing application objects both abstract and general as well as effective in solving the immediate problem. This is a difficult task, but this is where adherence to proper design rules, use of genericity and generalization, use of design patterns such as the ones mentioned, and abstinence from use of implementation inheritance help.

Activity 4: Modification of Design for Future Reusability

Reuse is great when one is reusing an existing artifact, but someone has to produce that artifact in the first place. A responsible designer is always conscious of this fact, and if higher priority requirements do not prevent it, strives to come up with a design in which future opportunity for reuse has been maximized. Some basic rules are important to observe:

1. Always strive to provide an abstract interface and concrete implementation subclasses.
2. As much as possible, use subtyping only and refrain from use of implementation inheritance.
3. Use genericity whenever plausible and possible.
4. Use a uniform naming convention across the entire API.
5. Separate the domain objects from interface and utility objects.
6. As much as possible, ensure that the classes, and particularly your abstract interfaces, satisfy only a minimum set of requirements adequate for the definition of a given class. Let all specialization be by the way of inheritance, aggregation, or through design patterns such as the decorator.
7. If at all possible, do not use multiple inheritance.

Activity 5: Class Specification

At this stage we are ready to shift our attention to each specific class. The design so far can be determined to be workable, in principle. The various design reviews and CRC sessions would have determined the necessity or redundancy of the various classes and associations worked into each class. What remains, at least for the moment, is deemed necessary. The design is now described in terms of a number of classes only, with associations and other artifacts absorbed into each relevant class.

The next step is to increase the visibility of each class to the degree that it would be possible for it to be implemented in a programming language. We need to do the following:

1. Identify and specify the type for each and every class, attribute, procedure call parameter, or function return.
2. Decide and justify the visibility of each and every attribute and operation.

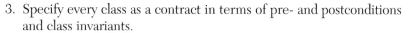

3. Specify every class as a contract in terms of pre- and postconditions and class invariants.

4. Specify all algorithms for all methods, for every class.

5. Identify, specify, and incorporate exceptions and means of handling each.

6. Identify and add each and every missing (should have been there already) or to-be-added (as a consequence of Steps 3 and 4) attributes and operations.

7. Perform a design review and ensure design validity and verifiability. Make all necessary changes.

8. Harvest for reuse and submit to a reuse library, potentially modifying some structures for better reusability.

The design should now be ready for a final review and implementation.

Conclusion

In this chapter we discussed the basic principles of good design and how one might incorporate them to produce a robust and high-quality design. In Chapter 6, we cover techniques for evaluating a design from the viewpoint of identifying defects.

Chapter 6

DESIGN DEFECT IDENTIFICATION

In Chapter 5 we concentrated on principles and techniques of good design as a context for prevention of design defects. However, given that very few processes are perfectly applied or completely error-free, it stands to reason that an object-oriented design and its corresponding document might contain defects, despite our attempts to the contrary at design time. These defects must then be identified and, if cost-effective, removed. This chapter therefore deals with the concept of design defect identification.

Design Defects

We saw earlier that in software engineering parlance the term *design* refers to both the design document and the intellectual content of that document. As such, in our treatment of design defects we must be mindful of the defects in the document in addition to the syntactic, conceptual, and technical defects of the design itself (i.e., the intellectual artifact).

We start with the design artifact first, postponing the treatment of the design document until later in the chapter.

Like any other artifact, a design may contain defects of omission and commission. Defects of omission in a design usually stem from lack of provision in design for a particular requirement, functional or otherwise. This means that there is no design feature that fulfills the given requirement, for example, when there is a requirement for password encryption but the design does not allow for encryption of the password. In this context, partial or incomplete design provision for a given requirement is not deemed a defect of omission, but one of commission.

Defects of commission can be categorized into a number of types:

- Incompletion: This defect occurs when a requirement is catered for but the design feature does not completely cover the requirement.
- Error: This is when in an attempt to cater for a requirement or part thereof, the design contains information or representation that is unable to fulfill the said requirement; for example, when the requirement is for a first-in-first-out organization but the design utilizes a stack instead of a queue.
- Ambiguity: This is when the design or design feature may be interpreted in multiple ways, not all of which represent the same solution to a requirement.
- Redundancy: This is when a design feature is present to cater for a requirement or part of a requirement that is already fulfilled through existing design features.
- Superfluicity: This is when a design feature is present but a corresponding requirement does not exist to make the presence of such design feature necessary or useful.
- Inconsistency: This is when two or more aspects of the design cannot logically coexist.

Adequate care must be exercised for defects in all these categories to be identified and removed if necessary.

Identifying Defects in Design

A design is represented through a number of diagrams and descriptions. An object-oriented design is usually depicted through a representation of its structural, causal or state sequential, and transformational models. There are usually therefore multiple models and diagrams that together depict a given object-oriented design. In a design depicted using UML, one might find one or several class diagrams and package diagrams depicting the structural aspects of the design; several sequence diagrams or collaboration diagrams depicting the dynamic and causal aspects; and context diagrams, activity diagrams, Object Constraint Language (OCL) statements, flow charts, mathematical expressions, and formulations or pseudocode depicting the transformational aspects. These are diagrams that depict the design, or the output of the design process. It stands to reason that all these diagrams must possess the following characteristics. They should be:

- Necessary. Without each, the design would be somehow deficient.
- Syntactically correct. They should correctly follow the UML language provisions.
- Internally robust. They should not contain any of the defects of commission or omission mentioned in the previous section.
- Clear and easy to read and work with.
- Mutually consistent.

In addition to these output-oriented diagrams, designers also work with a number of other diagrams and artifacts that might be collectively called in-process-oriented, input-oriented, or requirements-oriented. Among these one could mention usecases, usecase diagrams, context diagrams, architectural and topological diagrams, network diagrams, and so forth. These diagrams and artifacts do not form part of the final design of the software but are useful in deriving them. Needless to say, as sources of information for design, these artifacts also must possess a number of characteristics. They too should be:

- Necessary. They should depict a requirement or part of a requirement or feature without which the outcome of the design would suffer from internal defects.
- Internally robust. They should not contain any of the defects of commission or omission previously mentioned.
- Clear and readable.
- Mutually consistent when interrelated.

Note that the relationship of the latter category is with requirements of the system, not with its design. This means that although the characteristics enumerated for both categories read as the same list, their meanings are slightly different. Additionally, there has to be traceability and consistency between the two sets of artifacts. In other words, the artifacts in the second category (in-process artifacts) must underpin the design artifacts.

Now that we have identified the nature of defects that can occur and therefore the desirable characteristics in the design and design support diagrams, the question becomes: How do we determine whether such characteristics are extant?

There are basically two categories of techniques: design simulation and design inspection. Design simulation occurs when the design is exercised through a procedure by which the behavior and characteristics of each of its components is replicated or imitated by a role player, usually a person. Through such an exercise, defects, deficiencies, inconsistencies, and other design defects can be identified. Playing CRC with the design models as the basis is one such simulation technique.

Design inspection occurs when experts canvas through the design artifacts (diagrams, etc.) specifically to locate defects. They are usually guided by a number of inspection process artifacts such as checklists, reading rules, forms, and so on.

Design Simulation

The most popular and probably most cost-effective technique of design simulation is anthropomorphization of the design. Playing the CRC game can be of utility here.

The technique used is in a general sense the same as the one described in relation to the defect management of specifications, in that the game is played in the same way. The major difference is that this time, the CRC cards represent design artifacts and not domain abstractions. In other words, we are simulating a design by each participant playing the role of a given design-time object. Details of the CRC technique have been adequately described elsewhere in this book and further in other sources (Beck & Cunningham, 1989).

Design Inspection

As the name implies, design inspections are a form of inspection. Inspections, along with walk-throughs and reviews, belong to a category of defect management termed *static approaches* or *static evaluation*.

At times the terms *inspections*, *walk-throughs*, and *reviews* are used interchangeably (e.g., design review); they are in fact three distinct techniques, with only inspections having detailed defect identification as a primary objective.

An inspection may be applied to a number of different artifacts of the software process. These could be requirements, designs, code, or test suites, to name a few. Irrespective of the artifact being inspected, the process has a basic and uniform overall form that is modified based on the artifact that is to be inspected.

The basic procedure calls for the formation of an inspection team, and collection of a number of documents including the artifact or artifacts that are to be inspected; input documents and artifacts that provide an informational or semantic basis for the inspection; process guidelines (e.g., descriptions of reading techniques) that lead the members of the team through the inspection process; and various checklists, forms, and templates that allow the methodical conduct and recording of the findings.

On distribution of these documents, each inspection team member usually works independently to canvas through the artifact seeking to identify issues. In this context, an issue is defined as what the inspector deems a potential defect. Such issues are recorded and the process continues until no further issues can be detected. As implied earlier, the inspector is aided in this process by a number of inspection tools or aides such as checklists, process descriptions, and templates.

It is customary that once all inspectors have completed their independent inspections of the artifact, an inspection meeting is held. At this meeting all inspectors come together to review and discuss the product and each and every issue discovered by each of them when working independently. During this meeting, decisions are reached with respect to each issue, and they are either discarded as unimportant or accepted as a defect and therefore recorded and reported.

There has been much controversy with respect to the necessity or the form of inspection meetings. Opinions on this range from those who emphatically believe in the necessity of such meetings, to those who feel that a virtual (i.e., Internet-based) inspection meeting is as effective as an actual one or even more effective, to those who believe them to be completely unnecessary. The advocates of inspection meetings usually base their arguments on the assertion of synergy: During an inspection meeting new defects emerge as a consequence of the process of debate and collaboration that would otherwise go undiscovered. Opponents claim that this is largely not the case, and even if it were, the economies of time and resources spent on such meetings do not justify the incremental costs.

The number of people involved in a given inspection is also under dispute. Recommendations range from two to about seven, but four or five is the norm. Ultimately the choice of how many should participate in a given inspection also seems to be a function of number of other factors such as the criticality of the application, resources available, size of the artifact, pollution rate (defect density expected), the nature of the artifacts (e.g., is it a design or a segment of code?), and software engineering team size. This process is discussed further in Appendix C.

Inspecting Design Artifacts

In a typical inspection of an object-oriented design artifact, there are usually three to five inspectors involved. These inspectors are expected to be experienced designers with sufficient knowledge, skill, and background to identify a wide variety of design issues and problems. They are assisted in this endeavor by a well-defined process, usually available to them as a process description document, parts of which might be individual process descriptions or templates for each role. These describe the general activities that are to take place (see Appendix C). They might also be given guidelines to lead them toward what exactly to look for. These, in contrast, describe the potential defects that might exist or areas where they are more likely to be (see Appendix C). These guidelines may be prescriptive or descriptive. Prescriptive guidelines are usually called *reading rules*. They describe a step-by-step process of what to look at, how to do so, and how to identify anomalies. The Computer Science department of the University of Maryland, in conjunction with the Fraunhofer Institute-USA, has developed one such set of prescriptive rules for object-oriented design inspection (Travassos et al., 1999).

Descriptive guidelines are usually called *checklists*. They describe typical defects that might happen, and serve as a reminder for the inspector to look for similar flaws in the design being studied.

There is no reason both a descriptive and a prescriptive set of guidelines might not be used, or even one that is a mixture of both. In fact, it has been observed that in the absence of the availability of such guidelines, expert inspectors utilize an approach that is a combination of both.

With regards to the artifacts that might be inspected in relation to a typical object-oriented design, we might have the following:

- One or several class diagrams
- One or several sequence diagrams (usually several, but might not have been included in the presence of collaboration diagrams)
- One or several collaboration diagrams (might not have been included in the presence of sequence diagrams)
- One or several state diagrams

- One or several activity diagrams
- One or several algorithmic descriptions, algebraic formulations, OCL paragraphs, or equivalent transformational descriptions
- One or several module (package) diagrams
- One implementation diagram

The preceding list constitutes the design artifacts themselves. In addition we should have a number of design support artifacts such as the following:

- Context diagrams
- Usecases
- Usecase diagrams
- Architectural and topological diagrams
- A set of well-formed and defect-managed requirements

We use the latter set to examine certain external aspects of the artifacts in the former set.

To understand this process, we need to describe the intent and content of each of the artifacts in the first set and how they relate to the artifacts in the second set, and also to other artifacts in their own set. A good understanding of these artifacts and their essence can assist in identifying deviations that lead to defects.

Class Diagram

A class diagram depicts the structural view of the design model. In other words, it shows the model from a "what?" perspective; that is, what elements exist and what is the static or structural relationship between those elements? A class diagram therefore shows the individual classes, the objects of which are to collaborate for the system to be realized, the static relationships between them of the following kinds:

1. A is a kind of B. This is called inheritance in general and generalization in the UML parlance.
2. A is composed of B or, more generally, B is a part of A. This is called the whole–part relation in general and aggregation–composition in UML.
3. A's instances map to B's instances. This is called association.

Inheritance can be singular, multiple, or repeated. Inheritance depicts multiple levels of behavioral or descriptive granularity. In its recommended form, inheritance or generalization depicts the type–subtype relationship wherein the behavior of the subtype is an extension of the behavior of the parent type. There is type substitutability. For example, a mouse is a subtype of mammal and whenever we need to represent a mammal in general, a mouse can be used. A quarterly interest account, however, is not a type of daily interest account and cannot be substituted for it. Inheritance can also be multileveled.

Multiple and repeated inheritance can be utilized in many designs, as long as the target language accommodates these. Multiple inheritance occurs when a class inherits from more than one parent at a time, in other words, when a class has more than one immediate parent. Repeated inheritance occurs when a class inherits from the same parent more than once and in different contexts.

The whole–part relationship implies multiple levels of structural granularity. For example, one behavior of a given class can be taken as a context in itself and designed in terms of smaller grained collaborating classes. These lower level collaborating classes form the aggregands of the higher level class. For example, an ATM object may have a responsibility *read_card( )*. If we now took this operation as a context in its own, and say, wrote a number of usecases to determine what is involved in reading a card, we would soon identify a number of objects such as a card reader, a monitor, a keyboard, and so on. These are now lower level aggregand classes to ATM. Similarly, if we now concentrated on the individual behavior *read_password( )*, which might be a responsibility of the card reader aggregand object (as opposed to the ATM as a whole), we might find even finer grained classes such as card acceptor or ejector, magnetic strip reader, register, and so on, all lower level classes to a card reader, which in turn is lower level to ATM. Therefore aggregation may be multileveled.

There is dispute about what exactly an association is. Some methodologists argue that being a structural feature, an association is a mapping between an instance of a class and another instance of that same class (unary association) or with another class (binary association) or set of classes (n-ary). N-ary associations when n is greater than 2 are very difficult and often impossible to implement directly, so a design that contains a higher than binary association should be reevaluated.

Others argue that an association is actually the abstraction for the path through which messages are sent between objects of the classes for which a link needs to exist so that such communication may take place. Under such an assumption, an association can possess direction, whereas as mapping such directionality is meaningless. UML allows directional associations, therefore implying the latter definition of what an association might be. At the same time, such an assumption would make an association a dynamic artifact akin to the direction depicted of the occurrence of an event in a sequence diagram or the message transfer path between individual objects of a collaboration diagram. If we were to accept the second interpretation of what an association is, one can argue that either associations or sequence and collaboration diagrams would be at least partially redundant. In other words, if an association is a depiction of the system's dynamism, it should not be included as part of a structural model.

The designer needs to decide what paradigm is to be uniformly followed with regard to associations throughout a given design and abide by that decision. Classes themselves are template representations of the objects that might be instantiated from them. They are best thought of as representing a type of which—if possible—an object is an instance. I say *if possible* because not all classes are meant to be instantiated. Classes representing abstract types that collect and represent knowledge about parentage but do not represent a concrete type might not and are not instantiated. These classes are called *abstract classes*.

A class has a name that acts as a cognitive handle to identify the type represented by that class. Objects of a class are described by features described in that class. Features represent what an object of a class is and what it does. The former are referred to as attributes and the latter as operations or routines. Attributes may be thought of as questions about the structure or the state of an object, whereas a feature or operation may be thought of as what an object of this particular type can do for others (other objects that might ask for services). In this regard object orientation can be deemed a microscale client–server scheme. The UML depiction of a class has the name in the top compartment, attributes in the second compartment, and routines in the third compartment. At design inspection time, all three compartments must exist and be adequately populated. A good rule of thumb is that by design inspection time all the routines in the third compartment of a class should be depicted in following one of the following formats:

```
Create-X(init:Type)
Set-Y(value:Type)
Get-Y( ):Type
Do-W(parameters: Type)
Remove-X( )
```

where *X* is an object, *Y* a value, and *W* an operation.

There is also an optional fourth compartment defined in UML that contains the business rules, conditions, invariants, and the like that might impact the design model. As a good rule of design, such a compartment should not exist at design inspection time for any of the classes, as the assumption is that all such rules, conditions, and invariants have been operationalized and depicted as routines in the third compartment. Of course, certain target programming languages (e.g., Eiffel) that explicitly allow such artifacts may make the design exempt from this rule. In addition, UML allows a number of other adornments such as notes, qualifiers, and so on, on a class diagram. By the same token, none of these—or at most very few—should still remain in the diagram by the time it is ready for design inspection. Why? These items represent design decisions still to be made. If they still persist, they indicate that the design is not yet complete. For details of the syntax of UML class diagrams, please refer to appropriate sources (Rumbaugh et al., 1999).

Thus in a well-formed class diagram, each class must be represented not only by its name, but also through its features, which should contain all the necessary type information: argument types, return types, and so on. All routines should be in the form of short operations such as *create( )*, *get ( )*, and *set ( )* (discussed earlier). All business rules, invariants, pre- and postconditions, or other conditions should be made operational; that is, they should be expressed as routines or sets of routines. Public operations should have a public or some appropriate accessible scope, whereas all attributes (state information) in most cases should be made inaccessible (private scope) to clients. Routines that do not feature in the contract or profile of a server class (those routines that do not define what the object does or, in other words, those routines that do things for the object itself and not directly for the clients of the object) must be restricted in scope (usually private scope). All the public operations must correspond to at least one equivalent and identically named event or message in at least one sequence diagram or collaboration diagram. They should also be represented as activities to be performed within some state of at least one state diagram that corresponds to the state transitions of an object of the type this class represents. We discuss these latter diagrams at length later.

Inheritance should be as much as possible of the type–subtype form; in other words, generalization. A good test of generalization is to ask whether the subclass can be substituted for or can represent or act as the parent class. If the answer is negative, there is no subtyping. In a well-formed inheritance hierarchy, all the like features are collected and pushed up the hierarchy and all the dissimilarities are pushed sideways to form sister subtypes. During design inspection we must examine whether a given leaf class can be logically constructed through inheriting from parent classes in such a way that all its capabilities are correctly and adequately represented. Any class that has one or more of its features deferred is called an abstract class. All abstract classes in an inheritance hierarchy must be clearly marked. In UML this is done by italicizing the name of the abstract item.

Aggregation implies structural or compositional hierarchy. During the design inspection process the inspector must ensure that all aggregate classes define and declare all the aggregand classes that compose them as their features. Cardinality information would indicate how many of the aggregand objects need to be declared in the aggregate. See Figure 6.1 for an example.

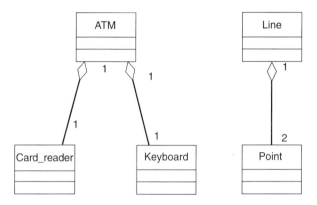

Figure 6.1
Aggregation.

In Figure 6.1, the two aggregand objects composing the ATM need to be created within the ATM. The ATM must know that only one of each is to be created, hence the 1..1 cardinality. For the diagram on the right, the line object has to know that it is defined by exactly two points. Whether the line creates the two points or the two points exist prior to the definition of the line is a design issue that needs to be considered carefully. In fact, it can be argued that the arrangement on the right is inappropriately modeled. The relationship between the two endpoints (as it is implied here) and the line is not best described as aggregation (composition) but as a relationship of A as defined by two specific Bs. Although a line is composed of many points, including the endpoints, the former is also defined by the two latter objects. This is a different relationship, as shown in Figure 6.2.

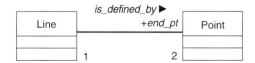

Figure 6.2
A better depiction of the line–point relationship.

Associations must be clearly labeled with a name and an indication of what direction in which to read the name. All higher than binary associations must, by design inspection time, be reduced to an equivalent set of binary ones. All one-to-one associations should correspond to a pointer to another class (a call with a parameter). One-to-many associations should correspond to a pointer to a container class such as an array, a stack, a set, a tree, and so on. Many-to-many associations might have been resolved to an indexed one-to-many association or left as many-to-many, in which case it may correspond to a table class or a set of ordered pairs of correspondence. It is important that at design inspection time no UML qualifiers or higher than binary associations remain. These are unimplementable modeling abstractions and must be resolved before a successful implementation is attempted.

In terms of overall characteristics sought in a well-formed class diagram, the following heuristics might be used:

1. Unless strictly subtyped, inheritance hierarchy should not be too deep, usually three or four levels at maximum. This depends on the application and circumstances.

2. None or very few classes on a class diagram should be named as roles (e.g., class DRIVER, EMPLOYEE, etc.). Such artifacts in reality represent an association between classes and not a single class at all. For example, an EMPLOYEE is a role depicting an association between a PERSON and a FIRM. DRIVER is best described as the diagram displayed in Figure 6.3 and not a single class.

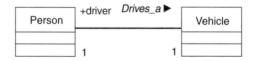

Figure 6.3
A better depiction of the driver situation.

3. There should be no controller type classes in a class diagram. Sometimes called *God classes*, their existence indicates poor understanding of object-oriented principles and the concept of distribution of control. A design that contains controller type classes would be in need of major rework.

4. Ensure that the lines of associations between classes are either all directionless (depicting mappings) or all with direction (depicting conduits of message passing). Particularly, there should be no directionless

associations left in a design class diagram that largely uses the directed graph approach.[1] This only indicates ambiguity, uncertainty, and incompletion of design.

Sequence Diagrams

Sequence diagrams are the diagrammatic representation of the sequence of events that occur within the system for an end-to-end task to be accomplished. It therefore depicts the causal, dynamic, or sequential aspect of the system. It answers this question: In what order or in what sequence? If the events and the time segments in between them were subject to measurement against real time, a sequence diagram's intent could be attempting to answer this question: When? A sequence diagram depicts the sequence of events between objects and not between classes. The latter would be meaningless.

A sequence diagram is usually closely related to a corresponding usecase. The relevant usecase captures the sequence to be traversed for the task to be accomplished in text, whereas the sequence diagram depicts the same thing diagrammatically.

Given this correspondence between usecases and sequence diagrams, it is important to mention that a primary purpose of the sequence diagram is to separate concerns. A sequence diagram does this in two ways. First, it separates the dynamic concerns from the static ones depicted in a class diagram and the transformational ones depicted in activity diagrams and other transformational artifacts. Second, it allows us to focus on a single end-to-end interaction with the system with one starting point, a singular path, and a singular outcome with no ifs, buts, cases, and conditions. It is unfortunate, therefore, that we see frequent misuse of sequence diagrams when users try to force things such as branching, conditionals, and so on onto an artifact that was created to separate out these concerns. These concerns are important, but they should not be depicted in a sequence diagram. If one has a conditional, one has at least two paths to consider with possibly different outcomes. This is not a single end-to-end interaction but several (at least two). It is best, in my opinion, to employ a separate sequence diagram to represent each case. This course of action might imply some diagramming duplication, but many years of experience and particularly significant gains in its ability to yield more reusable designs make it well worth the effort. This is much more so the case now with the availability of automated modeling and design tools than at any time before.

---

[1] Of course, this is not a necessary requirement for nondesign class diagrams such as requirements models.

In a typical sequence diagram we depict the sequence and direction of events as they occur between objects. Rectangular boxes labeled by the name of the individual object and the class to which it belongs represent these objects. There may be more than one object of a given type participating in a sequence of message exchanges. Each object has a lifeline from which events emanate and to which events are incident. The direction of the arrow is significant, implying who the client is and who the server is in this particular exchange. Each event should therefore correspond to an operation of the class of which the server object is an instance. Simultaneity (in the language of UML concurrency) or parallelism is implied when multiple events emanate at the same time from a client that might be incident on different objects (Events 6 and 7 in Figure 6.4). Chaining or succession is implied when multiple events emanate from the same object at different times but without an intervening incidence of a message (Events 3, 4, and 5 in Figure 6.4 are chained).

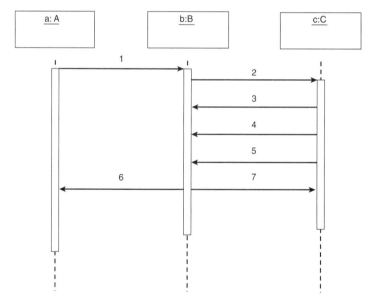

Figure 6.4
Chaining and synchronicity in a sequence diagram.

As a general rule, however, it is best that for each object (each lifeline) incident and emanating arrows alternate. Each arrow representing an event must carry a label that should correspond on the one hand with the event that is to take place (or the event occurrence that has been requested by the client) and on the other with the name of the operation that is to fulfill it. Such an operation needs to be one of the operations of the class to which the server object belongs. In a correct sequence diagram at design time,[2] every event has to correspond with an operation of the same name and footprint in the class representing the server object in the class diagram (see Figure 6.5). This is an instance of external validation.

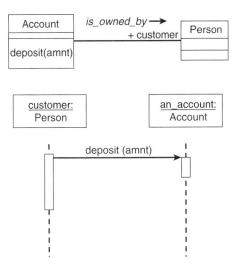

Figure 6.5
Correspondence of events and operations.

On certain segments of each lifeline there might be superimposed one or several long and thin rectangles (see Figure 6.5) called *activation regions*. These highlight the part of the life of an object during which it has focus.

There are other adornments and details with respect to sequence diagrams. For a better understanding of these diagrams and the details of the syntax please refer to relevant sources (Rumbaugh et al., 1999).

Collaboration Diagrams

Collaboration diagrams are also the diagrammatic representation of the sequence of events that occur within the system when an end-to-end task is accomplished. They also depict the causal, dynamic, or sequential aspect of the system. Similar to sequence diagrams, they also indicate in what order or in what sequence the events occur. Again, similar to sequence diagrams, collaboration diagrams also depict the sequence of events between objects and

---

[2]Such a stringent requirement may not be necessary for sequence diagrams drawn prior to design time, for example, as part of requirements modeling.

not between classes. Many users also attempt to misuse collaboration diagrams by trying to force them to represent situations for which they are not designed. Chief among these is the case of trying to depict conditions (ifs and cases). In short, a collaboration diagram represents largely the same information as a sequence diagram that can be deemed a possible substitute for it. The reverse, however, is not always the case, as in some situations a sequence diagram carries more information than a collaboration diagram. However, in situations when sophisticated causal and dynamic situations do not arise (e.g., a blackboard situation), a collaboration diagram might be sufficient.

A collaboration diagram contains icons for the individual objects that participate in the sequence of events. Any object that passes or receives a message from another object is connected to it by a line segment. Two arrows (one back, one forward) depict the direction of each message. Once all the objects to be connected together are so connected, the sequence of messages is placed against each arrow depicting the direction of the message in the order in which they appear, as shown in Figure 6.6. Simultaneous messages are labeled by letters of the alphabet (e.g., 6a, 6b), but the order of the alphabet is not significant.

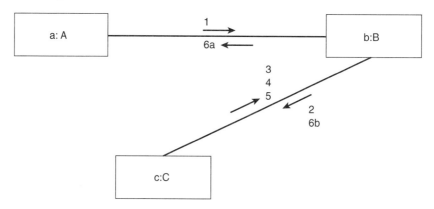

Figure 6.6
Collaboration diagram depicting chaining and synchronicity.

Each number representing an event must carry a label that should correspond with the event that is to take place (or the event occurrence that has been requested by the client) and with the name of the operation that is to fulfill it. Such an operation needs to be one of the operations of the class to which the server object belongs. As with a sequence diagram, in a correct collaboration diagram at design time, every event has to correspond with an operation of the same name and footprint in the class representing the server object in the class diagram.

There are other adornments and details of a collaboration diagram. For a better understanding of these diagrams and the details of the syntax please refer to relevant sources (Rumbaugh et al., 1999).

State Diagrams

Although still dealing with the dynamic aspects of the design model, state diagrams deal with the events that occur within the lifetime of a given object (or module) and how these events alter the state of that object or module. Therefore, unlike sequence and collaboration diagrams that deal with message passing between a collection of interrelated objects, state diagrams deal with the messages that are passed to a single object and how that object reacts to such stimuli.

It immediately follows from this argument that a complete state diagram of an object should depict the incidence of all events that are significant to an object and all the reactions of the object to every such stimuli. This means that all the events drawn on a state diagram (depicted as arrows) should correspond to events incident on all representations of that object from all its potential clients under all circumstances. The states drawn on a state diagram (depicted as circles, ovals, or rounded-edge rectangles) should contain all the capability that the object possesses to respond to such stimuli (see Figure 6.7). In other words, the actions implied by the event arrows should correspond to client calls made on the object and state activities should correspond to the operation that is invoked to fulfill that requirement.

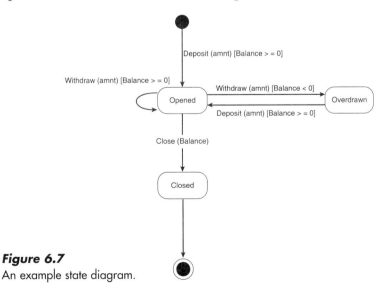

Figure 6.7
An example state diagram.

In practice, however, including all events and state activities would be impossible because not all demands or behaviors of an object can be predicted. When we deal with a system or object that displays some behavior, we expect some interaction with it. These interactions could fall into three categories:

1. Normal cases: What is predicted and expected of the object, the totality of which defines the role of the object. For example, an ATM exists to—among other things—provide the ability for customers to withdraw cash. This is expected and predicted, and is thus a normal case.

2. Non-normal cases: What the system or object is expected to be able to handle, even though the situation is one for which the system is not created. Banks do not install ATMs so that customers can check whether the card they are holding is a debit card by inserting it into an ATM. However, an ATM should have the capability to identify and reject inappropriate cards. The requirement for the ATM to recognize and reject an invalid card is a non-normal case.

3. Abnormal cases: When there is a situation that has been neither predicted or expected of the object to be able to handle.

It is the existence of this third category that makes the job of creating complete state diagrams impossible. There are an infinite number of these abnormal cases, and we could spend forever trying to predict and preempt them. The irony is that the number of cases correctly included and implemented has a direct relationship with the reliability of the system. Thus missing or omitted (or not predicted or included) state transition cases directly contribute to defects of reliability. A corresponding argument can be made within this very same context with regard to usecases, sequence diagrams, and collaboration diagrams. A given usecase or an individual sequence or collaboration diagram is meant to depict one end-to-end case. If the number of such cases is truly infinite, how many of these diagrams do we develop for a given design? The answer, of course, depends on the resources and the degree of criticality of the application, among other things.

As depicted earlier, a state diagram is made of arrows depicting events and nodes depicting states. At design inspection time, each arrow should be properly labeled by a statement that corresponds identically to the operation that is being invoked (it must match with corresponding ones in the sequence and collaboration diagram and also the class diagram). The types, footprint, and name must be checked to fulfill this requirement. Each state may or may not be named and would also contain a number of operations—called activities—

which are methods that must be executed by the object to fulfill the requirements of the client. Alternatively we can look at activities as invocations of messages that this object sends to other objects.

Guards or conditions may be placed on certain actions corresponding to a decision made as a consequence of the value of a parameter on the parameter list of the routine (in the class diagram) that implements that action (in the state diagram) or the return value of a function. Therefore it is possible to combine a number of actions with a similar nature but different outcomes into one and then control the differences of the outcome through a parameter or through the value returned. The need for such action arises when two or more similar usecases or variant sequence diagrams are combined. For example, when a vending machine calculates change, three conditions might arise (change = 0, change < 0, change > 0). Depending on the condition herein we must select a different target state, but the operation to calculate change is the same.

Actions might be synchronized. Depicted by a thick short bar (or a narrow rectangle), synchronization comes in two types. With fan-in synchronization, the bars indicate that all actions incident on the bar must take place before the event incident from the bar can be triggered. A fan-out synchronization indicates that on arrival of an action, a number of actions are triggered at the same time (see Figure 6.8).

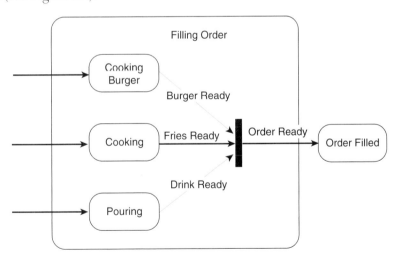

Figure 6.8
Synchronization using synchronization bar.

Although technically not necessary, a synchronization bar in either form can be depicted as a coordination (synchronization) state using the state notation. They are a convenient shorthand (see Figure 6.9).

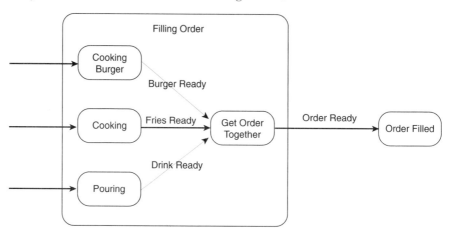

Figure 6.9
Synchronization using synchronization state.

Each arrow (event or action) must emanate from some state and should also land on a valid state. This immediately implies that all state diagrams must be closed loops or networks, but this is not always the case. Two special states are defined in UML (as in all other state diagram conventions): START and END. These two special states allow for the construction of open state diagrams. The astute reader would have surmised that the START node's activity should correspond with the creation or initialization of the object and the END node's activity with its removal and possibly garbage collection.

The following forms should be avoided unless specifically needed in an unusual situation.

Null Diagram (START–END)

Figure 6.10
A null diagram.

Null diagrams, as shown in Figure 6.10, should not occur, but if they did they would indicate the creation and removal of an object before it performs any useful work. Given this lack of utility, if null diagrams are included they signify a problem to which the designer has to attend.

Trap State

One of the most frequently occurring forms to avoid is the trap state. As Figure 6.11 indicates, a trap state is one that may be entered but never exited (Overdrawn).

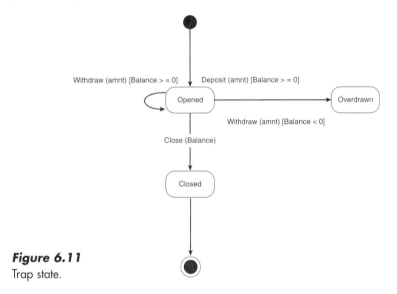

Figure 6.11
Trap state.

Such a state usually indicates a problem with the design, but this is not always the case. There are occasions, rarely, when an intentional trap state is designed so that the system halts and cannot transition to any other state lest there is an undesirable consequence. Usually however the designer should be wary of trap states.

Tightly Circular

A tightly circular or reflexive form occurs when a limited number of events lead to a limited number of states in a circular or reflexive manner. For example, in Figure 6.12, the collection of states S1, S2, and S3 and events E1, E2, and E3 forms such a loop.

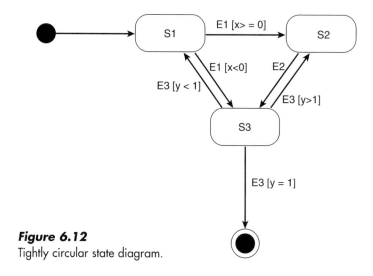

Figure 6.12
Tightly circular state diagram.

Tightly circular states are usually a sign of poor design at that locality. The tightly coupled states are either the same state or there is occasion to break the tight coupling by introducing other intervening states. These intervening states would represent other cases that might differ in the way they enter a succeeding state. Occasionally, however, a tightly circular set of states is intentionally introduced. There should be good reasons for such introduction however.

Disjoint States (Two or Several Independent Streams)

Largely independent streams are a sign of concurrency and parallelism, but completely independent streams are often signs of poor or flawed design (see Figure 6.13). Completely independent streams indicate that an object does more than one thing, which is an explicit violation of the requirement of cohesion. If an object lives a dual life, perhaps we need two objects.

Filling Order

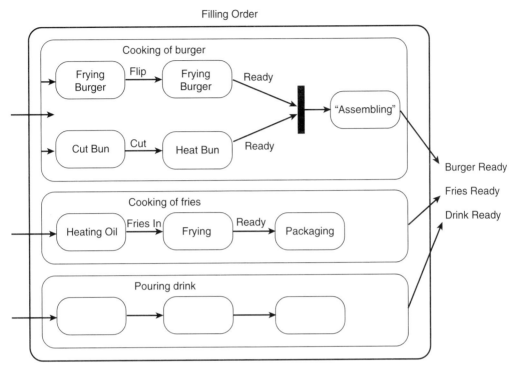

Figure 6.13
Disjoint states.

Deadlocks

A deadlock occurs when the next transition from a state cannot logically take place. A trap state is a special form of a deadlock. A deadlock halts the progression of state transition until it is resolved. Very rarely do we intentionally introduce deadlock situations into our dynamic models. Even when we do, there is usually a better solution to the problem. Usually they are a strong indication of a design flaw that needs to be rectified.

Conflict

A conflict occurs when a transition from a guard or synchronization point cannot logically take place. For an example, see Figure 6.14.

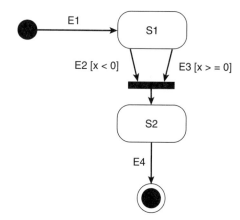

Figure 6.14
Conflict.

In Figure 6.14, state S2 cannot ever be reached because events E2 and E3 can never coexist. As both are required for the transition to take place, the system will be in conflict. Another form of conflict is the nonexclusivity conflict in which guard conditions for a transition are not disjoint (see Figure 6.15).

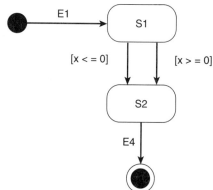

Figure 6.15
Nonexclusivity conflict.

God, Hub, and Minion States

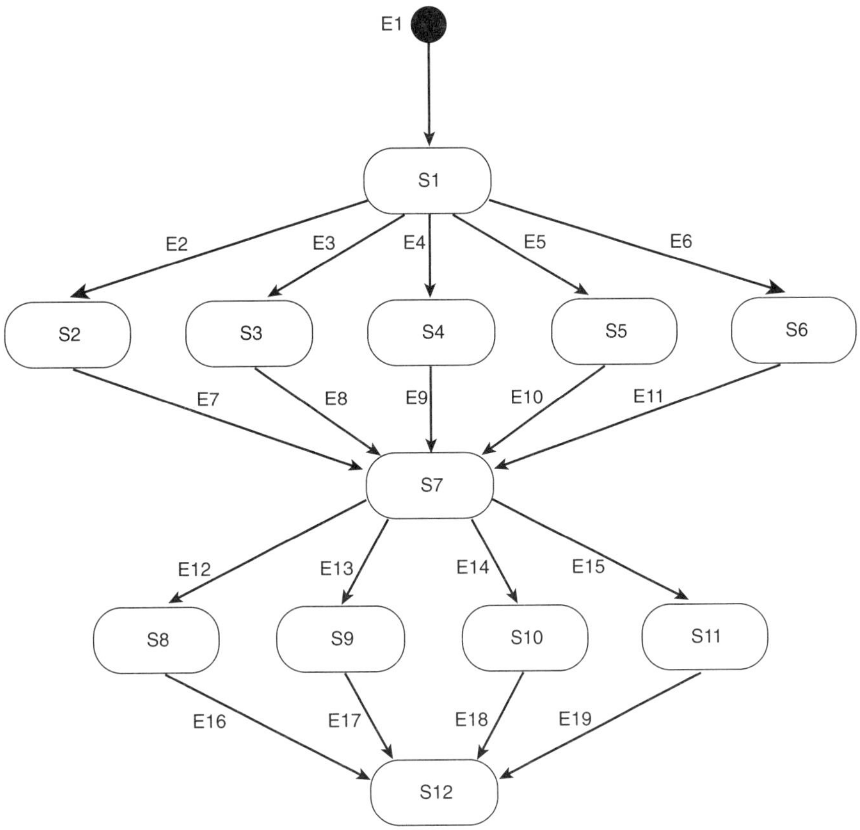

Figure 6.16
God, hub, and minion.

God states are those states that have a very small fan-in to fan-out ratio. As a general rule, the number of events incident on a state should be roughly the same as those emanating from it. When a situation arises in which a state has an event triggering it but then the activity of the state produces many events, that state is probably controlling too many other objects or features. It is omnipotent or at least polypotent. This is contrary to both the rule of maximizing cohesion—as the state, and therefore the object, is doing too many things—and that of minimizing coupling—as the state, and therefore the object, is communicating with too many other objects. This is displayed in Figure 6.16.

The reverse, the minion state, is the one that has many events incident on it and only one or a few states emanating from it. This situation is also in violation of the rule of minimization of coupling and probably in violation of cohesion rules.

The hub state is probably the worst. This is a single state that has many independent or nearly independent events fanning in and many independent or nearly independent events fanning out. The state is an arbiter or a controller, a hub of dynamic control if you will. This situation is undesirable because it violates virtually every rule of good design. See Chapter 5 for a description of these rules.

Activity Diagram

The stated purpose of an activity diagram is to depict the processing activities within a class (Rumbaugh et al., 1999). In other words, activity diagrams portray the transformation view of the design model. This view can be at any level of granularity. At the top level, where it depicts the entire system as one activity, it is usually called a context diagram. Multiple levels of abstraction may be portrayed using activity diagrams (as is true for state diagrams or even class diagrams). It seems, however, that activity diagrams are usually utilized to show the overall transformations in a system or process at a high level of abstraction. They can, for example, be used to show the high-level transformations of a software development process. Figure 6.17 is an activity diagram depicting the requirements workflow of the RUP.

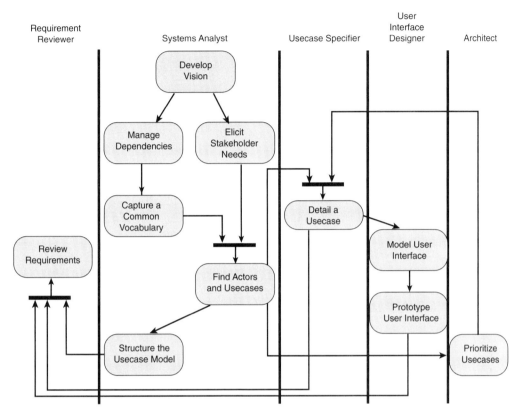

Figure 6.17
An activity diagram.

As such, used in this fashion, activity digrams tend not to be tremendously useful in design evaluation because they contain only high-level abstract information usually deducible from other aspects of the model anyway. They can also be used as a notation to describe the low-level transformations of a particular activity, action, or routine. In this sense, they are a useful transformational description that is essential to design (unless they are replaced by an equivalent modeling artifact such as transformational descriptions). In this latter sense, they are more akin to a flowchart. They depict the flow of control through the arrival of an information-carrying action that invokes a particular activity or process. On completion of this process, the output action or actions (subject to conditions and carrying information) become input actions to subsequent process nodes.

Conditions are shown as small diamond shapes with the possible conditions clearly labeled on the arrows that are incident from it. The condition to be tested may be written out as a guard label on the arrow coming into the condition diamond or within the body of the diamond. Synchronization is also available and works the same way as in state diagrams.

An activity diagram may be partitioned into *swim lanes*. These are areas of the diagram where activities and actions are semantically, logically, or operationally closer. Swim lanes are separated by vertical lines and must carry a label identifying them on the top. It is permissible for transitions to cross these lines, but the aim is to keep the crossing to a minimum.

As stated before, when activity diagrams are used in design they find greater utility as a descriptor of low-level behavior of individual actions, activities, or routines. In other words, they describe the transformational or algorithmic nature of the leaf-level operations and functions that together describe higher level states, events, routines, and ultimately objects. In the absence of such facility or its equivalent, the multiple levels of granularity would continue ad infinitum.

When dealing with an activity diagram in design, therefore, aim for it to describe a simple, leaf-level description of an algorithmic nature or a simple leaf-level process or operation that would not gainfully be divided into simpler, lower level modules. As a rule, we go to lower and lower levels of granularity in our models, along the way developing lower level usecases, sequence diagrams, state diagrams, and discovering aggregand objects until we are satisfied that our objects are described by operations that are simply understood or programmed. These operations, which should correspond to their equivalent actions, messages, and activities in the dynamic model, must now be described algorithmically; that is, operationally. An activity diagram can be used to do this. Therefore a number of observations or heuristics may be used when evaluating activity diagrams of a design:

1. An activity diagram should clearly describe the algorithm of the operation it represents in a language that can be directly translated into a programming language.

2. An activity diagram must be syntactically correct; that is, it must be composed of the elements that the UML vocabulary and grammar of such a diagram allows.

3. An activity diagram should for the purpose of design and at design evaluation time depict the low- (leaf) level simple operations and not abstract, complex, high-level ones.

4. Consequently an activity diagram should be simple and contain a small number of swim lanes, preferably one or two, and a small number of nodes and arcs, preferably 10 or fewer of each. An overly complex activity diagram is an indication of an operation that is trying to do too

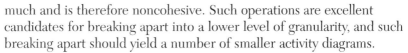

much and is therefore noncohesive. Such operations are excellent candidates for breaking apart into a lower level of granularity, and such breaking apart should yield a number of smaller activity diagrams.

5. An activity diagram should be devoid of trap transformations unless the transformation is an end transformation, a destructor. These are transformations that have inputs but no output.

6. An activity diagram should be devoid of conflicts and deadlocks.

7. An activity diagram should have no God, hub, or minion transformations.

Transformational Description

We stated earlier that at some stage, the designer needs to describe the transformational behavior of the leaf activities, actions, or other class routines. Drawing appropriate activity diagrams might be one such way. There are, however, other ways, such as writing pseudocode. OCL is a language within UML that lends itself to this purpose and presumably is the preferred language to use for this purpose according to the standard. However, there are many alternatives. Other pseudocoding languages, many formal languages (e.g., Z), truth tables, flowcharts, and mathematical equations are some of these techniques. Irrespective of which technique is used, the seven requirements stated earlier must be observed with all these techniques.

Module or Package Diagram

Module or package diagrams use artifacts called packages to group and organize model elements that are related semantically, logically, or otherwise.

They are therefore a structural diagram and are denoted by a rectangle with a small tab attached on the top lefthand corner. This tab usually bears the name—if any—given to the package. Abstract packages, the internals of which are not yet shown, might have their name written on the main rectangle as opposed to the tab (see Figure 6.18). Beware that such diagrams are of no use at design evaluation time, as by that stage the contents of packages and their interrelationships must be clearly and maximally indicated.

Figure 6.18
A UML package.

Packages may be thought of as higher or metalevel objects. They are, in other words, huge objects containing many lower level ones with their interactions clearly marked. In a way, this makes their existence—at least philosophically—rather redundant, because we somewhat arbitrarily choose our initial level of granularity to identify our initial set of objects, and we have seen repeatedly that an operation of a class at one granularity may be deemed as a class diagram at a lower level of granularity, then a package may be deemed and modeled using a class diagramming notation. Packages may contain lower level packages to the extent that the system can be thought of as the top package containing several lower level ones, which in turn may contain still lower level ones, and so on. In this sense the top package is the system object or a depiction of an instance of a system class that has the name, attributes, and behaviors we associate with the system in its entirety. Therefore it is a class after all. Nevertheless, package diagrams are used, and from the perspective that they indicate that the intention of the modeler has been to stop thinking of the abstractions at this level as classes or objects anymore, they might even be useful. They certainly are a good housekeeping tool whereby we can organize our collection of classes in a model and work toward minimizing coupling between the packages and increasing cohesion within them.

As such, a package diagram at design evaluation time must depict an abstraction of classes. Some packages must relate to some others. In other words, no isolated package should ever exist. The contents of each package must be clearly and adequately described as lower level class diagrams.

Implementation or Component Diagram

Despite their name, implementation diagrams are in fact design artifacts. They show what part of the design would be logically implemented with respect to other software components. It is therefore the diagram that captures, in UML, the logical topology of the software.

A component is depicted as a rectangle with two smaller rectangles projecting from its lefthand side, one on top of the other, as shown in Figure 6.19. The name and type of the component should be denoted on the component.

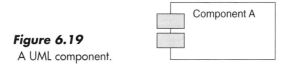

Figure 6.19
A UML component.

Components represent executable units and should exist at run time. They can be aggregated to form an aggregate component, as expected. Development-time relationships may be denoted between component diagrams using dotted arrows and appropriate stereotype labels.

Deployment Diagrams

Deployment diagrams are design diagrams that depict the configuration of processing resources with respect to the software. In other words, they depict the physical topology of the system.

Deployment modules, representing individual processing nodes, are depicted as projections in two dimensions of a rectangular prism (a box). The name of the node and its type are denoted on the box (see Figure 6.20). Communication and physical and logical links between deployment modules are shown as straight, solid lines. Compile-time, link-time, run-time, and support relationships between components that are attached to a particular deployment node may be denoted using dotted arrows and appropriate stereotype labels.

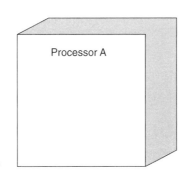

Figure 6.20
A deployment module in UML.

Of course, we must ensure that in a deployment diagram at design evaluation time, all components are accounted for and appropriately allocated. We
must ensure that the diagram depicts the physical topology and the architecture intended for the system in the first place and that such an arrangement is
actually possible and efficacious. In short, every class has to be included in a
package, packages must be arranged as component diagrams, and each component must be attached to a relevant deployment node.

The foregoing was a description of the various artifacts that might be
produced during the process of object-oriented design and some of their
desirable properties. During design evaluation, for example, doing a design
inspection, one can utilize these and similar principles as a guideline to seek
and detect design flaws and defects. In Appendix C, a design inspection checklist based on these principles is provided as an example.

Identifying Defects in a Design Document

We mentioned that our task in this chapter is twofold: (a) to provide guidelines
for design defect identification, and (b) to provide guidelines for the generation of defect-free design documents. Even if we assume a design is free from
defects, it does not follow that the document that depicts or presents it is
defect-free. We need to identify certain characteristics that together would
represent those of a good design document and evaluate a design document
against them. Fortunately, such a set of characteristics was developed and presented at the end of Chapter 5. What remains is to evaluate a design document
with those characteristics in mind. A design document should be correct, consistent, complete, concise, and comprehensible.

For a design document to be correct, it should depict the correct design;
that is, it should depict a design for the system for which it purports to be a
design document. Additionally it should contain correct diagrams and descriptions, as previously described. It should also be devoid of grammatical,
spelling, and other linguistic or referential errors.

Consistency in this context means that the document should contain information that is internally and mutually coherent. In other words, all elements
of the design document must logically coexist.

Complete means that all the necessary diagrams, models, narratives, lists,
indexes, appendices, and references are included and that each of these enumerated elements are internally complete in themselves. In other words, the
document must be a sufficient description of the design.

Concise means that the document reflects the necessary design information and nothing more.

Comprehensible means that the document is easy to read, understand, learn, and utilize.

Various organizations have developed and published templates for design documentation. Before one of these templates is used, it should be subjected to evaluation based on its ability to support the listed characteristics. In doing so, however, one should be careful that some of these characteristics are those of the design document instance and not of the template. For example, although a template might assist in ensuring correctness, it cannot guarantee it. If the designer omits a given requirement, no design document template can assist in identifying such a defect.

Conclusion

This chapter dealt with the corrective aspects of design defect management. Having started from a basis of defect prevention in design (Chapter 5), here we extended the idea that no design defect prevention technique or set of techniques may be deemed perfect. Therefore, design defects are to be expected in even the most meticulously designed product. As such, design defect identification is a necessary aspect of a good defect management strategy. We then went on to see that as the term *design* can be used to refer to both the design intellectual artifact and also to the document that captures and presents such an artifact, likewise design defect identification should also be considered a dual activity. We therefore seek to ensure that both the design and the document that presents it are examined for the purpose of identifying defects. It turns out that these defects are quite different from each other.

In Chapter 7, we deal with techniques that might be used with relation to the implementation of software, including code defect identification techniques such as testing and code inspection.

Chapter 7

PROGRAM DEFECT IDENTIFICATION

In Chapters 5 and 6, we discussed a number of principles and techniques of good design and design evaluation. However, it stands to reason that an object-oriented program and its corresponding document might contain defects, despite our attempts at design or programming time to the contrary. These defects must then be identified and, if cost-effective, removed. This chapter therefore deals with the concept of program defect identification.

For a variety of reasons, including those enumerated in the previous chapter, defect prevention even through utilization of formal methods, reuse, patterns, or good programming techniques cannot suffice as the only means of defect management. For example, it has been shown (Ghezzi et al., 1992) that formally derived or proven code can potentially contain defects. It is therefore necessary to enhance our software process through inclusion of defect management techniques designed to deal with existing defects. In our taxonomy we classify these techniques into two groupings: direct defect identification techniques, and failure detection and root cause analysis techniques. The next two sections describe each category in some detail.

Defect Identification Techniques

This category of defect management techniques is often called by a variety of other names such as *static verification* (Sommerville, 1995), *peer review* (IEEE 1028), or *software analysis* (Ghezzi et al., 1992). These techniques are based on the direct, static, and detailed study of the work product (e.g., source code) as opposed to the study of the performance of the software in the hope of identifying failures (e.g., testing). Unlike the latter case, the final code product does not need to be available for static verification (unless it is the code product itself that is being verified). Static verification can be applied to all software process work products (Strauss & Ebenau, 1995), so early detection and removal of defects becomes possible (e.g., design inspection).

In general, the terminology for defect identification techniques is both confused and confusing in that:

- Names often do not correctly or adequately describe a given technique.
- The same term may be used to refer to several different techniques.
- The same technique may be called by several different names.

Consequently, we offer a taxonomy that will assist both in establishing a basis for communication and for contrasting various techniques in this category. We base this taxonomy on the intent or the primary objective of each technique. To do so, we use the definitions provided by IEEE Standard 1028–1988, in which primary objectives of this category of techniques are enumerated as evaluation, education and examination of alternatives, and defect identification. Next we examine each category in turn.

Evaluation

The primary objective of a number of static verification techniques is to evaluate project progress, resource allocation, technical adequacy, and conformance to specification. We refer to these techniques as *reviews*. We place techniques described in IEEE 1028—Management Review, MIL-STD 1521B, and IEEE 1028—Technical Reviews, in this category.

IEEE 1028—Management Review

The management review technique described as part of IEEE 1028 does not have as its primary objective the detection and removal of defects. Management reviews are conducted to ascertain project progress, to recommend corrective action at the project level, and to ensure proper allocation of resources. As the name suggests, management and technical leadership of the project are involved in this management-led process in which a potentially high volume of material may be reviewed in a short period of time. This is in contrast with inspection techniques (to be introduced later), in which a low volume of material is inspected by a peer group for the purpose of defect identification at the work product level.

MIL-STD 1521B

This process is very similar to the IEEE 1028—Management Review process in many respects including its nature, objectives, volume of material reviewed, and the responsibilities and positions of stakeholders present. Where the two processes differ is in the team leadership: In MIL-STD 1521B review, this is shared by the representative of the contractor (customer) and that of the contracting agent. The number of people in a review team of this type could be tens of individuals. There is usually no formally specified process or specification for the type of data to be collected.

IEEE 1028—Technical Review

IEEE 1028 states the objective of technical reviews to be evaluation of conformance to specifications and project plans, and to ensure the integrity of the change process. Similar to the IEEE 1028—Management Review, technical reviews have no predefined number of participants and a high volume of material is usually studied during one sitting. Data collection is not a mandatory or specified process. Unlike management reviews, however, the composition and the leadership of the technical review team is of a technical nature, as are the process outputs and issues investigated. Management is usually absent.

The Efficacy of Review Techniques

As there is no specified recommended review team size, nor are the processes or their objectives and deliverables precisely specified, it is very difficult to measure the efficacy of review techniques. These techniques, however, have been deemed useful (Brykczynski et al., 1993; Remus, 1984) usually for purposes other than defect identification in work products.

Education and Examination of Alternatives

Walk-throughs belong to this category. A *walk-through* is a semiformal review of a product by a small team of peers, led by the product author, in which an attempt is made to meet a variety of objectives, including participant education, examination of alternatives (brainstorming), examination of readability and modularity problems, and defect identification.

Many walk-through techniques exist, but few are sufficiently described. The techniques discussed in the following section have a reasonably well-defined process model.

IEEE 1028—Walk-through

Although defect detection is a stated aim of IEEE 1028—Walk-through, it seems that the process is mainly used for examination of alternatives and as a process of peer education. Gilb and Graham (1993) stated that this walk-through technique is not precisely defined in the IEEE 1028 standard. The recommended number of participants is stated to be between two and seven composed of technical peers and the technical leadership of the project. The volume of the material considered, although relatively low, is still higher than that for the inspection process.

In addition, data collection and retention is optional and change incorporation is left as the prerogative of the work product producer.

Yourdon Structured Walk-through

Specified by Yourdon (1989), this technique is reasonably well defined in that the number and roles of participants, product size, walk-through duration, and management involvement are all specified reasonably precisely.

Freeman and Weinburg Walk-through

Freedman and Weinburg (1982) defined a walk-through process in which a stepwise work product execution is conducted using a specifically produced set of inputs. The process conforms with the minimum requirements of the IEEE 1028 standards but is not very precisely defined.

The Efficacy of Walk-through Techniques

Walk-throughs have been deemed useful for the following reasons:

- A large volume of work product can be evaluated in a reasonably short period of time.
- There is little specific training required to participate as part of a walk-through team.
- Participation in a walk-through is not very time consuming or intellectually demanding.
- Walk-throughs are often educational and are an effective forum for exchange of ideas.

Despite this, given the variety of objectives to be met and the usual lack of formal process model, the lack of requirements for data collection or change incorporation has made walk-throughs a useful yet somewhat inefficient technique (e.g., in comparison to inspection; Ackerman et al., 1989; Gilb & Graham, 1993). Lack of empirical data also has rendered impractical a meaningful comparison of the efficacy of various walk-through techniques with respect to each other.

Defect Identification

A number of techniques set as their primary objective the identification of defects in work products. These are central to our discussion, and we call these techniques *inspection*. There are many very good references that describe inspection techniques (Ackerman et al., 1989; Fagan, 1976, 1986; Gilb & Graham, 1993; Redmill, 1993; Strauss & Ebenau, 1995). These reports more or less describe the variants of a process first presented by Fagan (1976). We call these standard inspections or inspections for short, after Gilb and Graham (1993). I present a bit of history first.

Fagan Inspection

At the core of almost all software improvement is the Total Quality Management (TQM) technique of statistical quality management (Humphrey,

1989). Fagan Inspections—a technique developed by Michael Fagan at IBM Kingston Labs in the early 1970s—is one of the most successful applications of these principles in the domain of software process (Redmill, 1993). Having observed their utility in relation to hardware-oriented projects, Fagan decided to employ industrial statistical quality management techniques as an attempt to manage the quality of a particular IBM software project. This attempt culminated in the development of a technique named *code inspection,* which he described in Fagan (1976).

Although the name suggests that the practice was initially devised to be used in relation to the determination of defect content of code, subsequent development saw it applied to other software process artifacts such as requirements and design documents (Redmill et al., 1988; Reeve, 1991).

For a technique to implement statistical quality management successfully, it has to:

- Have constancy of purpose;
- Be precisely defined so it can be reproduced with results that are comparable; and
- Be measurement based, again, for the usefulness and comparability of results and for improvement purposes of the technique itself (Humphrey, 1989).

The superiority of inspection techniques in comparison to other review and walk-through techniques that have been widely reported (Bush, 1990; Dichter, 1992; Fagan, 1976, 1986; Graden & Horsley, 1989; Kelly et al., 1992; Kitchenham et al., 1986; Remus, 1984; Russell, 1991; Weller, 1992) is due to the adherence to these same principles. The following is a brief description of the Fagan style inspection process. Much more detailed discussion and description can be found elsewhere (Fagan, 1976, 1986; Gilb & Graham, 1993).

Fagan Inspection Process Description

- The inspection process commences with an inspection request by the author or another concerned stakeholder. An inspection leader is selected and notified.
- The inspection leader ensures that the entry criteria into the inspection requested are satisfied to prevent unsuccessful or ineffective inspections.
- The inspection leader then plans the inspection by selecting the participants, their roles, and their responsibilities within the framework of the inspection process description.

- The members of the team responsible for checking the product then work individually on the document in an attempt to find the maximum number of issues of the type for which they are selected to be responsible. In this, they are assisted by a number of logs, checklists, and other tools. These potential defects are recorded.

- During a logging meeting, issues found by individual checkers are debated and consolidated, more major issues are identified, and reports are produced.

- This report is then given to an editor to resolve. This is where it is determined whether the issue identified by checkers is a defect or not (for which an explanation is provided).

- The inspection leader then follows up the issue resolution process undertaken by the editor and an audit is performed to ensure the product now meets the inspection process exit criteria.

- Once exit criteria are met, the product is identified as inspected and is released.

- Inspection process data are kept for future reference.

Gilb and Graham Style Inspection

The Fagan style inspection still requires a feedback mechanism for improvement and extension of the process. The requirement is both in terms of root cause analysis (which deals with the improvement of other techniques in the software process to prevent the recurrence of defects of the type identified by inspection) and inspection process improvement (which deals with the improvement of the inspection process itself so better, improved inspection processes can be applied in the future).

Enhancements to this end were introduced by Jones and Mays at IBM (Jones, 1985) and adapted and incorporated into the Fagan inspection process by IBM as an effective defect prevention process.

Gilb and Graham (1993) based the inspection process described in their book on these enhancements. These defect preventions add the following to the base of inspection technique:

- A kick-off meeting in which in addition to distribution of documents and provision of a description of expectations from team members (all extant in the base practice) also provides feedback on process changes, training for inspectors on specific aspects or technologies, target setting, and strategizing for inspection productivity goal attainment.

- Root cause analysis (process brainstorming). During this meeting an attempt is made to identify the root cause of at least some of the issues logged and to generate suggestions for improvement of that aspect of the process (most probably a process other than that of inspection) that has led to that type of defect.
- Action database. The output of all brainstorming sessions is recorded in a quality assurance (QA) action database with proper assignment of ownership and deadlines, which will be tracked.
- Process change management team (action team). This is a team with the responsibility for seeing that the items logged within the QA action database are attended to by those responsible before the deadline is passed. Additionally, team members are responsible for effecting changes elsewhere (other processes) or within the inspection process to ensure improvement.

In-Process Inspection (Strauss and Ebenau Style Inspection)

The basic principles behind in-process inspections are the same as those initially intended by Fagan, but the perspective is enhanced in that in-process inspection is designed to be applied (with possible adaptation) to the improving of the quality of a much wider variety of products such as hardware (we have come full circle!), documentation, and courseware. In fact, any intellectual product may be subjected to an in-process inspection (Strauss & Ebenau, 1995). The emphasis in this approach is placed on the following:

- Early application of inspection during the development process,
- Application to a wider variety of products,
- Customization to fit particular project environments, and
- Customization to fit particular product types.

A balance between precision and uniformity of process definition and enactability (for the purpose of comparison, measurement, and improvement) and adaptability (to allow customization) had to be struck. Strauss and Ebenau struck this balance through defining the process of customization. Strauss and Ebenau (1995) contains a detailed description of this inspection process.

It should be mentioned that despite the foregoing enumeration of the differences of the three variants cited earlier, they are from an aim, procedure,

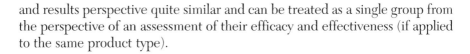

and results perspective quite similar and can be treated as a single group from the perspective of an assessment of their efficacy and effectiveness (if applied to the same product type).

Cleanroom Verification-Based Inspection

A verification-based static technique is at the core of the Cleanroom approach (Dyer 1991, 1992). As a balance between formality and efficiency, this technique attempts to demonstrate the correctness of the work product through a semiformal proof by executing basic constructs individually through a correctness checking set of questions.

Van Emden Style Inspection

Van Emden (1992) also described a development technique based on code inspection that uses a semiformal verification process. In this interesting technique, inline formal comments are used as a basis for paraphrasing the source code in an inspection meeting. During the inspection, it is determined whether the code conforms to the comments presented. Van Emden's work does not describe how this technique might be applied to work products other than code.

Automated Inspection

Automated inspection is the examination by a computer of a program through applying a certain number of good programming rules from a rule base. In other words, the computer conducts the inspection process. The rule set usually contains a number of rules derived from some theory of program correctness in addition to some other rules of good practice. The rule set and therefore the type of defects pointed out vary from theory to theory and from product to product. An example of such product might be PASS-C (1993).

Limited Scope Inspections

This class of techniques includes essentially limitations and variants of the inspection process as described earlier. These limitations and variations may be by direction, aspect, number of participants, and location of participants.

By Direction

Active design reviews (Parnas & Weiss, 1987) are really backward inspections. Initially, the inspection team overviews the modules presented to them and subteams are organized. The inspections are then conducted through the use of questionnaires supplied by the design team as a means to focus the attention of the inspection team. Subsequently, a meeting between designers and the inspection team is held, during which the inspection team presents their responses to the questions to the satisfaction of the design team.

By Aspect

Knight and Myers (1993) described an inspection technique in which inspections are targeted not toward identification of all defects, but only those related to certain aspects of the work product. These inspections are conducted by teams, the training and experience of the members of which are appropriate to the aspect under inspection. A collection of these inspections, each concentrating on a particular aspect, is claimed to be more effective in removing defects than the same level of standard inspection. Unfortunately, there is no further independent experimental evidence of the usability, efficacy, efficiency, or effectiveness of this technique on its own or relative to other techniques.

By Number of Participants

A typical software inspection requires three to seven participants (Gilb & Graham, 1993; Strauss & Ebenau, 1995), making it difficult to conduct inspections in cases where that many participants do not exist or are unavailable (e.g., small projects). Bisant and Lyle (1989) described a technique that limits the number of participants needed to two individuals. Humphrey (1995) introduced a technique that requires only one person (usually the author) to conduct an inspection. Unfortunately, empirical data based on sound experimental design are lacking in terms of the relative efficacy of such techniques, particularly in relation to mainstream type inspection techniques such as the one advocated by Gilb and Graham (1993). Nevertheless, application of the techniques presented by Bisant and Lyle and by Humphrey indicates that as they still are capable of identifying some defects, they can be deemed effective in an absolute sense. In other words, it seems that conducting an inspection with a limited number of people when sufficient numbers are not available is still better than not running one at all. To what extent this is the case in comparison to other techniques needs further investigation.

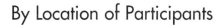

By Location of Participants

Another logistics consideration is whether to hold an actual inspection meeting at all (by colocating all participants) or to hold a "virtual meeting" through the use of technology. Votta (1993) proposed that inspections can be conducted without inspection meetings. It is unclear whether such a technique would succeed in the absence of an opportunity for group synergy. Again, robust empirical work to determine and compare the efficacy of this technique is needed.

Efficacy of Inspection Techniques

Although comparisons between individual process variants (e.g., Gilb & Graham vs. Ebenau & Strauss) are unavailable, there is a plethora of both experimental and experience-based reports in the literature indicating the efficacy and benefits of the inspection process (Bush, 1990; Dichter, 1987; Fagan, 1976, 1986; Gilb & Graham, 1993; Graden & Horsley, 1989; Kelly et al., 1992; Kitchenham et al., 1986; Remus, 1984; Russell, 1991; Strauss & Ebenau, 1995; Weller, 1992).

Inspection applied to software is now the second most popular technique of defect management (after unit testing) and the prime technique of static defect identification (Gilb & Graham, 1993).

Virtually all experience with inspection has been very positive. Fagan, in his original article, reported a 23% increase in code productivity[1] (Fagan, 1976) compared to the then existing IBM practices.

Gilb and Graham (1993) asserted that inspections are effective as they contribute directly to the following improvements:

- Development productivity improvement (30%–100%);
- Reduction of the development time scale (10%–30%);
- Reduction in testing time and costs (500%–1000%); and
- Reduction in cost of maintenance (up to 1000%).[2]

---

[1] The term is used in the original paper by Fagan, for which he gives a definition based on rate of defect identification. For further details the original paper should be consulted.
[2] The absolute validity (in terms of measurement theory) of some of these measures may be suspect.

Some of the most important indirect benefits of employing inspection techniques are making management defect and quality data available, increased likelihood of meeting deadlines, organizational improvement, and staff morale increase.

Due to the importance of inspections in defect management, we represent this category in our investigation of defect management. An inspection process belonging to the Strauss and Ebenau category is selected for this purpose.

Comparing Inspection and Testing (Failure Detection)

Inspection and testing are not to be viewed as competing alternatives (Kitchenham & Linkman, 1998; Russell, 1991; Weller, 1992). It should be noted that:

- There are specific categories of defects that are best managed by either technique (e.g., stylistic defects are best found through inspection, whereas integration faults are best located through testing).

- Test cases and test documentation are prone to defects and can themselves benefit from inspection (Larson, 1975; Remus, 1984).

Butler and Finelli (1993) agreed that testing has the propensity to locate the most commonly occurring faults. As defects causing these faults are removed, the time to discovery of the next fault dramatically increases. In terms of efficacy measures, this increase is at a much higher growth rate than the same effect in inspection. Butler and Finelli, unfortunately, did not provide any evidence in support of this argument.

Boehm and Papaccio (1988) also argued that the bulk of effort expended in testing only uncovers a small portion of the failures that occur most frequently. This is an argument for the effectiveness of static techniques in general and inspection in particular. Although testing effectively identifies the most frequent defects, the remaining defects must not be ignored because although not frequent, they could result in a severe failure when they eventually occur. Leveson (1986) pointed out that severity of a failure and the frequency of the occurrence of the fault that causes it are not related. This means that those defects not identified by testing might produce failures of such severity that ignoring them is impossible. They must either be identified through testing (now suffering from the law of diminishing returns) or through a different approach that has an equal chance of locating defects irrespective of their frequency of causing failure or their rework cost. Inspection is such a technique.

Ultimately the percentage of all defects discovered by a method and the stage when the method can be applied are the true determinants of a method's efficacy (Ackerman et al., 1989). In his seminal and still quite relevant work, Boehm (1984) identified that early detection of a defect can make its correction up to 100 times less expensive in comparison with a late detection. Inspection can be applied early and to early life-cycle artifacts, whereas testing can only be applied to the execution of the completed code. This makes inspection a good candidate for a high efficacy rating compared to testing. In terms of percentage of defects found and a similar measure of number of hours needed to identify and remove a defect, inspection has been reported to be almost invariably superior to testing. Reports (e.g., Ackerman et al., 1989; Gilb & Graham, 1993; etc.) indicate a factor of up to 300% in favor of inspection. Unfortunately it is uncertain whether such a claim is based on reliable data obtained through robust experimental design or empirical analysis. I therefore caution against extrapolation of such data.

However, postrelease defect reports tend to confirm the preceding assertion, where reductions of up to 67% in reported postrelease failure incidents have been recorded (Ackerman et al., 1989; Chaar, 1993; Kitchenham et al., 1986; Myers, 1978; Weller, 1992). This represents inspections as a very effective means of defect management in comparison with testing, at least in general terms.

Despite this, a confirmed predictive model of inspection efficacy in terms of the profile of the rate of defect removal per unit of time as time progresses during an inspection is still unavailable.

Inspecting Object-Oriented Code

As mentioned before, it is possible to apply inspection to a wide variety of artifacts, from hardware, to specifications, to design documents, to code, or event test suites and user manuals. The process is largely the same, with the difference being in the artifact being inspected and therefore the specific aspects of the artifact and how they will be examined. Procedures for these usually are captured in an inspection support document called an inspection checklist or inspection reading rules (see Chapter 6 for a discussion). It is these checklists or reading rules that make the difference in terms of what is inspected. It follows therefore that the same overall process as described for design or non-object-oriented program inspection (or any other inspection for that matter) can be used to inspect object-oriented code, as long as the checklists and reading guides used are specifically generated to examine code from an object-oriented perspective.

Such a checklist or reading guide should not only examine the code from the general programming perspectives, such as use of constants as constants, possibility of division by zero, and so on, but also specific object-orientation issues such as recursive inheritance, class and method scope violations, overloading, and the like.

Such a checklist has to deal with issues at multiple levels. These would be the level of the class, which is the unit of program construction in object orientation. Class interaction or module level would be at a higher level, whereby the interaction of instances of classes (objects) would be examined. At a lower level than that of the class, a checklist must also be effective at the method inspection level. An example checklist for object-oriented Java code inspection is provided in Appendix C.

Failure Detection-Oriented Defect Removal

Failure detection is the activity of exercising the software environment with the intent of identifying failures, or points of deviation from expectation. This approach can be subdivided into three distinct activities: failure detection, root cause analysis, and root cause defect removal.

In this sense failure detection is the activity that comes closest to the definitions that have traditionally been provided for the testing (Myers, 1979). At times differences may be detected between the intent and expression of these traditional definitions and that of the activity we term failure detection (Goodenough & Gerhardt, 1975), but there is sufficient proximity for the terms to be used interchangeably.

Root cause analysis is the activity of tracing the manifestation of a defect or series of defects (a failure) as discovered in the environment through failure detection or normal usage, through to the defect or defects in the source code that caused such failure. This is a nontrivial and time-consuming task.

Root cause defect removal is the activity of correcting the defect identified in the source code through the two preceding activities. The last two activities combined are usually termed *debugging*. A large number of debugging techniques exist, the most frequently cited of which are program tracing and scaffolding (Bently, 1985). Surveys and descriptions of effective debugging techniques are available elsewhere (McDowall & Helmbold, 1989; Stewart & Gentleman, 1997) and are not discussed further.

Testing Object-Oriented Code

We described object orientation as the encapsulation of the structural, causal, and transformational views of the situation being modeled (a program is also a model). In other words, an object-oriented software system is a set of objects containing a number of operations (methods) through the invocation of which they interact by sending and receiving messages. Thus in an object-oriented specification or design, we have class diagrams (structure models), sequence and state diagrams (causal or dynamic models), and algorithmic descriptions or activity diagrams (transformational models). When it comes to programming, the same views remain. The structure is reflected in the classes of a system, causality in the object call sequence, and transformations in the methods and their algorithms.

Three Categories of Object-Oriented Tests

An object-oriented system can also be tested along the same lines. We can therefore define structural testing, causal testing, and transformational testing:

- Structural testing: As the name implies, this is the testing of the structure of the program and thus deals with classes, objects, and their combinatorics. We use truth tables or other logical devices to conduct structural testing.
- Causal testing: This testing deals with the call sequences of the program and how individual objects transition from one state to another state. It can also be called state-based testing. Use of state diagrams and other dynamic model artifacts would allow us to conduct sequential testing between classes (who calls whom?) and modal testing within a given class (how many different states are logically allowed and entered into by the objects of this class?).
- Transformational testing: This form of testing is the closest to the traditional methods of testing non-object-oriented code. It concentrates on the correctness of how input values are turned into output values. It deals with the algorithmic correctness of the code within a method or between methods in a single object or indeed between objects.

It is possible to perform structural, causal, or transformational testing only to the exclusion of other methods. Yet similar to a UML specification that only has class diagrams but no sequence diagrams or algorithmic specifications, the story would be incomplete. All three forms of testing should be considered, planned, and conducted on object-oriented code.

Another important note is that like any other form of testing, testing object-oriented code based on this three-pronged approach does not guarantee the correctness of the end result product. Like any other testing approach, we can—as a result of testing—be convinced that we have discovered so many defects. There could even be more defects than before, as we could have introduced more defects than we removed. Some recent work however (e.g., Younessi et al., 2002) has shown that the likelihood of introducing more defects than removed is not great with most programming teams.

A third point of caution is that like any other testing scheme, this three-way approach is also a means of battling the combinatorial explosion that we would otherwise face when attempting to test all logical possibilities of a program. Like any other divide-and-conquer scheme, this one suffers from the problem that the parts do not add up to the whole. By that we mean testing structurally, followed by causally, and then transformationally would still leave a number of cases untested: those that fall through the cracks, so to speak.

Testing Levels and Testing Strategy

If object-oriented software systems are sets of objects containing a number of operations (methods) through the invocation of which they interact by sending and receiving messages, then we need to test them at the macro level in terms of the following:

- Classes,
- Cluster of classes or components,
- Groups of interacting components that provide a given and well-defined service (a framework), and ultimately,
- The system.

At the micro level, we need to test in terms of the following:

- Methods,
- Method interactions within an object,
- Classes, which themselves can be of three kinds:
  (base classes, derived classes, and reusable, generic, and abstracted class objects), and
- Class hierarchies.

Before we can proceed to describe each of these tests, we need to identify the oracle or basis against which each such test would find meaning and what artifact contains or defines such basis. See Table 7.1.

Table 7.1   Testing Basis

	Against		Using	
System		Specification		Req. Scenarios
				Acceptance Cases
Module		Architecture		High-Level Design
Class		Detailed Design		Objects
Method		Detailed Design		Algorithms
				Assertions

A system is tested against the requirements as stated or implied in the specification. This may be done as part of acceptance procedures and as such be performed against acceptance cases, which are a set of cases selected to determine the acceptability of the system. Such specification would yield a number of requirement scenarios, an end-to-end interaction with the system that generates a useful or interesting outcome. Requirement scenarios can therefore be seen as the instantiations of requirement-level usecases. However, they are not usecases; they are their instances. A usecase, in other words, would be an abstraction of a number of similar scenarios. For example, "customer withdraws cash from ATM" might be a usecase, but one corresponding requirement scenario might be "same customer as before withdraws $700 from ATM."

Modules or frameworks are tested against high-level design scenarios (cases), although they can also be verified against requirement scenarios individually with reuse in mind. In general, however, they are tested against the design document; for example, artifacts such as the design class diagram, design-level sequence diagrams, and the like.

A class is tested against the detailed object design and the contents of the design document that describes the class, its responsibilities, and its modes. Class hierarchies are similarly tested against the design document.

Methods are tested against the individual algorithms developed during the late stages of design. They are tested in terms of inputs–transformations–outputs, their pre- and postconditions, and method invariants, all of which should have been determined at design time.

Testing Strategies and Object-Oriented Artifacts

The class is said to be the unit of object-oriented software (Meyer, 1988) and therefore by extension, of object-oriented testing. Classes are composed of simpler units called structural headers, attributes, methods, and invariants. We therefore start, in Chapter 8, with the testing strategy for testing at the class level. This would include testing of base classes, derived classes and class hierarchies, generic classes and abstract classes. As part of this treatment we deal with testing strategies relating to the component artifacts of the class. Among these, of particular interest, are the techniques of method testing. Beyond that, in Chapter 9, we cover strategies for testing clusters of classes as they interact. These can be modules, frameworks, or entire systems.

To begin with, a class is a template and it cannot be tested because there is no class artifact in the compiled version of a program; there are instances (objects) created from that class template. However, we must test classes. We therefore need to engage in at least some of the following activities:

- Class testing,
- Class hierarchy testing,
- Method testing,
- Module testing (including regression), and
- System testing.

Conclusion

This chapter described the principles of both the static and dynamic approaches we might take to identify defects in program code. In the next two chapters we deal with the details of these techniques and provide specific guidance about how to conduct defect identification.

Chapter 8

TESTING CLASSES

In this chapter we discuss a number of strategies that allow us to test the structure and the behavior of a class in isolation or nearly so. By nearly so, we mean that we would also consider the case of a class that is derived through inheritance. The approach taken would be one in which testing adequacy in the artifact is built through reaching testing adequacy of its components and their combinations (Perry & Kaiser, 1990). For example, we might test a class by testing its attributes, its methods, its invariants, and then combinations of these in turn, knowing full well that reaching adequacy or indeed exhaustion in each of these individual cases would not necessarily lead to the overall correctness of the artifact.

Testing Base Classes

A base class is a class that contains all its own attributes and routines. In other words, it is not derived through inheritance. To begin with, a class (any class, including a base class) is a template and it cannot be tested because there is no class artifact in the compiled version of a program. There would be instances (objects) created from that class template. We therefore, based on our view, need to test the components that compose an object as described in the class that relates to it. These are class headers and footprints, attributes, routines, and class invariants.

We do so by providing a number of testing strategies, each belonging to the structural, causal, or transformation category of tests.

In general a class—in isolation—is correct if the following conditions are met:

1. All its intended instances can be correctly generated.

2. The attribute value set of all objects created from the class would at any one time represent a valid state of the object.

3. Each and every routine within these objects correctly alters the representation of the corresponding object.

No known single testing strategy can conclusively show that all these conditions have been satisfied, but we can discuss testing approaches that would raise our confidence in each of these three conditions.

Testing for Correct Generation of Instances

Classes in most object-oriented languages have within them a provision for instantiation. These are usually called constructors and they are in the form of routines. They might take initialization parameters and there might be more than one constructor for any one class.

We must create a set of tests to determine that each and every constructor can generate an intended instance of the class and also that in the case of multiple constructors, this is not order dependent (unless specifically required). A test case (a tester class) could be written that would test the following conditions:

1. All attribute values have been initialized correctly.

2. The order of initialization is correct.

Such a test case might check the self-consistency of the constructors. A simple structural way to do so is to follow this procedure:

1. Identify all constructors for the class under test.

2. Start with the first constructor.

3. Instantiate the class using this constructor.

4. Check the values of each attribute using an accessor (*get[x]*) routine.

5. Go to next constructor until exhausted.

6. Create several random orderings of constructor calls.

7. Compare the initialized attribute values after each construction of each object using any given constructor with all other such instantiations from other sequences. Ensure they are all consistent.

This approach, however, has the following problems:

- The available interface may disallow access to some attributes needed for state determination.
- The access methods (get methods) may produce side effects.
- The access methods may contain bugs and not report the correct value.

A second approach uses techniques of breaking encapsulation to look directly into the object to see how each attribute is set and used and in what order. This might be achieved, for example, using the friend facility of C++. Although this is a more reliable technique than the one discussed, it is somewhat contrary to the spirit of object orientation, as it breaks encapsulation and merges the evaluation of the state with its implementation. For a discussion of this issue, consult Chapter 1.

The preceding discussion implies that it is generally a good idea to design and code classes in such a way that their current state might be observed without necessarily having to deduce it based on the current attribute value set. The state design pattern may allow such access without breaking encapsulation.

Testing for Correct Attribute Values

The issue here is a reversed generalization of what was just discussed in the case of testing constructors. In the previous case we tested a particular category of routines (namely constructors) by trying to view the values of individual attributes. In this case, we are trying to ascertain the validity of an attribute value set (a state) after the invocation of a given routine (constructor or otherwise). We offer two approaches. The first, belonging to the causal category, uses the state diagram for the object to determine the next state and then once the state is identified, it determines the attribute values.

State-Based Attribute Value Testing

The life of an object may be depicted in a state diagram. In the state diagram each event (transition) implies a change of value of at least one attribute and implies at least one test. The outcome of that test may then be compared with the expected response as per the specification. Such a response set may be created by constructing an $n \times m$ matrix where n is the cardinality of the set of all transitions and m is the cardinality of the set of all states. Each cell of a matrix such as this would then represent the set (more than one in general) of attribute value sets expected. This is the case, as a transition may have a guard or condition on it, necessitating the inclusion of multiple possible outcomes per event–state pair. Techniques to deal with such possibilities are discussed shortly during our treatment of method testing. See Table 8.1.

Table 8.1.   A 2 × 4 Table of States and Events

		Transitions			
		E1	**E2**	**E3**	**E4**
States	S1				
	S2				

Another somewhat similar approach makes an assumption of coverage based on the potential impact of n routines on one attribute. This is a structural test that examines the changes of value of a single attribute as a consequence of the impact of each and every routine that has a potential to change it. This approach uses the concept of a *slice* (Bashir & Goel, 2000), which is the set of one attribute and all routines that can potentially impact it. Of course slices may overlap, as they can share routines (never attributes). An $n \times m$ matrix can be created where n is the cardinality of the set of attributes of the class and m is the cardinality of the set of all routines that transform the attribute. For each cell, if the routine can potentially manipulate the attribute, we can define at least one test that involves that routine–attribute pair. The class can be tested for all possible sequences of routines one slice at a time. Comparing the result of each test (a particular attribute value for a given attribute) with the expected attribute value determines the "correctness" of that slice. The assertion is that if all slices are correct, then all individual attribute values are manipulated as specified, so all states are reached as required.

The astute reader, however, would note that some combinations of routines within a slice might be redundant. For example, if Routine A simply calls Routine B, then the attribute values manipulated by Routine B need not be redundantly evaluated in relation to Routine A. To reduce the combinations to the essential ones only, a call graph may be used in combination with the matrix. A *call graph* is the sequence of routine calls that lead to the utilization of a particular attribute. All such sequences may be relatively easily drawn for a particular class, given the structure of that class.

Testing if Routines Correctly Alter the Representation of the Corresponding Object

The preceding test strategies simultaneously test attribute value correctness and whether accessor and transformer routines set them correctly. We have also dealt with constructor routines and deal with destructor routines shortly. All that remains is to treat the case of reporter routines (procedures), but this is quite simple. Given access to the attribute values implying the state (or the state directly), we can determine the value of every attribute after invocation of a routine that plays a reporter (procedure) role with respect to it. None can change.

Assertion-Based Testing of a Class

Assertions, or more precisely, structural assertions,[1] are logical facts about the structure of a class that, although not part of the operational specification of it, do define necessary conditions for its correct execution. Structural assertions include preconditions, postconditions, and invariants.

A precondition is a logical condition or set of conditions that must be true before a routine can execute. For example, when we pop a stack, we would require that the stack has at least one element before we pop it.

A postcondition is a logical condition or set of conditions that must be true at the end of the execution. For example, when we pop a stack, we want to be assured that the number of items in the stack is reduced by exactly one. The postcondition for pop therefore might include a statement to that effect.

An invariant is a condition that must be true at all times. A class invariant, the most prevalent type of invariant in object orientation, is a condition or set

---

[1] I introduce state-based assertions later.

of conditions that must remain true for all objects of a class throughout the life of an object. Violating the class invariant makes the object no longer an instance of the class from which it was initially derived. A class invariant for a stack might be that the size of the stack can never be negative.

Assertions are logical statements and therefore it is possible to design programming languages that allow assertions to be written integrally as part of the source code and allow compilation of such code along with the operational body of the program. Eiffel is one such language wherein routines are written that include pre- and postconditions and loop invariants, and classes can contain class invariants. For example, we might write the precondition that there should be an element in the stack to pop to begin with for a stack's pop operation, as follows:

```
pop   is   -- remove the top item
require
Has_Item: not is_empty
```

where `is_empty` is a function that returns a binary value of *true* if the stack is empty.

Similarly, the postcondition that the size has to be one less than it was before pop can be written as:

```
:::::
ensure
one_Less: stack_size = old stack_size -1
end;   --pop
```

where `stack_size` is a function that returns an integer with a value equal to the number of elements in the stack.

An invariant might be as follows:

```
:::::::
invariant
Non_Negative: stack_size >= 0;
end   --class STACK
```

Of course multiple pre- and postconditions for each routine and invariant statements for a class can be written. If such assertions can be made to switch on

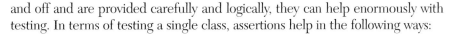

and off and are provided carefully and logically, they can help enormously with testing. In terms of testing a single class, assertions help in the following ways:

1. Many annoying yet logically easily avoidable errors can be identified very early. For example, a precondition that requires a number to be positive would catch an error that calls the said routine with a negative number or zero.

2. It removes the necessity of antiencapsulation to check states and the values of private attributes.

3. Errors emanating from the interaction of multiple objects of the same class can be trapped more easily.

4. Server class defects are pinpointed when a server class precondition rejects a valid message.

5. Class invariants can identify many cases of state corruption.

Assertions are also of enormous help in interobject testing, and we deal with those issues later in the book. From a software process perspective, assertions have these additional advantages:

1. Help in at least partial automation of a relatively large class of tests.

2. Assist in encouraging reuse.

3. Assist in practicing reliable reuse.

4. Help with documentation and code understandability.

5. Facilitate extraction of test cases.

6. Assist in better (less error-prone) implementation of an object design.

As mentioned earlier in the chapter, many of the concepts discussed here may apply at the class or the routine level. In the case of structural assertions, class invariants are treated at the class level, whereas pre- and postconditions and loop variants and invariants are treated at the routine level. We discuss these later. In our treatment, we assume the availability and utilization of a language that permits inclusion and compilation of assertion as an integral part of the code.

Class Invariants and Assertions at the Class Level

The class invariant is the common element shared by all preconditions and postconditions provided that the latter two are completely specified. In other words, a class invariant represents what must not change—and therefore must appear at all times—as part of all pre- and postconditions. Thus a class invariant can flag the violation of all the predicted conditions that might be transgressed as a consequence of some inappropriate implementation or utilization of any instance of the class.

A large degree of automated testing can thus be performed through employment of executable class invariants. These tests often are able to identify usage violations or logical contradictions of how an object should behave. In short, they concentrate on R-type defects. F-type defects, such as the incorrect calculation of a result that is not yet in violation of an invariant, might go undetected. For example, if a *stack_size* operation of a stack is written incorrectly to always return a positive number, irrespective of whether the stack is empty or not empty, our invariant as presented before would probably not trigger a violation when a *pop* operation also incorrectly pops the nonexistent "zeroth" element. Similarly, most incorrect algorithmic calculations would not be detected unless they impact the logical condition of the invariant. The fact that the value of the interest added to your account was calculated to be $4.60 as opposed to $46.00 would go undetected. To safeguard against F-type defects, we must perform method-level transformational tests, which are discussed later.

Routine Scope, Preconditions

Preceding discussion indicates that the actual precondition for any routine is actually:

$$Pre = Pre_d \bullet Inv$$

where *Pre* is the actual logical precondition effective, Pre_d is the declared preconditions declared with the routine, *Inv* is the logical set of class invariants, and $\bullet$ is the logical AND operator.

The meeting of a precondition is the responsibility of the client to the object whose class is under test. Preconditions can therefore identify many interobject defects, a fact we discuss later. In terms of intraobject impact on testing, a precondition can provide a "converse" scheme for testing, meaning a tester might attempt to intentionally violate the preconditions of a routine. The routine should then prevent progress. An appropriate assertion violation message or behavior should be generated.

Routine Scope, Postconditions

Similar to preconditions, the actual postcondition of a routine can be obtained by:
$$Post = Post_d \bullet Inv$$
where *Post* is the actual logical postcondition effective, $Post_d$ is the declared postconditions declared with the routine, *Inv* is the logical set of class invariants, and $\bullet$ is the logical AND operator.

The postcondition verifies that—given the precondition—the contract has been fulfilled. This is often declared as a set of logical statements about the attribute values of the object that define its final state of interest. Thus a complete postcondition should declare what the change has been in what needed to change, and what did not change as it should not have changed. It is often the latter condition that is difficult to express logically.

Postconditions can automatically detect many defects of both R-type (e.g., state violations) and F-type (e.g., miscalculation). For example, a postcondition that requires the value of $s = \sum_{i=1}^{n} i$ obtained through code written as a loop be sufficiently close to the value of T calculated as $T = \frac{n(n+1)}{2}$ would catch a large class of result miscalculations.

Routine Scope, Loop Invariants

A loop invariant is a Boolean condition that relates the iterations of a loop and must always be true, irrespective of on which iteration in the loop we are focused. In other words, a loop invariant must be correct under these conditions:

1. If no iteration was made.
2. After the last iteration.
3. Before the first iteration.
4. After the nth iteration when $0<n<$last.

Such a loop invariant can assist in removing many loop-related defects, such as overflows and underflows.

Routine Scope, Loop Variants

A loop variant is a logical expression that relates an iteration of a loop to a previous (or successive) one. We can assert the necessary condition that a loop must terminate through a loop variant. The loop variant must move toward its target with every iteration; if it does not, there is a chance that the loop is not progressing.

Constraint-Based or Assertion Constraint Coverage-Based Testing

We said earlier that testing adequacy could be established based on state transition coverage. We can similarly establish a constraint or assertion coverage-based test. This form of testing would require that for every routine, we cover every logical combination of the pre- and postconditions that might occur and present test cases that realize that given condition. Again, a table would come in handy.

For example, if we have a routine with two preconditions, a and b, and one postcondition, q, then we would have the truth table shown in Table 8.2.

Table 8.2   Test-Set Determination Based on Pre- and Postconditions

a	b	q	TEST
T	T	T	Test-set1
T	T	F	Test-set2
T	F	T	Test-set3
T	F	F	Test-set4
F	T	T	Test-set5
F	T	F	Test-set6
F	F	T	Test-set7
F	F	F	Test-set8

Modal Testing of a Class

The preceding testing strategies are based on a central premise that messages may arrive in any sequence and all message sequences are permitted and meaningful. In most situations, however, this is not the case. Most objects only accept a subset of their message set in any one state. In other words, past history or present state is also a determinant of what messages may be accepted to transition into a new state. Such objects are said to be modal in nature (Binder, 1995a, 1995b). In other words, the assumption thus far has been that the class invariant is the only allowed state constraint allowing all sequences of messages. Restriction in terms of acceptability of particular sequences of messages but not others are not explicitly considered. Testing strategies that ignore such effects must be exhaustive to have all such potential sequences as a subset of all sequences tested and explicitly reject nonregular sequences. Otherwise, we need to devise strategies that accept the fact that classes may be modal and thus accordingly verify the following:

1. Messages that are sent to an object appropriately and legally in a given state are accepted.

2. Messages that are inappropriate or illegal in a given state are rejected when the object is in that state.

3. The transition effected as a consequence of Item 1 leaves the object in the correct resultant state.

4. Nonaction or rejection action taken as a consequence of Item 2 leaves the object in a correct state.

State Invariants

The concept of object modality can be viewed from the perspective of state invariants (D'Souza & Wills, 1999; Kemmerer, 1985; Schuman & Pitt, 1987). State invariants are similar to class invariants in that they are assertions constraining an object, definitionally. Unlike class invariants that hold for all methods and constrains the entire state space of the object, a state invariant is an assertion about the object in a given state and constrains that state only. This makes the state invariant equally or more restrictive (stronger) than a class invariant. For an object that is nonmodal, the class invariant and the state invariant are identical. For modal objects, the class invariant is weaker or at the same strength as each state invariant, and the domain of the state invariants together must cover that of the class invariant.

Accepting or Entering Conditions

It is expected that the same relationship between a class invariant and state invariant be extensible to preconditions and their state counterparts, called accepting or entering conditions. For each method there is one or more accepting conditions defined. Each has the responsibility for checking if the incoming call is acceptable given the current state, as a precondition does with

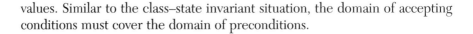

values. Similar to the class–state invariant situation, the domain of accepting conditions must cover the domain of preconditions.

Resulting Conditions

A resulting condition is the state counterpart of the postcondition. It confirms that once a call is accepted and honored in a state, the ensuing state is valid. Again, the domain of the resulting states must cover the postconditions domain.

Modal Testing

One can utilize state assertions (i.e., state invariants, accepting conditions, and resulting conditions) to represent sequential constraints, thus making testing of modal objects more manageable. The behavior of the object as a collection of states that represent sequential constraints must be defined and each such state must be represented with a state invariant.

A mode might fail when the following occur:

1. A call is accepted when it should have been rejected. This is called a *sneak path* (Binder, 1995b).
2. The object is in a valid state but a valid call is rejected.
3. A method is correctly accepted but produces the wrong state (an R-type defect).
4. A method is correctly accepted but produces the wrong response (an F-type defect).

We then start with the state diagram of the object and the code for the class showing the state assertions. We derive a transition tree from the state diagram as follows:

1. We start with the initial state for each transition.
2. For each transition out of the initial state we draw a branch to a resulting state.
3. For each intermediate state, we repeat the process until we reach final states or loop back.

Using the transition tree, we determine all event paths, which are full or partial paths through the transition tree starting from the root.

For each conditional transition, we determine all combinations of possible input modes and develop additional test cases for each newly discovered condition that we add to the tree. We then test each case by determining the various modalities defined for each method involved. The modal information (state invariants, accepting and resulting conditions) determines the tests to be run. This tests conformance, and when illegal messages are sent, it tests sneak paths.

Transformational Testing of Methods

The modal strategy concentrates on the state behavior of the object. It is ineffective in dealing with incorrect output when it is within the bounds of a valid state. For that, other techniques might be used and transformation-based strategies might be of value here.

Transformation-based techniques rely on the algorithmic nature of class routines. They are applied mainly at the routine level and test an individual routine. In other words, they are based on the input–transform–output model of a routine. Another way of looking at the differences between the various classes of testing we have been discussing is that if structural testing relates to the specification provided of the object at the class level, and state-based and modal testing are based on the state diagram of the entire object, then transformational testing is based on the individual routine's flow diagram.

Transformation-based testing, by concentrating on the individual routine's flow of control, is better placed to catch many of the F-type defects that are not found by testing schemes that rely on state validity or domains.

The essence of transformational testing is to ensure that a given routine can produce the required outputs given the necessary inputs. In this sense transformational testing comes closest to traditional non-object-oriented testing schemes developed and described in the 1960s, 1970s, and 1980s and applied to much of the non-object-oriented code available today. The difference is that in our discussion we advocate applying these techniques to an individual routine rather than a code segment several pages long or an entire application.

The first feature of our advocated transformational testing is the small size of the artifact to which it would apply. As already mentioned, transformational tests apply to individual routines of a class one at a time. In a well-designed and well-written object-oriented system, such routines fall into a small number of categories.

Creator routines must not exceed a few lines of code each, usually one to three lines. They should create the object and set the initial values.

Accessor routines should be even smaller. A *set* routine should generally be a one-liner. These routines should just set the value of the attribute (in this discussion we are not including the code written in the routine for pre- and postconditions and modal assertions). A *get* routine may be a bit longer, but still only one to five lines. It should cohesively only get the value of a given attribute.

Mutator routines may be a bit longer still. They actually manipulate the state of the object and are the routines that are responsible for the implementation of the specification. Mutators also have to be kept on the small side. No more than 20 lines of code are expected here. Longer mutator code can usually be broken down to smaller, more cohesive individual routines. Some of these may be new creators, new *gets* and *sets*, and some lower level mutators. The total number of lines of code may exceed the original number, but each individual routine would be within the prescribed limits. For detailed discussion about routine size in object-oriented code, consult Henderson-Sellers (1996).

Another feature of our advocated transformational testing is that well-designed object-oriented routines are not only small; they are also cohesive. They are usually designed to clearly do only one thing. Applying transformational techniques to object-oriented routines contrasts with non-object-orientation applications, where such testing schemes usually have to be applied to code with considerably lower levels of cohesion.

Cohesion is important because it reduces the potential space of a given code segment and thus improves testability. For example, a cohesive code segment does not have more than one entry or exit condition. Everything else being the same, a less cohesive code that has two entry and two exit conditions would require at least four times more testing than a cohesive routine of one entry and one exit condition. Needless to say, the testing in the former would also be considerably more complicated and error and omission prone.

At any rate, given the small size and cohesion of each object-oriented routine, we can much more easily and successfully apply these "traditional" testing approaches.

Transformational techniques can be divided into two subcategories, each divisible into further subcategories themselves, as follows:

- Partitioning or subdomain testing
  - specification based or functionally based,
  - program based,
  - defect based or evolutionary based, and
  - analytically based.

- Statistical testing
  - random testing, and
  - error seeding.

Descriptions of these techniques and details of their utility are given in the following sections.

Partitioning or Subdomain Testing

A popular approach employed as an attempt to control the combinatorial explosion problem in transformational testing is to subdivide the input domain into a number of logical subsets called subdomains, according to some criterion or set of criteria, and then to select a small number of representative elements from each subdomain as potential test case candidates (Frankl et al., 1997). The criteria usually employed can be classified as being:

- Specification based or functionally based,
- Program based,
- Defect based or evolutionary based, or
- Analytically based.

We consider each category briefly.

Specification-Based or Functionally Based Approaches

Sometimes also referred to as *functional testing*, these techniques concentrate on selecting input data from partitioned sets that effectively test the functionality included in the requirements specification for the routine. The partitioning is therefore based on placing inputs that invoke a particular aspect of the routine's functionality into a given partition.

In such techniques testing involves only the observation of the output states given the inputs, and as such no analysis of the structure of the routine is attempted (Hayes, 1986; Luo et al., 1994; Weyuker & Jeng, 1991). Individual approaches to input domain partitioning include those described in the following sections.

Equivalence Partitioning (Frankl et al., 1997; Myers, 1979)

This is where each input condition is partitioned into sets of valid and invalid classes called *equivalence classes*. These are used to generate test cases by selecting representative values of valid and invalid elements from each class. In this approach one can reasonably assume (but not be certain) that a test of a representative value of each class is equivalent to a test of any other value. That is, if one test case in a class detects an error, all other test cases in the class would be expected to do the same. Conversely, if a test case did not detect an error, we would expect that no other test case in the class would find an error. This assumption does not necessarily hold, however, and its truth is a function of the care with which equivalence classes have been selected and if they are truly equivalent.

The major deficiency of equivalence partitioning is that it is generally ineffective in testing combinations of input circumstances. There is also considerable variability in terms of the number of resultant test cases or testing effectiveness depending on how and at what granularity the equivalence classes are determined. In most typical situations, however, defects are interdependent and it is hard to predict the correct level of granularity for the equivalence classes prior to testing. These two deficiencies have a significantly detrimental effect on the defect identification efficacy of testing strategies based on equivalence partitioning (Beizer, 1991; Frankl et al., 1997).

Cause–Effect Graphing

Probably initially proposed by Elmendorf (1974) and popularized by Myers (1979), cause–effect graphing is a method of generating test cases by attempting to translate the precondition and postcondition implications of the specification to a logical notation with satisfaction by the routine that can be ascertained (Myers, 1979).

Cause–effect graphing can be useful when applied to simple cases. It has the interesting side effect of assisting in discovery of potential incompleteness or conflict in the specification. Unfortunately, it suffers from a number of weaknesses that make its utility of limited scope. The major weaknesses are as follows:

- It is difficult in practice to apply, as it still suffers from combinatorial explosion problems.
- It is difficult to convert the graph to a useful format (usually a decision table).

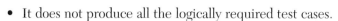

- It does not produce all the logically required test cases.
- It is deficient with regards to boundary conditions.

Boundary Value Analysis

A potential resolution to the last stated deficiency with cause–effect graphing is boundary value analysis, to be used in conjunction with the aforementioned. Boundary value analysis (Myers, 1979) is a method similar to equivalence partitioning in that it subdivides the domain into equivalence classes. The differences are as follows:

- Test cases are derived by considering both input as well as output equivalence classes.
- The test element selection is made in such a way that each independent logical path of execution of the class is subjected to at least one test.

In terms of efficacy, boundary value analysis suffers from exactly the same weaknesses as equivalence partitioning (Omar & Mohammed, 1991).

Category-Partition Method

This method (Ostrand & Balcer, 1988) decomposes the functional specification of the routine into independently testable functional units. For each functional unit, parameters that affect the execution of that unit (i.e., the explicit inputs) are identified and their characteristics determined, each forming a category. Each category is then partitioned into distinct groups, each containing sets of values that can be deemed equivalent. These sets are called *choices*. To develop test cases, the constraints between choices (e.g., Choice X must precede Choice Y), are determined and a formal test specification is composed for each functional unit.

Somewhat similar to equivalence partitioning, the advantage of category partitioning is in the facility with which test specifications can be modified. Additionally, the complexity and the number of cases can also be controlled. The major disadvantages of this method are those enumerated for other equivalence partitioning type methods.

The Efficacy of Specification-Based Testing Approaches

The number and dates of the publications cited here indicate that the short-comings of specification-based methods were recognized early and have been criticized by many authors. The main criticism is that they generally are unable to find nonfunctional failures (Haung, 1975; Howden, 1982; Myers, 1979; Ntafos & Hakimi, 1979). They are also often imprecise in terms of rules for identification or the level of granularity for selection of partition classes (Howden, 1982). They are usually hard to automate, as human expertise is often a requirement, at least for subdomain class selection (Ostrand & Balcer, 1988). Another major issue is that of the rapid proliferation of test cases needed for adequate coverage (Haung, 1975; Myers, 1979; Ntafos & Hakimi, 1979).

There are two other major shortcomings of this category of techniques:

- The assumption of disjoint partitions. This is the assumption that it is sufficient for the partitions or subdomains created to be disjoint. In reality, however, subdomains might not be all disjoint and hence the special case of disjoint partitions does not reflect the characteristics of the general case (Frankl & Weyuker, 1993).

- The assumption of homogeneity. This is the assumption that subdomains are homogeneous in that either all members of a subdomain cause a program to fail or none do so. Therefore, the assumption proceeds that one representative of each subdomain is sufficient to test the routine adequately. This assumption is unjustified, however, in that it is generally very impractical, if not impossible, to achieve homogeneity. Thus frequent sampling of subdomains is still required.

Much of the recent work in the analysis of the efficacy of subdomain testing has attempted to challenge these assumptions and provide frameworks that do not include them. Weyuker and Jeng (1994) challenged the homogeneity assumption but still assumed subdomains to be generally disjoint. Chen and Yu (1994) carried on from this, generalized this work, and demonstrated that under certain conditions, subdomain testing is at least as efficacious as random testing (to be discussed later). Further work by Chen and Yu (1996) challenged the second assumption (that of subdomains being disjoint) as they included in their analysis both joint and disjoint subdomains. The work again identifies a number of cases (albeit small in practice) in which subdomain testing might be a superior technique to use compared with random testing. In general and in the absence of a scheme by which specific conditions are built into the subdomains, the efficacy of subdomain testing remains very close to that of pure random testing and usually, it seems, not worth the extra effort

(Chen & Yu, 1994; Duran & Ntafos, 1984; Hamlet & Taylor, 1990; Weyuker & Jeng, 1994).

Program-based techniques that concentrate on the way the routine has been built have been proposed as a complementary technique to those just described.

Program-Based Testing Approaches

When the basis for the subdivision of the domain is not the functional specification of the routine or what the routine should do, but what the routine actually does, then it is possible to devise subdomain partitions that attempt to provide "coverage" by exercising necessary elements of the routine. These elements might relate to the structural elements of the routine such as statements, edges, or paths, or the data flow characteristics of the routine. Often termed *white box testing* or *glass box testing* (Haung, 1975; Myers, 1979; Ntafos & Hakimi, 1979), the basic requirement is the execution of each routine element at least once. The inputs that execute a particular element form a subdomain.

Statement Coverage

Statement coverage is deemed useful on the basis that by observing a failure on execution of a statement, we can identify a defect. As such, it is necessary to execute every statement in a routine at least once. Based on this, therefore, white box testing methods have been devised relying on the criterion that test sets must be selected such that every statement of the routine is executed at least once. The main problem with statement coverage as an approach (aside from the basic logical problem of all program-based approaches) is that it is not clear what is meant by a statement whether we need to deal with blocks or individual elementary statements. Another problem is how to deal with recursion; that is, whether to consider a recursive block as one series of statements or several nested ones, and if the latter, how many nestings, and so on.

Control Flow Coverage

If we consider a program or routine as a graph of nodes and edges, with nodes representing decision points and edges representing the path to the next decision point, the preceding statement coverage criterion calls for coverage of all nodes. Control flow coverage (also known as edge coverage), on the other hand, calls for coverage of all the edges between nodes. This is reasonable because in such a graph as described previously, edges describe the control flow of the program and test cases make each condition generate either a true or a false value. Thus, a test that gives full edge coverage tests all independently made decisions in the routine.

Hidden edges exist in the form of logical conditions. Simple control flow coverage will miss these. However, control flow coverage may be further strengthened by addition of the requirement that all possible compound conditions also be exercised at least once. This is called the *condition coverage criterion*.

Path Coverage

Combining statement and control flow coverage requirements, one can define a coverage criterion that states that test sets must be selected such that all paths within the routine's flow graph are traversed at least once. It is clear that this requirement is stronger than either the statement or the control flow coverage criteria individually or both conducted separately. The problem is, however, that traversing all control paths is infeasible, as it suffers from the explosion of state space problems. It might be feasible to cover all the "independent" paths within a routine.

Data Flow Oriented

Data flow coverage methods (Rapps & Weyuker, 1985) subject the routine to data flow analysis (Weiser, 1984) and identify certain data flow patterns that might be induced. The way these data flows might be induced are then used as the basis for creation of test subdomains and subsequently of test sets. Boundary interior testing (Howden, 1989), for example, requires selection of two test sets for each loop; one that enters the loop but does not cause iteration, and one that does.

The problem with data-flow-oriented approaches is that "they produce too many uninteresting anomalies unless integrated with a tool to evaluate path feasibility and subsequently remove un-executable anomalies" (Clarke et al., 1989, p. 1319).

The Efficacy of Program-Based Approaches

All program-based approaches suffer from a number of logical shortcomings. As highlighted earlier, program-based techniques rely on the implication that by observing a failure on execution of a program element (statement, edge, path, etc.) we can identify a defect. Alternatively, if a failure is encountered when executing a particular program element, then a defect is present in that program element. This statement can be written in the form of $p \rightarrow q$. The implication in itself is sound. The problem stems from the fact that this simple implication is frequently misrepresented in a number of generally incorrect forms such as these:

- Not $p \rightarrow$ not q, which states that if a failure is not encountered when executing a particular program element (in our case an object-oriented routine), then a defect does not exist in that program element. This is clearly not logically equivalent to our initial implication statement, but is the aspiration on which program-based testing in particular and partition testing in general is based.
- $(p(X) \rightarrow q(x)) \rightarrow (p(Y) \rightarrow q(y))$. This can be interpreted as follows: If a failure encountered during testing of a program element using data set (X), yields a defect (x), then using dataset (Y) results in a similar failure that in turn will yield defect (y). This again is not a logical consequence of our original implication, as confidence in the true equivalence of our equivalence sets must be first established.

Aside from the logical shortcomings, there remains the combinatorial weakness of these coverage-based techniques. Although addressed by many authors (Clarke et al., 1988; Frankl & Weyuker, 1988; Goldberg et al., 1994; Hutchins, 1994) using a variety of approaches (Bicevskis et al., 1990; Chilenski & Miller, 1993; Clarke, 1976; Lindquist & Jenkins, 1988; RTCA Inc., 1992), these still remain.

Defect-Based Approaches

Defect-based approaches were introduced and studied during the 1970s and 1980s as a potentially more effective approach to testing compared with specification-based approaches (DeMillo & Offutt, 1991; DeMillo et al., 1978; Howden, 1982; Morell, 1988; Offutt, 1992; Richardson & Thompson, 1988; Weyuker, 1983; Weyuker & Ostrand, 1980). These techniques rely on the hypothesis that programs (and in our case routines) tend to contain defects of a specific kind that can be well defined, and that by testing for a restricted class of defects we can find a wide class of defects. This is based on these hypotheses:

- Good programmers write routines that contain only a few defects (i.e., they are close to being correct; Budd, 1980; DeMillo et al., 1978).

- A test data set that detects all simple defects is capable of detecting more complex defects (coupling effects; DeMillo et al., 1978).

Thus if we create many different versions of a routine (mutations) by making small changes to the original, intending them to correspond to typical program defects that might be introduced, then test data that identifies such a defect in a mutation are also capable of identifying the same type of defect in the original program. It is further assumed that due to coupling effects, a test set that identifies a mutant will also reveal more complex defects than the type just discovered. Inputs that kill a particular mutation form a subdomain. Mutation testing (Budd, 1980; Hamlet & Taylor, 1990) is the implementation of these ideas and is closely related to the method of detecting defects in digital circuits.

It should be noted that despite the superficial resemblance between mutation testing and the technique known as error seeding (Mills, 1972) the two methods are strictly distinct. Error seeding is a statistical method that works on the basis of ratio of detected versus remaining defects. It is an indicator of when to stop testing and not a testing strategy in itself, whereas mutation testing deals with sensitivity of test sets to small changes in the program and as such makes no assumption or requirement on the statistical distribution of errors.

The Efficacy of Defect-Based Approaches

Mutation testing is currently the only technique known to me that falls into this category. As such, it is the only representative of this category for comparison purposes in this section.

Budd (1980) made a cursory comparison between various techniques falling under the categories of specification and program-based approaches and concluded that all testing goals stated by these approaches are also attainable through employment of mutation testing.

On the negative side, the following may be extended as criticisms of this approach:

- Mutation testing requires the execution of a very large number of mutations.
- It is very difficult (often impossible) to decide on the equivalence of a mutant and the original program, even for very simple systems.
- A large number (up to 80%) of all mutations die before contributing any significant information (Budd, 1980).

- The last remaining mutants (2%–10%) take up a significant number of test case applications (> 50%; Budd, 1980).

Statistical Testing Approaches

Statistical testing is the use of the random and statistical nature of defects to exercise a program or routine with the aim of causing it to fail (Thevenod-Fosse & Waeselynck, 1991). There are basically two approaches.

Use of a Probability Distribution to Generate Test Inputs

The extent of the effectiveness of this strategy is directly related to the distribution utilized to derive the input test set. Extreme variability therefore exists in terms of which distribution is utilized, ranging from a uniform distribution (Duran & Ntafos, 1984) to very sophisticated distributions derived formally from the structure or the specification of the routine (Higashino & von Bochman, 1994; Luo et al., 1994; Whittaker & Thomason, 1994).

There are essentially two directions one can take:

1. Use an informally selected distribution and then test each element many times. In other words, leave the composition of the input distribution to the tester's intuition. This is by far the most prevalent method of software testing and is popularly termed basic or simple random testing (Beizer, 1991; Humphrey, 1995; Myers, 1979). With this technique the tester generates and uses random inputs that are envisaged to uncover defects without the formal use of probability distributions but with a knowledge of the structure or the required functionality of program. This is a very simple and easily understandable strategy. However, its efficacy has been demonstrated to be generally too low for the production of commercially robust software, at least when utilized in isolation (Duran & Ntafos, 1984; Frankl et al., 1997; Woit, 1992). However, its popularity persists, making this approach a standard stock technique of testing practiced practically everywhere, at least as one of many methods (Cobb & Mills, 1990; Humphrey, 1995).

2. Search for test distributions that are better approximations of the operational profile or the structure of the routine and then reduce the number of tests for each element (e.g., Whittaker & Thomason, 1994). This is a theoretically attractive but practically arduous approach because the true operational profile of a software product and therefore its individual routines would usually be unknown prior to commissioning.

Another issue is the intricacy of the relationship between the structure of a routine and the test input distribution. This can become impractically complicated as the size and complexity of the routine grows (Frankl & Weyuker, 1993; Hamlet & Taylor, 1990). Fortunately, for object-oriented routines, if we manage to keep them cohesive and small, this might not be such a big issue.

Error Seeding

This is the very old but interesting technique of knowing when to stop testing. In this technique a known number of carefully devised known defects are seeded into a routine that is to be tested. The program is then tested and a number of these previously known and unknown defects are identified. Assuming that the seeded defects are typical defects, it stands to reason that the ratio of the known defects found to the total number of known defects is the same as the ratio for unknown defects. This allows us to statistically estimate the number of remaining defects in a routine (Endres, 1975; Mills, 1972, 1989). This technique can be applied at the routine, class, cluster, or system level.

A Comparison of the Effectiveness of Subdomain-Based and Statistically Based Approaches

As previously discussed, a number of authors have compared the defect-removal abilities of partition testing with the statistical method of simple random testing (Chen & Yu, 1994, 1996; Duran & Ntafos, 1984). They conclude that despite varying the combination of sample sizes, subdomain sizes, or the likelihood of execution from each subdomain, simple random testing proved more effective in terms of finding at least one failure during the testing process. Hamlet and Taylor (1990) and Weyuker and Jeng (1991) also concluded that partition testing does not increase the effectiveness of testing in comparison to random statistical testing means unless at least one subdomain has a relatively high failure probability, and low execution likelihood. It is not clear what proportion of "average" industrial object-oriented software possesses these properties, although the occurrence of such programs is not very high (Hamlet, 1989). Also due to the low execution likelihood requirement, it is logical to conclude that the defects found under those conditions will not have a significant effect on reducing the number of failures.

In accepting these findings, one must pay particular attention to the premises at the core of the experiment, and so has to satisfy oneself that the measure of finding at least one failure is an appropriate measure of test effectiveness.

Testing Derived and Abstract Classes

We have included the treatment of class hierarchies and therefore of derived and abstract classes in this chapter because one can demonstrate that logically a derived class can be reconstructed from its ancestry plus the content of the class itself. There are, of course, some rules and a number of complications. These were discussed in Chapter 1. The reconstruction of a class based on its content and what it inherits from its ancestors is called class flattening (Meyer, 1992). A flattened class is therefore a derived class that is being considered as a base class as if all its inherited features were local to it.

One type of class that may appear in the ancestry of a derived class is an abstract class. An abstract class is a class that has the implementation of at least one of its features postponed to a subclass. Therefore, testing derived classes and abstract classes belong to the same domain of discussion.

Testing Derived Classes

A derived class can be flattened and tested as if it were a base class. This makes the testing of a derived class logically the same as testing a base class. However, is it really necessary—or more correctly, to what degree is it really necessary—to test the parent classes of a derived class that participate in forming its flattened version, if they have already been tested?

Not testing them at all would expose us to the danger of not catching many defects that emerge from the interaction of classes and their subclasses. Testing them as an integral unit would require redoing many tests that have already been applied. This would waste time and project funds. The trick therefore is to come up with a strategy of testing only those combinations that need testing.

As part of their coverage-based structural testing strategy, Bashir and Goel (2000) provided for extending their technique to cover derived classes. We highlight such a strategy next.

Their approach assumes the task to be the testing of a derived class, the base class of which has already been tested. The strategy is to derive an enhanced call graph that captures the interrelationship between local and inherited features of the class concerned. The attribute call matrix of the derived class is then determined in a fashion similar to the testing of a base class, as discussed earlier. We add a row for each attribute that has been redefined in the derived class or are first defined in that class. We similarly add a column for each routine that has been introduced or redefined by the derived class. Special markings and notations are used to distinguish between inherited (belonging to the base) and local (introduced or redefined) features. The matrix thus obtained would have four quadrants.

Quadrant 1 shows the relationship between inherited attributes and inherited routines. It is essentially the same as the nonreduced matrix for the base class. By nonreduced we mean that all the redundant entries that were removed when testing the base class are still shown, as there might be—in other quadrants—an indirect usage of them.

Quadrant 2 shows the relationship between the inherited attributes from the base class and the routines of the derived class. This is one area where much new testing should be done.

Quadrant 3 shows the relationship between attributes of the derived class and the routines inherited from the base class. Initially, it might be envisaged that this quadrant should be empty, but this is not necessarily the case. Entries are made in this quadrant if a case exists that a routine of the base, say A_b, calls another routine B_b, and then B_b is redefined in a derived class as B_d. Now consider a call on an object of b type that invokes A_b. A_b in turn invokes B_b and we have no problem. However, if the method A is invoked on an object of d type, it would invoke B_d, which would manipulate the attributes of the derived class d!

Quadrant 4 shows the relationship between local attributes of the derived class and its routines. These are also new relationships that must be scrutinized closely.

We now determine the nonredundant slices and test for defects in each slice by testing permutations of routines that manipulate each attribute. It stands to reason that if a given combination determined by the permutation is already tested, it is skipped. Otherwise new tests are performed. The more interesting cases involve the interaction between new features (those redefined or originating in the derived class) or between them and features of the base class. These must all be tested whenever the context of slice is modified. In other words, a routine of the base class must be retested if the entries in its row have changed, particularly when the number of such entries has grown.

Testing from a Causal Perspective

The issue here is the need for conformance of the states of a derived class with those of its base class. In other words, if D is derived from B, then D must conform to all states of B as well as the new ones D has introduced. Given a modal situation, many faults may occur as a consequence of subclassing.

From a design perspective, a new feature extending a base class should only introduce new states. A redefined feature should only present states that are extensions or substates of the original. Neither should ever be allowed to alter the state of the superclass. Yet a base class might have state faults that only come to the fore in a substate context, maybe one presented by a redefined routine or a new one in the context of a subclass. A rerun of all base class state-based test suites is usually recommended. Branch coverage on the flow graph of the flattened class is a minimal requirement.

Testing Abstract Classes

The trouble with abstract classes is that—being abstract—they cannot be instantiated. To test a class, we must have an instance of it, and this is impossible with abstract classes. The best course of action to manage defects of abstract classes is to use a static approach such as inspection or automated analysis rather than execution-based testing.

This said, however, there are a number of approaches that might make some type of execution-based evaluation of abstract classes possible. One way is to create a concrete version of the abstract class by ensuring that all abstracted routines are stubbed appropriately (see Figure 8.1).

By appropriately we mean that pre- and postconditions must be provided for these stubs to conform with exactly how these stubs might be implemented in a derived class. This is sometimes not possible, as we might not know what sort of extension might be made of the abstract class. Even when there is clarity, it is often very difficult to write such assertions for anything other than very simple cases.

Another problem with this approach is its lack or difficulty of extensibility down the class hierarchy. For this strategy to work for more than one layer, we must have repeated or multiple inheritance available to us, but this is not always the case with many object-oriented programming languages.

Another possibility is to test the abstract class with its descendants in a flattened class form. To do so, the abstract class must be tested repeatedly with every flattening possible. This approach is usually adopted.

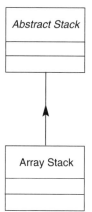

Figure 8.1
Deriving a concrete subclass from an abstract type.

Conclusion

In this chapter we discussed a number of testing techniques applicable at the class level. This included techniques that applied at the level of the individual class itself (in fact at the level of the individual object that was an instance of the class concerned) and its components. The discussion also logically extended to the discussion of derived and abstract classes. In the next chapter, we continue with this topic by discussing testing of clusters of classes as we integrate individual objects into an application and then conclude with a discussion of system testing.

Chapter 9

Integration, Integration Testing, and System Testing

Despite the fact that the topics of integration and system testing are usually mentioned and handled together by many writers in software engineering, the two are separate concerns and are usually only put together because the volume of discussion on one or the other would not merit a separate chapter or section. Here also I have combined the discussion of both topics in this chapter, but I do recognize the differences in the spirit and conduct of these two activities.

An important issue to be conscious of relates to the first of the two topics, to distinguish between integration and integration testing. *Integration* is the act of combining individual units to get a composite module; for example, to combine a number of classes to obtain a package or subsystem. This is part of implementation and although how integration is achieved does have an impact on defect management practices, it is not in itself a defect management practice. Integration testing, on the other hand, is the defect management strategy of pursuing potential defects that might emerge as a result of interaction of software units and that would not manifest themselves with respect to a single unit's composition or operation.

Integration, therefore, is realization of the design of the system and its evaluation would be of design artifacts such as sequence diagrams and design class diagrams. System testing is, on the other hand, the evaluation of the degree and limits of if and how the complete collection of all software units and modules combined after integration would satisfy the stated or implied requirements. As such, system testing is done with respect not to design (although it may be informed by it) but of the specification. Artifacts such as usecases therefore are utilized instead.

It should be clarified further that there are in some opinions two different stages of system testing. One resembles integration testing and can be thought of as the very last stage of integration testing when the last module or unit of software is incorporated and tested. This we call *system integration testing*. It is in our opinion the natural end result—and therefore a part—of integration and integration testing against the design of the software product in question. The other is true system testing because it is done against customer requirements and is performed after all modules are integrated and integration testing has ended. Customer acceptance procedures may be thought of as being one such true system test. It is this latter kind that we discuss as system testing in this chapter.

Components and Integration

Integration testing has to do with the integration of components. A component for the purpose of this discussion is any unit of software that can be decomposed into smaller cohesive units. The concept of cohesion is important here because emergent properties must exist before a unit is considered a component. In an object-oriented system, for example, a class is a component. It has properties that would not exist if it were taken apart. A class is also the unit of object-oriented software. As such, although it would be possible to think of individual routines and attributes of a class as units, they would lack cohesion and therefore we do not consider them components. At any rate, integration and integration testing deal with combining classes and groups of classes. The individual classes are assumed to have been already adequately tested and sufficiently free of defects. Integration is, however, not necessarily only at the level of combining individual classes. Several previously integrated (and integration-tested) clusters of classes could be put together to form a larger cluster, and so on, until all necessary components of the system are integrated and tested (see Figure 9.1).

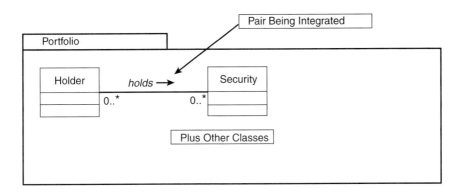

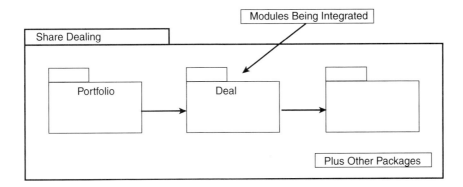

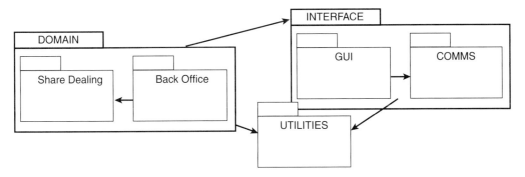

Figure 9.1
Multiple levels of integration.

Another important issue is to make a distinction between components and their more restricted subtypes, subsystems. A component is merely a cohesive collection of modules; it does not need to implement any particular or distinguishable end-to-end part of the specification (e.g., the Utilities component in Figure 9.1). For a component to be a subsystem, on the other hand, it is necessary for such a condition to exist. For example, look at Share Dealing in Figure 9.1. Integration testing can and does apply to all components, whether they form subsystems or not. Subsystem testing, however, does not and cannot apply to all types of components, only those that are subsystems. Subsystem testing is, of course, testing the lower level elements of a component that is a subsystem with respect to the specification. In other words, subsystem testing is testing of a component subsystem as if it were the entire system against that portion of the specification that is relevant to it.

Component Interaction

The essence of object orientation is message passing. Interaction among components therefore is critical in every aspect of object orientation, particularly in integration and integration testing. However, object-oriented components being interdependent, the sequence of integration of such components is critical from the perspective of its integration testing. A defect in the interface between Modules B and C that may be easily observable when A is integrated with B and then AB with C may not be as easily detectable when C is integrated with A and then AC with B! Therefore choosing the sequence of integration is critical. Unfortunately, determining the correct sequence of integration, if possible, is almost as hard as proving the program correct in a formal sense. However, there are a number of popular and sensible strategies, although not all are suitable in all cases or in relation to all types of integration testing techniques. One challenge of integration testing is to choose the right combination of integration strategy and integration testing technique. To be able to provide such guidance, we first need to examine the various integration techniques and then the different types of integration testing strategies available.

Integration Strategies

There are a myriad of ways to integrate components. The following are a few of these ways, selected for their power, simplicity, or popularity:

1. Collective integration, sometimes called the big bang approach, integrates all components at the same time and then proceeds to detect defects.

2. Top-down integration utilizes the system's control hierarchy. In an object-oriented system this is possible only if such hierarchy actually and "naturally" exists; for example, when there is a head or control class. Given that the spirit of object orientation encourages distribution and is the antithesis to designs that contain privileged or special classes, top-down integration has only limited utility.

3. Usage-based or bottom-up integration is the technique of testing according to the control structure but in a constructive fashion, from leaf level up. Again, such techniques are only useful in systems that possess a hierarchical structure.

4. Layered integration considers the system as layers and performs integration based on the interaction between these layers. A layered architecture should prevail for this technique to be applicable.

5. Progressive or collaborative integration is probably the most appropriate form of integration in the case of most object-oriented integration testing situations. It uses the collaborative essence of object orientation in that it assumes no special characteristic for any of the modules that are to be integrated. The only guidance is what is dictated by the collaboration requirements of the modules being tested as available in the design. Client–server integration is a particular instance of collaborative integration in that the interaction of a number of clients and one server is taken as the basis for integration testing.

It should be noted that these interaction strategies are largely independent of the scope of their application. By that we mean that integration using such techniques can be made at any cohesive level of granularity, be it a collection of classes, a collection of packages, or a collection of large subsystems.

Orthogonal to these integration strategies but not to each other in terms of defect detection capability are a number of integration testing techniques, discussed next.

Integration Testing Techniques

Jüttner et al. (1994) indicated the necessity of using multiple approaches to integration testing. In agreement with Jüttner et al.'s assertion, I introduce various techniques of integration that apply at various levels:

1. Binary or couple testing is the technique of testing the impact of a client component's operations on the state of the server component.

2. Scenario testing follows a use scenario to ensure that correct states are reached.

3. Modal testing tests the behavior of subsystems with behavior that is defined sequentially and modal.

Adequate integration testing would probably benefit from a combination or sequence of these techniques together.

Binary or Couple Testing

This approach basically builds on the structural testing technique discussed in Chapter 8. You might recall that the approach discussed related the attribute values of an object with the routines of the same class (or a subclass) that alter them. Here, the idea is extended to encompass the impact of the routines of a client object on the attributes of a server object. Once these relationships are identified, slices are selected and tests are performed (Bashir & Goel, 2000).

Let us look at an interaction between the client object **c:C** and the server object **s:S**. Let us further assume that Object **c** has m routines and n attributes. Similarly Object **s** we assume to have p routines and q attributes. We also assume that both Objects **c** and **s** have been unit tested adequately. We now reconstruct the $n \times m$ matrix representing the interaction of the attributes and routines for Object **c** and the $p \times q$ matrix for Object **s**. We then proceed to construct an $m \times p$ matrix to capture and represent the interrelationship of the routines of **c** and **s**. If a routine of Object **c** calls a routine of Object **s**, the intersecting cell in the $m \times p$ matrix is marked.

Now, for each attribute, having determined a slice, these would yield the sequence of test cases, as per the $n \times m$ matrix of Object **c** already available.

Next, we bring in the impact of the routines of Object **s**. Thus for each routine of Object **c** that calls any routine of Object **s** we make substitution reflecting that fact. For example, if m_1 calls p_1, we substitute $m_1(p_1)$ for slice n_1. All test cases are then rewritten in this fashion. We then distill the sequences to only the routine sequences from the server object. This can potentially yield several redundant sequences that must be eliminated. Once the set of test sequences is reduced to its essential cardinality, we represent each routine of Object **s** by the routine or routines in Object **c** that call it. This gives us the test set we need to run. An example follows.

Let us assume that two classes **C** and **S** have been adequately unit tested. Let us further assume that Class **C** is instantiated to Object **c**, and Class **S** to Object **s**. Let us also assume that Object **c** has three attributes (n_1, n_2, and n_3) and five routines (m_1– m_5). Object **s** has three attributes (q_1, q_2, and q_3) and four routines (p_1– p_4). Let us also assume the relationships between the various entities as marked in Tables 9.1 and 9.2.

Table 9.1   Object c:C, the Client Object

		ROUTINES				
		m_1	m_2	m_3	m_4	m_5
ATTR	n_1	✓	✓		✓	
	n_2		✓	✓		✓
	n_3	✓			✓	

Therefore, for n_1, the test sequence would be:

$$m_1 , m_2 , m_4$$
$$m_1 , m_4 , m_2$$
$$m_2 , m_1 , m_4$$
$$m_2 , m_4 , m_1$$
$$m_4 , m_1 , m_2$$
$$m_4 , m_2 , m_1$$

Note that m_3 and m_5 do not participate.

Table 9.2   Object s:S, the Server Object

		ROUTINES			
		p_1	p_2	p_3	p_4
ATTR	q_1	✓			✓
	q_2		✓	✓	
	q_3				✓

The $m \times p$ matrix depicting the interaction between the client and server objects is shown in Table 9.3.

Table 9.3   The Call Relationship Between the Client and the Server

		ROUTINES-C				
		m_1	m_2	m_3	m_4	m_5
ROUTINES-S	p_1	✓				
	p_2			✓		✓
	p_3					
	p_4		✓			
	p_5					

We now use the matrix in Table 9.3 to reflect the impact of the client routine calls on the server. For the slice n_1, the sequence would be:

m_1, m_2, m_4	$\rightarrow m_1(p_1), m_2(p_4), \phi$	$\rightarrow$	$m_1(p_1), m_2(p_4)$
m_1, m_4, m_2	$\rightarrow m_1(p_1), \phi, m_2(p_4)$	$\rightarrow$	$m_1(p_1), m_2(p_4)$
m_2, m_1, m_4	$\rightarrow m_2(p_4), m_1(p_1), \phi$	$\rightarrow$	$m_2(p_4), m_1(p_1)$
m_2, m_4, m_1	$\rightarrow m_2(p_4), \phi, m_1(p_1)$	$\rightarrow$	$m_2(p_4), m_1(p_1)$
m_4, m_1, m_2	$\rightarrow \phi, m_1(p_1), m_2(p_4)$	$\rightarrow$	$m_1(p_1), m_2(p_4)$
m_4, m_2, m_1	$\rightarrow \phi, m_2(p_4), m_1(p_1)$	$\rightarrow$	$m_2(p_4), m_1(p_1)$

where ϕ stands for null participation, as m_4 does not call any server routines, p.

Distilling by removing redundant sequences, we get: $m_1(p_1), m_2(p_4)$ and $m_2(p_4), m_1(p_1)$, which imply test sequences m_1, m_2 and m_2, m_1, for slice n_1. Other slices need to be treated similarly.

Scenario Testing

As its name indicates, scenario testing uses an end-to-end sequence of state transitions to ensure that the states that need to be reached in each scenario are indeed correctly reached. An end-to-end scenario depicts a part of the system that corresponds to a logically cohesive segment of the specification in terms of states and transitions between them. Instances of one or several classes may be involved in an end-to-end scenario that may or may not be aligned directly to any specific usecase. In fact, such scenario testing is best performed against specific instances of sequence diagrams and not instances of usecases. This statement does not ignore the fact that there is often a correspondence between sequence diagrams and usecases.

The essence of scenario testing is therefore the extraction of individual test sequences in the form of a control flow model from the design dynamic model of the system.

In earlier chapters we saw that a well-formed sequence diagram depicts the sequence of events as they are exchanged between collaborating objects to achieve a concrete and cohesive task. It is customary among designers and practitioners to draw sequence diagrams that, in addition to dynamic information, contain transformational information. Use of sequence diagrams in scenario testing is yet another argument for limiting such practice. A sequence diagram should contain the dynamic behavior of the sequence and should be cohesive in itself. In other words, it should concentrate on one sequence, not several that might have some sequence in common but deviate transformationally. For example, it is probably best to draw two distinct sequence diagrams for these cases. First, when a coin is inserted in a vending machine, the machine asks for more coins, a minimum sum is reached, and the machine asks for a selection. The user makes the selection but the machine indicates that the item is not available. Second, when a coin is inserted in a vending machine, the machine asks for more coins, a minimum sum is reached, and the machine asks for a selection. The user makes the selection but the machine indicates that the item is not available. These two cases, although they might have many steps in common, are fundamentally different sequences with different occasions of use, different consequences, potentially different classes involved, and most fundamentally, in need of a transformation (e.g., a decision point) to select between them.

Such selection has nothing to do with sequences and states, but with transformations and decisions, and it belongs to a separate model—a transformational model. As such, each sequence diagram should depict a single and cohesive end-to-end sequence of events and no conditionals or iterations. This might increase the number of individual sequence diagrams, but at the same time it renders them simpler and more useful. We assume that we are dealing with this type of sequence diagrams.

A scenario, in our discussion, is therefore one instance of going through such a cohesive sequence diagram. It is important to distinguish between a scenario and a sequence. A sequence is the abstract version of a scenario. This means that several scenarios can be extracted from a given sequence. For example, a sequence may indicate that a sum of money is inserted and an item is successfully selected and dispensed. It does not say what sum was deposited and what item was selected and whether the same item was dispensed. To test such a system we need to cover these individual cases as much as possible rather than just suffice with an abstract case. This means that the sequence diagram needs to be viewed as a sequence of routine calls between collaborating objects. We need to test the correctness of such sequences but also each individual routine call in terms of the range of possible values that may correspond with the preconditions of each routine. This means that we need to identify individual paths through each sequence diagram from end to end. If the sequence diagrams are of the type we have advocated, this should be trivial. Each sequence results in one linear flow graph. Otherwise, we convert each sequence diagram to a flow graph by inserting decision and iteration points where needed. Additionally, each condition or guard on an event also becomes a decision point. We then identify individual paths in the flow graph derived and identify the input sets that would cause the selection of each path. Each path would now correspond to a set of tests, and each set of tests would represent adequate testing of the various partitions of the input set of each routine in the path. The outcome of each test can then be compared with the outcome expected as per the sequence diagram.

Modal Testing

This is a test of an integrated subsystem or system. When there is a definable, cohesive, and modal subsystem or system with equally definable interaction with the outside (the rest of the system or the outside world), we can model the behavior of such a subsystem or system to assist us in testing issues such as rejection of valid states for that subsystem, production of invalid end states, and incorrect acceptance of events when they should be rejected.

The basis of such testing is the determination of the collective state of the subsystem and how it is changed as a consequence of stimuli received by it. In other words, we can view the subsystem under test as an individual cohesive unit (like a single object) and determine its state model as it interacts with stimuli that it receives.

One effective way of viewing this scheme is to initially look at what amounts to a sequence diagram of this cohesive unit and the objects with which it interacts. The MVC model is one appropriate way of envisaging this. Under such a view, our subsystem under test is the model and the interacting objects are the controller and view.

Having obtained such a set of sequence diagrams, we can use them to construct an integrated (collective) state model of the subsystem as it interacts.

The next step is to form a transition tree (see Chapter 8) that covers the state model by tracing out each and every root-to-node path that in turn would represent a test case. This demonstrates conformance for the subsystem. The converse also needs to be tested. This means that we also need to test for situations when incorrect events are accepted when they should have been rejected. Modal testing to determine sneak paths may be employed with the subsystem taken as the model object considered a single entity. Basically this means countertesting (trying those events that are not allowed) of all transitions except those that are valid or not feasible.

System Testing

This chapter so far has been about testing integrated components. These tests, as mentioned, were done with respect to the design of the application, even if it was ultimately the specification that drove the testing process. System testing, on the other hand, can be with respect to the design—as the last stage of integration and integration testing—or directly with respect to the specification. It is principally the latter that we discuss now.

For system testing to take place, first a system must exist. Here we recall the distinction given previously of components and systems or subsystems. These systems are tested against the requirements for that system as a cohesive unit. It is further assumed that the units and subsystems of such a system have been tested and integrated correctly and such integration adequately scrutinized.

Such a state of affairs should indicate that the system should conform to its design. To the extent that the design in question reflects the requirements—a fact that should have been confirmed during design defect management—the system by extension should therefore reflect the requirements stated against it. However, be aware of the following:

1. Not all requirements may have been explicitly expressed.

2. This is our last chance to identify deviations—if any—from the requirements and therefore to improve the quality of the system before it is handed over to the customer.

3. Not all requirements may have been adequately incorporated in the design, particularly those nonfunctional requirements such as capacity, load, and recovery requirements.

4. Not all requirements may have been adequately tested at the design test stage.

It is for these reasons—and many more—that we need to do system testing.

System requirements against which testing is to be performed may be viewed (nonorthogonally) in terms of attributes such as functionality, reliability, usability, and maintainability. For a system in which a high degree of confidence is to reside, such attributes must be ultimately tested at the system level.

Functional testing at the system level encompasses considerations such as these:

1. Maintenance of the abstract system state in accordance with the requirements, stated or implied, and

2. Generation of correct output given correct inputs and state.

Reliability testing at the system level encompasses considerations such as these:

1. Maintenance of the abstract system state in accordance with the requirements stated or implied,

2. Correct state transition from one valid state to another, and

3. Consistent startup, restart, and recovery.

Usability testing in turn requires:

1. Correct behavior under varying degrees of data volume,

2. Correct behavior under varying degrees of transaction volume,

3. Correct behavior under varying degrees of user volume,

4. Consistency of the user interface—if one is present, and

5. Consistency and logicality of task groupings.

Maintainability testing requires only the conformance of system documentation and system behavior.

Usecase-Based Testing

Many aspects of the functionality and reliability of a system may be tested using the set of usecases developed as part of the software system specification. It is probably more effective to have a two-pronged approach to such testing: both top-down and bottom-up, which relate to the location of the individual usecase selected in the usecase diagram hierarchy. Therefore, this represents a possible approach:

1. Select and rank (see Chapter 3) high-level usecases that collectively demonstrate the general operation of the system. These are the usecases at the top one or two levels.

2. Identify the requirement to which the usecase refers.

3. Start with the usecase on the top and determine a sufficient number of scenarios (event traces) as instances of the selected usecase. Category partition on initial states and boundary condition analysis may help in selecting these scenarios.

4. Execute each scenario and compare results with expectation (the requirement).

5. Once overall functionality is assessed, shift attention to leaf-level (lowest level) usecases. Select and rank these.

6. Perform Steps 2 to 4 for leaf-level usecases.

7. Shift attention again to moderately high-level (immediately below the top level ones selected already) and repeat Steps 2 to 4.

8. Continue until all usecases have been exercised.

System Temporal Boundary Testing

This test refers to procedures used to determine correct system behavior during initial startup, restart and recovery.

The test for initial startup must be done in accordance with startup requirements if such requirements exist (they should). Such requirements may be in the form of state diagrams, usecases, or some similar artifact. The advantage of this approach is that it tests the startup behavior with respect to both the design and the specification of the system. The testing method is simply to execute the system at startup and to observe and compare the behavior to expectations. In addition, we need to ensure that the startup process is in accordance with the documented startup procedure.

Restart and recovery must be from a known and logical state. This condition must be tested at least with respect to normal expectations and what has been specified. To assure successful restart we must examine the class and state invariants of all objects as they are restarted. The restart sequence must also be checked.

Performance and Load Testing

There are generally several categories of performance testing, including the following:

1. Data volume testing,
2. Transaction volume testing,
3. User volume testing,
4. Memory utilization testing, and
5. Network volume testing.

To begin testing of any of these categories we must first determine a performance measure. In other words, we must first know what constitutes adequate performance. Once performance measures are available, performance testing can continue. As performance assesses functionality of the system, usecases again are very useful. Follow this procedure:

1. Select and rank basic, top-level usecases that together encompass the functionality of the system that might be sensitive to volume variations.
2. Select the top usecase.
3. Develop specific scenarios from these usecases.
4. Select one mode (initial state) and test the scenario based on that mode.
5. Alter each of the following over a predetermined range to represent typical and extreme stress on the system:

   a. Transactions
   b. Storage accessibility
   c. Memory accessibility
   d. Network load
   e. Number of concurrent users accessing (logged on but not using) the system

f. Number of concurrent users utilizing (actually performing tasks on) the system

g. Number of concurrent database accesses

h. Number of concurrent invocations of the same functionality

Usability Testing

Human factors and usability are also very important attributes of a system and their adequacy must be assessed. The HCI literature is rich with advice regarding various methods of usability testing, so we do not discuss this aspect as part of our work here.

System Acceptance

System acceptance is an important late-stage technique within the development life cycle involving both the developer and the customer. Often incorporating a series of tests and demonstrations, we define system acceptance as determination of the degree of conformance of the proposed product with the current version of the user requirements as demonstrated by the developer and perceived by the procurer.

System acceptance is, however, often mistakenly equated with acceptance testing, which is only a possible subactivity of system acceptance. System acceptance is (or should be) a life-cycle technique, but acceptance testing is one possible approach that might provide some evidence toward the determination of the degree of conformance of software being demonstrated and the intended requirements the software is to fulfill. It is important to note that, to this end, approaches other than testing can also be used. For example, once it is determined that some requirement is to be fulfilled, the conformance of the system code with this requirement may be demonstrated through a formal proof.

It should also be noted that, as a process-oriented technique, system acceptance is fundamentally different in nature to testing because whereas testing is conducted with the intent of discovering nonconformance, acceptance is generally intended to demonstrate conformance.

Before a system can be accepted, it should be available to be shipped (i.e., finished and ready to go), at the right price, and of adequate quality. At the time of system acceptance, it is highly likely that price expectation and the system availability to ship are already satisfied. The central issue of system acceptance is therefore the assessment of the quality of the proposed system.

However, as system acceptance is a demonstration of the extent of conformance of software to the requirements, it is important for it to be conducted in an environment that assures both the coverage of all important areas of requirement, and the establishment of quantitative acceptance success factors.

To ensure that both these requirements are fulfilled, I recommend an approach that recognizes that the activity of software acceptance is, in fact, identical to that of product quality determination in that they both refer to the degree of satisfaction of the customer with the software product.

In Chapter 3 we presented a coherent and systemic process for the determination of the quality attributes deemed important in a system to be developed. At that time we advocated that such determination be made early in the life-cycle process and before system design is underway. We saw a five-stage process of determining a reconciled set of measurable quality attributes of a system as envisaged by the various stakeholders of that system. Armed with such a set of quality attributes and measures, we can extend the process into a system acceptance procedure.

The initial five stages (in brief) were as follows (see Chapter 3 for details):

Stage 1. Construct a quality matrix.

Stage 2. Fill (complete) the matrix.

Stage 3. Test for coverage.

Stage 4. Document.

Stage 5. Update.

We can now add a sixth stage, **Enact:**

1. At the time of system acceptance, use the latest version of the acceptance document produced in Stage 4 to obtain a list of all requirements you are testing for conformance and the details of the corresponding methods and success criteria for each such demonstration.

2. Obtain (or at least schedule) and arrange all resources needed to perform each demonstration.

3. Determine the interdependencies particularly between:

   a. Requirements (e.g., Requirement 26 is predicated on satisfaction of Requirement 22).

   b. Evaluation techniques (e.g., test to demonstrate conformance to Requirement 20 requires a structure or result that is developed or obtained when formally proving Program Y, the proof of which is a success factor for demonstrating Requirement 55).

   c. Physical resources required (e.g., tests for Program X and Y both have to run on the same machine and utilize the same peripherals and sensors).

4. Using the information in Steps 2 and 3, produce a project activity network and a project plan for the system acceptance activity.

5. Perform each acceptance activity (demonstrate, test, analyze, prove, etc.) as stated in the acceptance document and evaluate the result (this should be easy because explicit success factors are available).

6. Sign off with the customer.

Beta Testing

An effective way of ensuring that a system is going to be acceptable to the user base is to involve some of them in evaluating the system prior to its general release. This is most effective in the case of "shrinkwrapped" software; that is, systems that are not developed for a specific client and are to be marketed to a wide customer base (e.g., Microsoft Windows XP). This is called *beta testing*.

There is more to beta testing than just putting the product out to a subset of customers who volunteer. There are a number of important issues that have to be considered, including those covered next.

Identify a Purpose for Beta Testing

One major issue that leads to failed or less than successful beta testing is that often there is no specific statement of purpose for the testing procedure. In other words the developer does not state the following clearly:

- What aspects of the product do they want evaluated? Is there an order of priority they want observed? Not stating this requirement clearly can lead to an evaluation made in piecemeal fashion with some important aspects missed or not considered of any consequence. For example, users might evaluate and like the user interface but never bother to check the "backup" facilities. It should be noted, however, that if the beta sites are selected correctly (discussed later), this problem should not arise, as correct selection of beta sites should ensure evaluation of every aspect of the product.

- What level of precision or detail do they want the participants to apply to the product evaluation? Different individuals or sites might have different priorities and might evaluate the product at differing levels of criticality. This can potentially create confusion in utilizing the results of the beta test.

- What feedback does the developer want from the beta sites and in what form? In the absence of the provision of guidelines about form or level of feedback required, the developer might receive anything as a beta test evaluation ranging from one that simply says "We liked it!" to a multivolume document of everything and anything the system did or did not do.

Select Your Sites Carefully

Not everyone who volunteers is an appropriate beta site. Often, in desperation to maximize the number of participants in the beta testing exercise, developers do themselves a great disservice by including inappropriate evaluators. Note the following:

- Select your sites to be statistically representative of your target market. A product developed for the "general" market is likely to be contemplated or purchased by a wide array of potential users. These users define a spectrum of various needs and wants. During beta testing, ensure that this is taken into account when selecting beta sites. Otherwise you will run the risk of losing a segment of your market or not having certain aspects of the system adequately evaluated.

- Select sites that are "capable" of beta testing your product. For a myriad of reasons ranging from lack of time to lack of expertise, some sites are not capable of adequately evaluating your product. Avoid wasting your time and theirs by conducting an initial screening of their abilities, commitments, and objectives.

- Do not deliver your product into the hands of the "enemy." If your trade secrets are important to you or you wish to "surprise" the market, then be very careful about who you allow to beta test your product.

Decide What to Do Next

- Use the information you get from your beta sites. It is surprising how many developers ignore a lot of feedback from their beta sites! If you have selected your sites carefully and correctly, and if the feedback data you have received are in a useful and statistically significant form, then they should be used.

- Decide whether to enhance or modify now, to send back for more beta testing, or to keep the modification suggestion for a future version. Use the information to make enhancements or modifications to the product or to decide when such modification or enhancement should debut, perhaps in a future version. If you have carefully selected your beta sites and have specific statements of purpose, sending software back for more beta testing should not be necessary.

Conclusion

Once the components of a system are developed and evaluated individually, they need to be integrated to compose a system. In this chapter we discussed the issues, potentials, and problems associated with integration and how components—once integrated—need to be evaluated in terms of the adequacy of their interoperability.

Once a system is put together and the interoperability of its components is evaluated, we still need to do two more things before we develop adequate confidence in the product:

1. Evaluate the system with respect to its requirements and ensure it fulfills them, and

2. Demonstrate such conformance to customers in a meaningful and irrefutable (or at least acceptable) manner.

The first of these activities is called system testing and the second is system acceptance. We also described both these activities in this chapter.

Appendix A

A TAXONOMY OF DEFECT MANAGEMENT

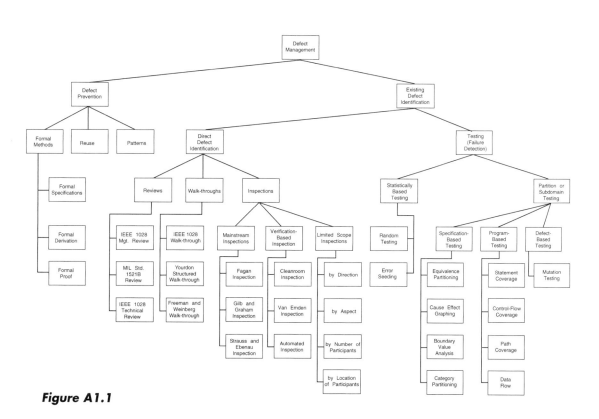

Figure A1.1

Appendix B

SYNTAX OF OBJECT Z

Sets and Types

[X]	Type X
data type $::= m_1 \vert m_2 \vert \ldots \vert m_n$	
X = = Y	X stands for Y
Z	Set of integers
N	Set of natural numbers (≥ 0)
N_1	Set of positive integers (≥ 1)
$t \in S$	t is an element of set S
$t \notin S$	t is not an element of set S
$S \subseteq T$	S is contained in T
$S \subset T$	S is strictly contained in T ($S \neq T$)
$S \not\subset T$	S is not contained in T
$S \cap T$	Set of intersection of S and T
$S \cup T$	Set of the union of S and T
$\mathbb{P}S$	Powerset of S: the set of all subsets of S

$\mathbb{F}S$	Finite powerset of S: the set of all finite subsets of S
$\cap SS$	The distributed intersection of all sets in SS
$\cup SS$	The distributed union of all sets in SS
$\varnothing$ Or { }	The null or empty set
S\T	Difference: elements that are in S but not in T
#S	Size or cardinality: number of elements in S
{D|p.t}	Set of t's such that given declaration D, P holds
disjoint Sq	The sets in the sequence sq are disjoint
sq partition S	The sets in sq partition the set S

Logic

true, false	Logical constants
$\neg P$	Not P
$P \wedge Q$	Conjunction: "P and Q"
$P \vee Q$	Disjunction: "P or Q"
$P \Rightarrow Q$	Implication: "If P then Q"
$P \Leftrightarrow Q$	Equivalence: "If P then Q and if Q then P"
t=r	Term t is equal to term r
$t \neq r$	Term t is not equal to term r; that is, $\varnothing(t=r)$

Predicates

$\forall x{:}T.P$	For all x of type T, P holds
$\exists x{:}\ T.P$	There exists an x of type T, for which P holds

Relations

X × Y	The set of ordered pairs of Xs and Ys
X ↔ Y	The set of relations from X to Y; = = $\mathbb{P}(XY)$
x R y	x is related to y by R; (x,y) εR
dom R	The domain of relation R; = = {x:X	(∃x:X . x R y) . x}
ran R	The range of a relation R; = = {y:Y	(∃x:X . x R y) . y}
S◁R	The relation R is domain restricted to S
R▷S	The relation R is range restricted to S
R~	The inverse of R

Functions

X ↦ Y	The set of partial functions from X to Y
	= = {f:X↔Y	(∀x:X	x∈ dom f. (∃₁y:Y.x f y))}
X → Y	The set of total functions from X to Y
	= = {f: X ↦ Y| dom f = X.f}
fx or f(x)	Function f is applied to x

Sequences

seq X	The set of sequences with elements drawn from X
	= = {S:N ↦X	dom S = 1...#S}
seq₁ X	Set of nonempty sequences of X
iseq X	Set of nonduplicate sequences of X
#S	The length of sequence X
< >	The empty sequence

<x$_1$,...x$_n$> The sequence of x$_1$ through to x$_n$

<x$_1$,...x$_n$>^<y$_1$,...y$_n$> concatenation

$$= = <x_1,...x_n,y_1,...y_n>$$

head S $= = S_1$

last S $= = S_{\#S}$

tail S^S$_1$ $= = S$

frontS^<x> $= = S$ where <x>$= =$last S

rev S   The sequence S in reverse order

Schemas

Class Schema

```
___Class Name[generic parameter] _____

 inherited classes
 type definitions
 constant definitions
 state schema
 initial state schema
 operation schemas
_____

 history invariant
```

State Schema

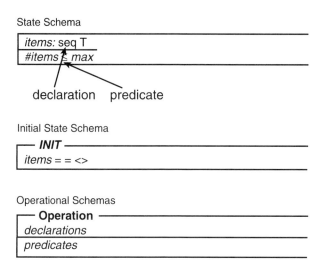

declaration   predicate

Initial State Schema

```
 ┌─ INIT ────────────────────
 │ items = = <>
```

Operational Schemas

```
 ┌─ Operation ────────────────
 │ declarations
 │ predicates
```

Figure A2.1

Schema Decorations

| *name*: T	*name* is a constant of type T
item ?: T	*item* is an input or accepts input
item !: T	*item* is an output or holds an output
item'	New state of *item* after change
Δ(*item*)	The schema effects change on *item*

Appendix C

SOFTWARE INSPECTION PROCESS

1. Inspection Process Script

1.1 Definitions

Please refer to script I-1.

1.2 Introduction

Formal inspections are rigorous and formal techniques for the peer examination of work products held to identify and remove defects injected into newly developed or revised artifacts as a result of developer error. They may be applied to all phases of development and a wide variety of work products including those of requirements, high-level and low-level design, code, and test procedures. Inspections are designed to remove defects early in the development phase and when such removal is relatively inexpensive.

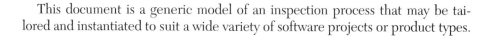

This document is a generic model of an inspection process that may be tailored and instantiated to suit a wide variety of software projects or product types.

1.3 Statement of Purpose

The purpose of conducting formal inspections is to reduce the number of defects transmitted from one development stage or phase to the next. As it is a generally held view that early detection of defects minimizes the cost of their removal, formal inspections thereby reduce the cost of improving product correctness and quality. Another aim of software inspection is to assure adherence to project coding and documentation standards. In fact each instance of the lack of such adherence may be deemed a maintainability defect, and as such detectable and removable through the inspection process.

1.4 Process Description

A typical software inspection process consists of six distinct stages. Please refer to Script I-2X (where X stands at a minimum for either S, D, or C, in turn standing for specification, design, or code). The following is a short description of each stage:

1. Inspection Planning
    The author or the author's proxy works with the coordinator to collect the necessary inspection material (the input) and ensure that they meet all the entry criteria. They then select a moderator for the inspection team. The moderator and the author or his or her proxy then select the remaining team members and schedule a meeting time at least a week in advance, ensuring that all selected team members are available and can attend the inspection meeting scheduled. The moderator then duplicates and distributes the necessary input material to all inspection team members.

2. Inspection Overview
    Optionally, and when it is deemed necessary or useful to educate the inspection team members in some aspect of the process or the material to be inspected, an overview session is held. This usually takes the form of the author, or his or her proxy making a half-hour to one-hour presentation on the aspect that requires special attention. The moderator arranges and schedules an overview that is attended by all team members.

3. Inspection Preparation

   On receipt of the inspection material and before the inspection meeting, each inspection team member studies the inspection input material and thoroughly familiarizes himself or herself with what is provided, so that they can better find defects during the inspection. Guided by appropriate checklists and guidelines, each inspector is responsible for his or her own adequate preparation and is required to record the time spent in preparation. During such preparation, an inspector may come across what is deemed to be a defect. At this stage, the inspector notes down the details of the defect on the Inspection Preparation Notes Form (e.g., Form I-3X where X stands at a minimum for either S, D, or C, in turn standing for specification, design, or code), the contents of which may then be discussed during the inspection meeting.

4. Inspection Meeting

   This meeting is scheduled by the moderator and is attended by all inspection team members. At the start of the meeting, the moderator who is in charge of conducting the meeting reviews the agenda, highlights the purpose of the meeting, and ensures that all team members have completed their preparation. During this meeting, the purpose of which is to locate defects, the reader presents and paraphrases the work in small segments. As the material is presented, each inspector looks for defects or identifies defects noted on Form I-3 during preparation. As defects are recognized and accepted, they are recorded and classified on the inspection defects list (Form I-4X where X stands at a minimum for either S, D, or C, in turn standing for specification, design, or code). At the end of the meeting the moderator ensures that all inspectors are unanimous on the number and the nature of all defects identified and arrive at a "disposition" for the output work product.

5. Rework

   The Inspection Defects List (Form I-4X) will be presented to the author or the person responsible for making the changes necessary to remove the defects, who carries out this task or organizes the list so that the changes can be carried out to the satisfaction of the exit criteria.

6. Follow-up

   Once the defects have been removed, the moderator follows up the revisions and may or may not call another inspection meeting to ensure adequate proximity of the work product to the requirements of the exit criteria. Once satisfied, the moderator submits an Inspection Summary Report (Form I-5) to the coordinator.

1.5 Process Roles

The following roles are present during inspections:

1. Author/Author's Proxy
   This is the individual who has either produced the work product (e.g.,
   a designer or programmer) or is responsible for its production (e.g., a
   team leader) or for effecting any changes or someone sufficiently
   familiar with the work to act as a proxy. The role of the author or proxy
   is to work as part of the inspection team to identify defects based on
   his or her special understanding of the material being examined. This
   role may not be combined with that of moderator, scribe, or reader.

2. Moderator
   The moderator organizes and conducts the inspection meeting. This is
   a central role, and the success or failure of any inspection exercise is
   very sensitive to the quality of the moderator. In general the role of the
   moderator is to plan the inspection, ensure that all other team members have completed their preparatory tasks and that all input material
   meets their respective input criteria. The moderator also must ensure
   that during the meeting:

   a. Attention is focused on effective defect identification and
      no other task such as discussions on style or approach, trivi-
      alities, solution provision, and so on.

   b. Bias is avoided and that all participants are treated equally
      and their contributions received and considered equitably.

   c. Focus is kept on inspecting the work product and not find-
      ing faults with the author, and that comments are directed
      to the scribe and not the author or the proxy, particularly
      critical ones.

   d. Resources, particularly time, are used effectively and defect
      finding effort is maximized. The moderator is also the liai-
      son person with all other stages of the process and other
      stakeholders and at the conclusion of the meeting it is he or
      she who collects, collates, and reports on the inspection.
      Following up on defect resolution is also a moderator task.

3. Reader
   The reader, a person other than the moderator, the author or proxy, or
   the scribe, is responsible for presenting and paraphrasing the work
   product to the rest of the team during the inspection meeting. The
   reader must be thoroughly familiar with the work product and have

organized a logical order for its presentation. The reader should also work with the moderator to determine a pace for presentation in concert with the inspection rate intended. The reader is also responsible for answering all questions about the work product but may refer to the material or the author or the proxy if need be.

4. Scribe
   The scribe is responsible for recording all the necessary data generated during an inspection.

1.6 General Procedures for Inspectors

The first person to commence activities for an inspection is the author or his or her proxy who works with the inspections coordinator to select a moderator. As a member of an inspection team, your participation commences when notification is received that your participation in an inspection is requested. If for any legitimate reason you are unable or unwilling to participate, now is the time to decline. Simply return the material with a notice of decline and possibly reasons why.

1. Overview
   You may be requested to attend an overview meeting. This is generally an optional tutorially oriented meeting conducted by the author, the proxy, or at times the inspection coordinator or a combination of some of these individuals. During this meeting a review of some overall and general aspect of the work product or of the process is conducted for the purpose of educating the team members. This might be in relation to some specific aspect of the functionality, organization, technology, or techniques used in relation to the work product. The duration is usually the same as that of an inspection meeting, rarely exceeding three hours. Any obvious defects should be noted by the moderator, who should already have been selected, and discussed at the inspection meeting. An overview is usually conducted when:

   a. The work product is complex, large, convoluted, or unfamiliar to the inspection team.

   b. The work product incorporates or utilizes new or unfamiliar technology.

   c. The work product is critical to the project.

   d. Inspectors differ significantly in their areas of expertise or level of experience.

2. Preparation

   In addition to the specific roles of moderator, scribe, and so on, the role of every team member is also to be an inspector. The purpose of the preparation stage is to enable this task to be conducted more effectively. As a team member you will receive copies of the work product and all the associated checklists and scripts required at least several days before a meeting is scheduled to be held. Each inspector is to use all resources reasonably available to attain an adequate understanding of the work product. It is quite likely that potential defects will be identified during preparation. These should be noted on the Preparation Notes Form (Form I-3X), but with the understanding that defects will only be officially accepted once they emerge during the inspection meeting as a result of the synergy developed by the group dynamics. It should be noted that although the purpose of the preparation session is to understand the work product, potential defect identification opportunity should not be ruled out.

   The duration of such preparation is usually around one hour and should not exceed that of an average inspection meeting, never more than three hours for each inspection. Excessive time expended in preparation will be nonproductive as a limit of effective return is eventually reached.

3. Inspection Meeting

   Initiated, scheduled, and conducted by the moderator, the inspection meeting is the central activity of the inspection process. Its sole purpose is to identify, agree on, and classify work product defects. It is specifically not an opportunity for education, nor is it intended to evaluate, review anyone's performance, or impress anyone. As such, management must be excluded from this meeting at any cost.

   The moderator uses a dictated format (Script I-6) to conduct the meeting. He or she reviews the agenda, introduces the participants if necessary, assigns each their role(s), and opens the inspection activity by requesting the reader to commence presenting the work product. As discussions about potential defects or any other matter ensue, the moderator keeps the meeting focused on defect detection.

   As a result of discussions during this meeting a number of defects are identified, discussed, agreed on, and classified according to type. This information is then recorded on the Inspection Defects List (Form I-4) by the scribe. Classification of defect type is in accordance with the Defect Classification Scheme (Form I-7X where X stands at a minimum for either S, D, or C, in turn standing for specification, design, or code.) provided as part of the inspection input.

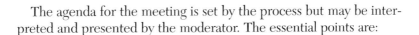

The agenda for the meeting is set by the process but may be interpreted and presented by the moderator. The essential points are:

a. Introduction

The moderator introduces the inspectors, assigns each their roles, and describes each role briefly. The moderator then acknowledges the work of the author and states that the purpose of the meeting is to find work product defects and not faults of the author. The moderator then emphasizes the important fact that the meeting must remain focused on defect detection, recording, and classification and that all other discussions should be postponed until after the meeting.

b. Establish preparation

The moderator then verifies that each inspector present has spent sufficient time preparing for the meeting. This is done by each inspector stating their total preparation time and a brief description of the outcome of the preparation activity. The meeting will proceed if the moderator is convinced of the adequate preparedness of all participants, otherwise the meeting is postponed. As a guideline the total amount of preparation of all inspectors (the sum) should not be less than the intended duration of the meeting or two thirds of what the moderator expected to have been spent.

c. Conduct defect detection

Once the moderator is convinced that the meeting should proceed, the reader commences the paraphrasing of the work product. This is to be done in a logical sequence prearranged by the reader while preparing for the meeting. Note that if roles have not been assigned to each inspector before preparation is to be done, each team member must arrive at the meeting assuming that he or she will fill any role that may be assigned. This implies preparing to present the material as the reader.

As the material is presented the inspectors identify defects, make comments regarding defects, or ask questions. These questions must be directed to the reader and not the author or the proxy as the case may be. The reader may choose, however, to refer the question back to the author or the proxy.

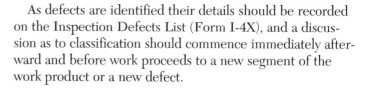

As defects are identified their details should be recorded on the Inspection Defects List (Form I-4X), and a discussion as to classification should commence immediately afterward and before work proceeds to a new segment of the work product or a new defect.

d. Review
Once all of the work product has been examined and all defects identified are classified and recorded, the recorder reviews the Inspection Defect List with all participants to ensure completeness, accuracy, and consensus.

e. Determine disposition
The inspection team then uses the Inspection Defect List to determine what course of action is to be taken with the work product. This is not an opinion of the inspection team of the quality of the product, simply a recommendation of the procedure to be followed after the inspection meeting is completed. The dispositions recommendable are:

A: Accept the work as complete
C: Conditionally accept the work with rework to be made to the satisfaction of the moderator
R: Reinspect after rework

1.7 Individual Task Scripts

1.7.1. Author's or Author's Proxy's Scripts
Please refer to Forms I-A1 to I-A6

1.7.2. Moderator's Scripts
Please refer to Forms I-M1 to I-M6

1.7.3. Reader's Scripts
Please refer to Forms I-R1 to I-R6

1.7.4. Scribe's Scripts
Please refer to Forms I-S1 to I-S6

1.7.5. Other Inspector's Scripts
Please refer to Forms I-O1 to I-O6

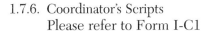
1.7.6. Coordinator's Scripts
Please refer to Form I-C1

Script I-2X
Inspection Process Scripts

Please refer to Scripts I-2S, I-2D, and I-2C.

Author's or Author's Proxy's Task Scripts

FORM IA-1
AUTHOR'S OR PROXY'S PLANNING TASKS

1. Make an initial determination that the work product meets the inspection entry criteria.
2. Work with the moderator to jointly ensure this fact.
3. If not, work with persons necessary to bring the material into compliance with the requirements.
4. Otherwise, provide the moderator with a copy of the input material.
5. With the help of the moderator, select the team members and allocate them roles.
6. Determine, with the moderator, if an overview meeting is required.

FORM I-A2
AUTHOR'S OR PROXY'S OVERVIEW TASKS

1. Prepare a logical sequence for the presentation of the material.
2. Prepare a presentation as if a technical presentation is to be given to technical staff other than your immediate peers.

3. Ensure that all material required for adequate understanding of the work product or the process aspect for which the overview was recommended is clearly presented.

4. Ensure that all questions asked are clearly or adequately answered.

FORM IA-3
AUTHOR'S OR PROXY'S INSPECTION PREPARATION TASKS

1. Ensure that all material to have been received has been received and that the input work product package is complete.

2. If not, inform the moderator.

3. Keeping the recommended preparation rate in mind, study the input work product to gain an in-depth understanding of it and using the appropriate Defect Classification Scheme (Form I-7X) also to note candidate defects. Do this for approximately the time recommended on the Inspection Notice.

4. Complete the Preparation Notes Form (Form I-3X).

5. If a specific role is assigned to you, make any preparations that might be necessary. If not, assume that you may be given the role of the scribe or the reader. Specifically you should consider how you would present the material as the reader.

6. Surrender a copy of the completed Preparation Notes Form (Form I-3X) to the moderator prior to the inspection meeting.

FORM I-A4
AUTHOR'S OR PROXY'S INSPECTION MEETING TASKS

1. Answer any questions directed to you by the reader and try to answer them objectively and clearly.

2. Inspect the work product as if an inspector on someone else's work product inspection session.

3. Do take note of comments made by the inspection team that might help in more effective removal of defects, particularly comments that may not be noted by the scribe.

4. Remain objective and realize that this is not an exercise in evaluating you, or even your work product. This is an exercise in locating defects in the work product being examined.

FORM I-A5
AUTHOR'S OR PROXY'S REWORK TASKS

1. Receive and review all material, particularly the Inspection Defects List.
2. Remove or cause to be removed all defects regardless of classification and at a time and place outside the inspection process framework.
3. Liaise with the moderator and inform him or her of the successful removal of all defects.
4. With the help of the moderator, coordinate the follow-up action to be taken.

FORM I-A6
AUTHOR'S OR PROXY'S FOLLOW-UP TASKS

1. If the original work product disposition was a C, then review the work with the moderator and assist him or her to arrive at an appropriate decision.
2. If the original work product disposition was R, then work with the moderator to convene a reinspection session. Go back to Form I-A1.
3. Send a thank-you note or e-mail to all participants.

Moderator's Task Scripts

FORM I-M1
MODERATOR'S PLANNING TASKS

1. Receive the work product and decide whether it meets entry criteria.
2. If the work product does not meet entry criteria, refer it back to the author with an explanation of what shortcomings exist. Await their removal and resubmission of the work product.
3. With the help of the author, determine if an overview meeting is required.

4. With the help of the author, select all other team members and assign them roles.

5. Schedule the overview meeting at least several days before the intended inspection meeting and invite all team members. Ensure that there is sufficient preparation time between the overview meeting and the inspection meeting.

6. Distribute the inspection input material, preferably before the overview meeting if one is held.

7. Schedule the inspection meeting.

8. Determine an appropriate preparation rate.

9. Estimate the preparation time required using the rate determined above.

10. Determine an appropriate inspection rate.

11. If for any reason, the inspection of the work product is to exceed three hours in duration, decide on a natural break point and split the inspection into multiple meetings, each not exceeding three hours.

12. Inform all parties concerned by sending each an inspection meeting notice. If any of the invitee team members cannot attend, recompose the team and continue.

13. Ensure that all logistics matters such as selection and availability of a meeting room are attended to.

FORM I-M2
MODERATOR'S OVERVIEW TASKS

1. As part of your planning task, you would have arranged (optionally) and announced an overview meeting

2. Commence the meeting, introduce the purpose of the meeting, and hand over to the author or his or her proxy, who will give the overview.

3. Steer the meeting toward exchange of information and education and not defect detection.

FORM I-M3
MODERATOR'S PREPARATION TASKS

As in Form IA-3: AUTHOR'S OR AUTHOR'S PROXY'S INSPECTION PREPARATION TASKS

FORM I-M4
MODERATOR'S INSPECTION MEETING TASKS

1. Act as the coordinating, presiding team member.
2. Ensure that all logistics are adequately in place.
3. Ensure that all input material required is available and sufficient copies are available.
4. Start and end the meeting and ensure that the meeting adheres to all time aspects and schedules.
5. Ensure that the meeting agenda is closely followed.
6. Ensure that the inspection rate is adhered to and that the inspection process is conducted effectively.
7. Ensure that a sufficient amount of material is inspected. Disallow inspection of too much material.
8. Encourage cooperation and synergy, counteracting any inappropriate physical or emotional activity or condition.
9. Ensure the complete, timely, and accurate recording of inspection data.
10. Review and help the team arrive at consensus on the contents of the Inspection Defects List.
11. In consultation with the rest of the team, arrive at a disposition for the work product.
12. Duplicate the Inspection Defects List and provide it with instructions to the author or the proxy.

FORM I-M5
MODERATOR'S REWORK TASKS

There are no specific tasks to be performed.

FORM I-M6
MODERATOR'S FOLLOW-UP TASKS

1. If the disposition of the product is C, then review the rework with the assistance of the author or his or her proxy.

2. Either accept the product or advise reinspection.

3. If the disposition is R, then prepare for reinspection by reinvoking task Script I-M1.

Reader's Task Scripts

FORM I-R1
READER'S PLANNING TASKS

There are no specific tasks to be performed.

FORM I-R2
READER'S OVERVIEW TASKS

1. If an overview session is scheduled, attend it and participate actively.

2. Try to fully comprehend the material, technology, approach, and processes employed. The reader (if the role is already assigned to an individual) must pay particular attention as it will be he or she who would paraphrase the work product.

FORM I-R3
READER'S PREPARATION TASKS

As in Form IA-3: AUTHOR'S OR AUTHOR'S PROXY'S INSPECTION PREPARATION TASKS

FORM I-R4
READER'S INSPECTION MEETING TASKS

1. Discuss your plan of presentation with the moderator prior to the meeting.

2. At the meeting, describe the work product comprehensively by paraphrasing the work and "adding value" through your presentation. Do not be tempted to ask for everyone's comments or a list of potential defects, segment by segment.

3. Avoid personal interpretation or discussion of personal preference. Remain objective and neutral.

4. Attempt to answer all questions asked but do refer them to the moderator or the author if necessary.

FORM I-R5
READER'S REWORK TASKS

There are no specific tasks to be performed.

FORM I-R6
READER'S FOLLOW-UP TASKS

There are no specific tasks to be performed.

Scribe's Task Scripts

FORM I-S1
SCRIBE'S PLANNING TASKS

There are no specific tasks to be performed.

FORM I-S2
SCRIBE'S OVERVIEW TASKS

1. If an overview session is scheduled, attend it and participate actively.

2. Ask questions and try to understand the work product as fully as possible.

3. Particularly question the assumptions and specific representations, if applicable.

4. Do not be tempted to discuss or suggest alternatives.

FORM I-S3
SCRIBE'S PREPARATION TASKS

As in Form IA-3: AUTHOR'S OR AUTHOR'S PROXY'S INSPECTION PREPARATION TASKS

FORM I-S4
SCRIBE'S INSPECTION MEETING TASKS

1. Be thoroughly familiar with the input material.

2. Particularly be familiar with the inspection defect classification scheme.

3. Record all defects, as soon as the team arrives at consensus about them. Note all the details required and as specified in the particular development phase work product inspection process instantiation scripts (e.g., for code inspection you may wish to record line number, type, severity, description, etc.).

4. Ensure that a copy of the work product with all defects found clearly highlighted is handed in at the conclusion of the meeting.

5. Ensure that all defects are accurately classified as soon as they are officially recognized.

6. Check all output material to ensure their internal integrity prior to handing over to the moderator.

7. Hand over all completed output material to the moderator.

FORM I-S5
SCRIBE'S REWORK TASKS

There are no specific tasks to be performed.

FORM I-S6
SCRIBE'S FOLLOW-UP TASKS

There are no specific tasks to be performed.

Other Inspector's Task Scripts

FORM I-O1
OTHER INSPECTOR'S PLANNING TASKS

There are no specific tasks to be performed.

FORM I-O2
OTHER INSPECTOR'S REVIEW TASKS

As in FORM I-S2: SCRIBE'S OVERVIEW TASKS

FORM I-O3
OTHER INSPECTOR'S PREPARATION TASKS

As in Form IA-3: AUTHOR'S OR AUTHOR'S PROXY'S INSPECTION PREPARATION TASKS

FORM I-O4
OTHER INSPECTOR'S INSPECTION MEETING TASKS

1. Ensure adequate preparation has been done and that all your inspection preparation notes are correctly filled in and available.

2. Be objective, impersonal, and professional.

3. Actively participate in the meeting.

4. Bring to attention of others all potential defects you may identify during the meeting or may have identified while preparing prior to the commencement of the meeting.

5. Work with the moderator to keep the meeting on schedule and paced according to the recommended progression rate.

6. Avoid personalization. Do not criticize the generator of the work, only inspect the work product.

7. Avoid the temptation of educating others, providing solutions, or alternative approaches. Remain focused on identifying defects.

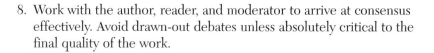

8. Work with the author, reader, and moderator to arrive at consensus effectively. Avoid drawn-out debates unless absolutely critical to the final quality of the work.

FORM I-O5
OTHER INSPECTOR'S REWORK TASKS

There are no specific tasks to be performed.

FORM I-O6
OTHER INSPECTOR'S FOLLOW-UP TASKS

There are no specific tasks to be performed.

Script I-1
Definitions

- Defect. An issue considered by the consensus of the members of the inspection meeting to detract from the quality of the work product.
- Entry criteria. The preconditions that must exist before an inspection meeting may commence.
- Exit criteria. The postconditions that must be met before an inspection may be concluded.
- Inspection. A software engineering process of defect management in which a work product is examined physically by a number of experts called inspectors, each playing a specified role in the process. The outcome of an inspection is a list of identified and confirmed defects discovered in the work product under inspection.
- Inspection meeting. A meeting of all inspectors, each playing a specified role, during which a work product is examined in order to find, classify, and report defects in it.
- Inspection preparation. The activity engaged in by each inspector individually and prior to the inspection meeting, during which the work product is examined for discovery of issues that may be raised at the inspection meeting.

- Issue. A potential defect identified by an inspector during inspection preparation work.
- Work product. A software engineering artifact produced as a result of the software process. This may be code, documentation, design, a test suite, or any other such artifact.

FORM I-3X
INSPECTION PREPARATION NOTES

Please refer to Scripts I-3S, I-3D, and I-3C.

FORM I-4X
INSPECTION DEFECTS LIST

Please refer to Scripts I-4S, I-4D, and I-4C.

FORM I-8
INSPECTION MEETING CHECKLIST

Before the meeting:

1. Has an adequate meeting location been booked?
2. Have all inspectors been selected?
3. Have all inspectors been notified of the meeting?
4. Have all inspectors committed to attending?
5. Have they all committed to preparing for the meeting?
6. Are all input materials required available and are sufficient copies available?

During the meeting:

7. Is everyone present?
8. Is the agenda being closely followed?
9. Is the inspection rate adhered to and is the inspection process being conducted effectively?
10. Is all inspection data being recorded in a complete, timely, and accurate manner?

11. Is the team capable of arriving at consensus on the contents of the Inspection Defects List?

12. Has a disposition been arrived at for the work product?

After the meeting:

13. Has the Inspection Defects List been duplicated and provided, with instructions, to the author or the proxy?

FORM I-5
INSPECTION SUMMARY REPORT FORM

INSPECTION SUMMARY REPORT

Meeting Date: [ ]   Project: [ ]

Work Product Identifier: [ ]   Version or Release No: [ ]

Work Product type: [ ]

Meeting type: Inspection [ ]   Reinspection [ ]

Disposition: [ ]

Total Number of Defects: [ ]

Total Number of F-Type defects: [ ]

Total Number of R-Type defects: [ ]

Total Number of U-Type defects: [ ]

Total Number of M-Type defects: [ ]

Notes:
Work product type may be one of the following:

User Requirements Definition (RD)
Requirements Specification (RS)
° Other Requirements Document (OR)
High-Level Design (HD)
Detailed Design (DD)
° Other Design Document (OD)
Code
Unit Test Plan (UP)
Unit Test Oracle (UO)
Unit Test Case (UC)
° Other Unit Test Document or Product (OU)
Integration Test Plan (IP)
Integration Test Oracle (IO)
Integration Test Case (IC)
° Other Integration Test Document or Product (OI)
Acceptance Plan (AP)
Acceptance Test Oracle (AO)
Acceptance Test Case (AC)
° Other Acceptance Test Document or Product (OA)
Configuration Management Plan (CP)
° Other Work Product (OW)

If work product selected is marked by "°" in the list above, please specify.

Work product: [ ]

FORM I-7X
PRODUCT DEFECT TYPE CLASSIFICATION SCHEME

Please refer to I-7S, I-7D, and I-7C.

Script I-6
Moderator's Inspection
Meeting Agenda

1. Introduce the inspection meeting.

    1.1. Introduce the inspectors.

    1.2. Identify and briefly describe each inspector's role.

    1.3. State the purpose and scope of the inspection.

2. Ensure that inspectors are prepared.

    2.1. Ask each inspector for their total preparation time and record this.

    2.2. Make a judgment as to the sufficiency of the time spent and if satisfied allow meeting to proceed. Otherwise postpone meeting and ask the inspectors to arrive prepared the next time.

3. Conduct meeting (identify defects).

4. Review and determine product disposition.

Script I-2S
Specification Inspection
Process Script

2.1. Purpose

The purpose of specification inspection is to ensure that the specification document is a true specification of the requirements and is complete and free of defects.

2.2. Inputs

The following input materials are required:

1. A page—and if possible paragraph—numbered copy of the specification document to be inspected including all relevant usecases, models, and diagrams.
2. A list of individual requirements for the system.
3. The to-be-developed product's envisaged quality requirements and their success measures (acceptance criteria).
4. An appropriate Specification Defect Type Classification Scheme (Specification Checklist; Form I-7S).
5. All relevant task scripts for all role players.
6. Blank copies of Inspection Preparation Notes (Form I-3S), Inspection Defects List (Form I-4S), and Inspection Meeting Checklist (Form I-8), all compatible with the Specification Defect Classification Scheme (Form I-7S).

2.3. Entry Criteria

1. All sections of the specification document are prepared and present.

2. All models, usecases, and diagrams are available. At a minimum, and in an early stage of the process, there is at least one UML diagram (e.g., a class diagram, a sequence diagram, etc., is present). For a specification inspection that inspects the specification as a candidate final product, all such models and other artifacts must be available.

3. All forms and checklists are appropriate, compatible, and correct, and have been duplicated in sufficient quantities and are available.

4. Preferably all inspectors are thoroughly familiar with the product requirements and are experienced analysts.

2.4. Roles

The roles are to be conducted as per the task scripts. The moderator is usually a senior or lead technical staff member with day-to-day contact with the specification task. The author is either an author of the specification document, an analyst responsible for the model, or someone sufficiently familiar with the specification to act as proxy. The reader role may not be shared, and the scribe role may be performed by the moderator.

2.5. Procedures and Rates

Inspect the document in accordance with the General Inspection Procedures and the task scripts given earler. Utilize the Inspection Meeting Checklist (Form I-8). The preparation rate should be approximately 20 to 50 pages of design per hour, which is also the rate for inspection during the inspection meeting.

2.6. Exit Criteria

1. All defects identified have been recorded and classified.

2. Disposition has been recommended.

3. Rework has been completed to the satisfaction of the Inspection Process Script as determined by the moderator.

4. All output products have been generated and are complete to the satisfaction of the moderator.

2.7. Outputs

1. Individual Inspection Preparation Note Forms.
2. Inspection Defect List.
3. Inspection Summary Form.
4. Improved (Defect Corrected) Work Product (Specification).

Script I-2D
Design Inspection Process Script

2.1. Purpose

The purpose of design inspection is to ensure that the design is a true interpretation of the specification and is complete and free of defects.

2.2. Inputs

The following input materials are required:

1. A page—and if possible paragraph—numbered copy of the design document to be inspected including all models and diagrams.
2. The specification of the product.
3. The traceability matrix.
4. An appropriate Design Defect Type Classification Scheme (Design Checklist); (Form I-7D).
5. All relevant task scripts for all role players
6. Blank copies of Inspection Preparation Notes (Form I-3D), Inspection Defects List (Form I-4D), and Inspection Meeting Checklist (Form I-8), all compatible with the Design Defect Classification Scheme (Form I-7D).

2.3. Entry Criteria

1. All sections of the design document must be prepared and present.
2. The specification for the product is properly defect-managed and current.
3. All models, usecases, and diagrams are available. At a minimum, and in an early stage of the process, there is at least one UML diagram (e.g., a class diagram, a sequence diagram, etc., is present). For a design inspection that inspects the design as a candidate final product, all design artifacts must be available.
4. All forms and checklists are appropriate, compatible, and correct, and have been duplicated in sufficient quantities and are available.
5. Preferably all inspectors are thoroughly familiar with the project and its specifications and are experienced designers and programmers.

2.4. Roles

The roles are to be conducted as per the task scripts. The moderator is usually a senior or lead technical staff member with day-to-day contact with the design task. The author is either the author of the design document, a designer, or someone sufficiently familiar with the design to act as proxy. The reader role may not be shared, and the scribe role may be performed by the moderator.

2.5. Procedures and Rates

Inspect the design in accordance with the General Inspection Procedures and the task scripts given earlier. Utilize the Inspection Meeting Checklist (Form I-8). The preparation rate should be approximately 10 to 20 pages of design per hour, which is also the rate for inspection during the inspection meeting.

2.6. Exit Criteria

1. All defects identified have been recorded and classified.

2. Disposition has been recommended.

3. Rework has been completed to the satisfaction of the Inspection Process Script as determined by the moderator.

4. All output products have been generated and are complete to the satisfaction of the moderator.

2.7. Outputs

1. Individual Inspection Preparation Note Forms.

2. Inspection Defect List.

3. Inspection Summary Form.

4. Improved (Defect Corrected) Work Product (Design).

Script I-2C
Code Inspection Process Script

2.1. Purpose

The purpose of code inspection is to ensure that the code is a true implementation of the design and is complete and free of defects.

2.2. Inputs

The following input materials are required:

1. A line-numbered listing of the clean compiled code to be inspected.

2. The last compiler report pertaining to the listing to be inspected.

3. The current detailed design document pertaining to the particular code implementation being inspected.

4. An appropriate Code Defect Type Classification Scheme (Form I-7C).

5. All relevant task scripts for all role players.

6. Blank copies of Inspection Preparation Notes (Form I-3C), Inspection Defects List (Form I-4C), and Inspection Checklist (Form I-8), all compatible with the Code Defect Classification Scheme (Form I-7C).

2.3. Entry Criteria

1. There are no remaining syntax errors in the code as proven by the compiler report.

2. The detailed design has met the exit criteria of a detailed design inspection.

3. All forms and checklists are appropriate, compatible, and correct, and have been duplicated in sufficient quantities and are available.

4. Preferably all inspectors are thoroughly familiar with and experienced in writing programs in the programming language in which the code is written.

2.4. Roles

The roles are to be conducted as per the task scripts. The moderator is usually a senior or lead technical staff member with day-to-day contact with the programming task. The author is either the author of the code or someone sufficiently familiar with the code to act as proxy. The reader role may not be shared and the scribe role may be performed by the moderator.

2.5. Procedures and Rates

Inspect the code in accordance with the General Inspection Procedures and the task scripts given earlier. Utilize the Code Inspection Checklist (Form I-8). The preparation rate should be approximately 150 to 200 lines of code per hour, which is also the rate for code inspection during the inspection meeting.

2.6. Exit Criteria

1. All defects identified have been recorded and classified.
2. Disposition has been recommended.
3. Rework has been completed to the satisfaction of the Inspection Process Script as determined by the moderator.
4. All output products have been generated and are complete to the satisfaction of the moderator.

2.7. Outputs

1. Individual Inspection Preparation Note Forms.
2. Inspection Defect List.
3. Inspection Summary Form.
4. Improved (Defect Corrected) Work Product (Code).

SPECIFICATION INSPECTION PREPARATION LIST

Specification Identifier: [ ]   Meeting Date: [ ]

Moderator: [ ]

Your Name:

Total Preparation Time:

Other Members:

Name	Role

LIKELY DEFECTS

LOC.	TYPE	DESCRIPTION	TIME

LEGEND:

LOC: Location of the defect given as page number and paragraph in which the defect appears (e.g., pg. 31-para. 3).

TYPE: Defect type according to the Defect Classification List. Include the defect type code (e.g., C1).

DESCRIPTION: A short description of the defect as found, not as classified in the defect classification scheme.

TIME: The number of minutes into the preparation time when the defect was first identified and recorded (e.g., 35).

Please supply comments (if any) on the back of this form.

Page   of

DESIGN INSPECTION PREPARATION LIST

Design Identifier: [　　　　　　]

Meeting Date: [　　　　　　]

Moderator: [　　　　　　]

Your Name:

Total Preparation Time:

Other Members:

Name	Role

LIKELY DEFECTS

LOC.	TYPE	DESCRIPTION	TIME

LEGEND:

LOC: Location of the defect given as page number, diagram, or paragraph in which the defect appears (e.g., pg. 31-para. 3).

TYPE: Defect type according to the Defect Classification List. Include the defect type code (e.g., C1).

DESCRIPTION: A short description of the defect as found, not as classified in the defect classification scheme.

TIME: The number of minutes into the preparation time when the defect was first identified and recorded (e.g., 35).

Please supply comments (if any) on the back of this form.

Page   of

CODE INSPECTION PREPARATION LIST

Program Identifier: [   ]

Meeting Date: [   ]

Moderator: [   ]

Your Name: [   ]

Total Preparation Time: [   ]

Other Members:

Name	Role

LIKELY DEFECTS

LOC.	TYPE	DESCRIPTION	TIME

LEGEND:

LOC: Location of the defect, given as code line in which the defect appears (e.g., 31).

TYPE: Defect type according to the Defect Classification List. Include the defect type code (e.g., C1) and the number of defect from sample defect numbers (e.g., C1-1 is division by zero or other impossible computation).

DESCRIPTION: A short description of the defect as found, not as classified in the defect classification scheme (e.g., X=M/Y, Y assumes value of 0 when Z=3).

TIME: The number of minutes into the preparation time when the defect was first identified and recorded (e.g., 35).

Please supply comments (if any) on the back of this form.

Page ___ of ___

SPECIFICATION INSPECTION DEFECT LIST

Specification Identifier: [　　　　　　]

Meeting Date: [　　　　　　]

Moderator: [　　　　　　]

Disposition:

　　A: Accept　　　　☐

　　B: Conditional　　☐

　　C: Reinspect　　　☐

Total Inspection Time:

Other Members:

Name	Role

DEFECTS

LOC.	TYPE	DESCRIPTION	TIME

LEGEND:

LOC:　　　　　　Location of the defect given as page number and paragraph in which the defect appears (e.g., pg. 31-para. 3).

TYPE:　　　　　Defect type according to the Defect Classification List. Include the defect type code (e.g., C1).

DESCRIPTION:　A short description of the defect as found, not as classified in the defect classification scheme.

TIME:　　　　　The number of minutes into the preparation time when the defect was first identified and recorded (e.g., 35).

Please supply comments (if any) on the back of this form.

Page　　　of

311

DESIGN INSPECTION DEFECT LIST

Design Identifier: [   ]   Meeting Date: [   ]

Moderator: [   ]

Disposition:

    A: Accept ☐

    B: Conditional ☐

    C: Reinspect ☐

Total Inspection Time:

Other Members:

Name	Role

DEFECTS

LOC.	TYPE	DESCRIPTION	TIME

LEGEND:

LOC: Location of the defect given as page number and paragraph in which the defect appears (e.g., pg. 31-para. 3).

TYPE: Defect type according to the Defect Classification List. Include the defect type code (e.g., C1).

DESCRIPTION: A short description of the defect as found, not as classified in the defect classification scheme.

TIME: The number of minutes into the preparation time when the defect was first identified and recorded (e.g., 35).

Please supply comments (if any) on the back of this form.

Page   of

CODE INSPECTION DEFECT LIST

Program Identifier: [   ]   Meeting Date: [   ]

Moderator: [   ]

Disposition:

   A: Accept ☐

   B: Conditional ☐

   C: Reinspect ☐

Total Inspection Time:

Other Members:

Name	Role

DEFECTS

LOC.	TYPE	DESCRIPTION	TIME

LEGEND:

LOC: Location of the defect given as code line in which the defect appears (e.g., 31).

TYPE: Defect type according to the Defect Classification List. Include the defect type code (e.g., C1) and the number of defect from sample defect numbers (e.g., C1-1 is division by zero or other impossible computation).

DESCRIPTION: A short description of the defect as found, not as classified in the defect classification scheme (e.g., X=M/Y, Y assumes value of 0 when Z=3).

TIME: The number of minutes into the code inspection meeting when the defect was accepted and registered (e.g., 35).

Please supply comments (if any) on the back of this form.

Page   of

Script 17-S Specification Inspection Checklist

1. Does the specification document convey a comprehension of the essence and context of the problem situation or issue at hand?
2. Does a common dictionary exist? Does it contain all the necessary entries?
3. Have all the stakeholder classes and the individual stakeholders been identified?
4. Are all support diagrams included?
5. Does the document specify the quality requirements of the system and measures for each quality requirement and acceptance goals?
6. Is the feasibility of the system in question?
7. Are the requirements as stated consistent?
8. Are the requirements as stated clear?
9. Is there a valid Requirements Traceability Table (RTT) available?
10. Is there a system synopsis available?
11. Are graphical specification models (UML) included? Is there at least one class diagram and one dynamic diagram (e.g., sequence diagram)?
12. Are the UML models syntactically correct?
13. Are formal specifications (if needed) included? Are they internally consistent?
14. Are there any omitted requirements?
15. Is the system boundary adequately defined?
16. Are there any missing attributes or operations?
17. Are there any structural abstractions that are missing, incorrect, inaccurate, or unclear?
18. Does the dynamic model (e.g., state model or sequence diagrams) support the usecase model and vice versa?
19. Does the dynamic model support the structure (class diagram) model and vice versa?
20. Does the usecase model support the structure model and vice versa?

21. Is the specification document:

    i. Clear?

    ii. Complete?

    iii. Concise?

    iv. In conformance to stated, required, or adopted standards?

22. Are there any sections that are omitted intentionally? Why?

23. For each usecase:

    i. Is the usecase redundant? That is, is the essence of the usecase captured by another usecase elsewhere?

    ii. Is the usecase incorrectly composed? Specifically, is it a description of the processing needed rather than the exchanges required to ensure an interaction with the system?

    iii. Does the usecase represent capability not required of the system?

24. For each potential class:

- Does the provisional class/object (PCO) relate to the purpose for which the system exists? Otherwise, discard.
- Is information retained within the relevant system about this class/object? Otherwise discard class.
- Does this PCO have a behavior that is needed by the system? It should, otherwise it would not be needed.
- Does this PCO have more than one attribute and/or behavior? It should, otherwise it would be an attribute or an operation (see following).
- Identify all PCOs that have identical or semantically close names.
- Investigate if these names actually refer to the same entity. This may not always be the case: Clerk, LoanClerk, or TaxationClerk, for example.
- In such situations rename all for clarity.
- Investigate if different PCOs have the same name. Resolve.
- Isolate PCOs that have only one attribute or function.
- Isolate PCOs whose name is a quantity that is simply derived by computation.
- Absorb these PCOs into other PCOs that can logically contain them.

25. Have all required attributes been identified? If not:
    - How would anyone in this domain describe this class?
    - How would anyone in this domain recognize this class?
    - What questions would this class be responsible to answer in this domain?

    Good attributes should possess the following characteristics:
    - Relevance: An attribute must relate to the universe of discourse (e.g., color of check not relevant in a banking system).
    - Atomic: An attribute must contain one value at any one time.
    - Encompassing: An attribute must be characteristic of the entire object, not a component of it (e.g., diameter is an attribute of a tire, not of a car).
    - Local (nonrelational): The attribute of an object must not attempt to capture a characteristic of a relationship (e.g., permission_value is an attribute of permission, not of either a person or a file).

26. Have all required operations been identified? If not:
    - How would anyone in this domain describe what this class does?
    - What would this class be responsible to do in this domain?

    Good operations should possess the following characteristics:
    - Relevance: An operation must relate to the universe of discourse (e.g., the fact that the font on a check can be changed is not relevant in a banking system).
    - Cohesive: An operation must do only one thing at any one time.
    - Encompassing: An operation must be characteristic of the entire object, not a component of it (e.g., change diameter is an attribute of a tire, not of a car).

Script 17-D
Design Inspection Checklist

General Design and Design Document Considerations

1. Does the design document convey a comprehension of the essence and context of the solution proposed?
2. Does the common dictionary contain all new terms introduced during design?
3. Have all the design time stakeholder classes and the individual stakeholders been identified?
4. Are all support diagrams (e.g., architectural schematics, hardware topologies, etc.) included?
5. Does the document directly address the quality requirements of the system and measures for each quality requirement and acceptance goals?
6. Are the elements of the design consistent?
7. Are the elements of the design clear?
8. Is there a valid Requirements Traceability Table (RTT) available? Have all the sections relevant to the design process completed accurately?
9. Are graphical specification models (UML) included? Is there at least one class diagram and one dynamic diagram (e.g., sequence diagram)?
10. Are the UML models syntactically correct?
11. Is there a formal derivation (if needed) included? Is it proven correct?
12. Are there any requirements not supported by a design feature?
13. Are there any structural abstractions that are missing, incorrect, inaccurate, or unclear?
14. Does the dynamic model (e.g., state model or sequence diagrams) support the usecase model and vice versa?
15. Does the dynamic model support the structure (class diagram) model and vice versa?
16. Does the usecase model support the structure model and vice versa?

17. Are there any database considerations? If so, has a database model been developed? Is it accurate, concise, implementable, and robust?

18. Is there enough redundancy in the design model?

19. Are there any sections of the design document that are omitted intentionally? Why?

20. For each usecase added at design time:

    i. Is the usecase redundant? That is, is the essence of the usecase captured by another usecase elsewhere?

    ii. Is the usecase incorrectly composed? Specifically, is it a description of the processing needed rather than the exchanges required to ensure an interaction with the system?

    iii. Does the usecase represent capability not required of the system?

21. For each potential class added at design time:

    - Does the provisional class/object (PCO) relate to the purpose for which the system exists? Otherwise, discard.
    - Is information retained within the relevant system about this class/object? Otherwise discard class.
    - Does this PCO have a behavior that is needed by the system? It should, otherwise it would not be needed.
    - Does this PCO have more than one attribute and/or behavior? It should, otherwise it would be an attribute or an operation.
    - Identify all PCOs that have identical or semantically close names.
    - Investigate if these names actually refer to the same entity. This may not always be the case: Clerk, LoanClerk, or TaxationClerk, for example.
    - In such situations rename all for clarity.
    - Investigate if different PCOs have the same name. Resolve.
    - Isolate PCOs that have only one attribute or function.
    - Isolate PCOs whose name is a quantity that is simply derived by computation.
    - Absorb these PCOs into other PCOs that can logically contain them.

22. Have all required attributes been identified? If not:

    - How would anyone in this domain describe this class?
    - How would anyone in this domain recognize this class?
    - What questions would this class be responsible to answer in this domain?

Good attributes should possess the following characteristics:

- Relevance: An attribute must relate to the universe of discourse (e.g., color of check not relevant in a banking system).
- Atomic: An attribute must contain one value at any one time.
- Encompassing: An attribute must be characteristic of the entire object, not a component of it (e.g., diameter is an attribute of a tire, not of a car).
- Local (nonrelational): The attribute of an object must not attempt to capture a characteristic of a relationship (e.g., permission_value is an attribute of permission, not of either a person or a file).

23. Have all required operations been identified? If not:
- How would anyone in this domain describe what this class does?
- What would this class be responsible to do in this domain?

Good operations should possess the following characteristics:

- Relevance: An operation must relate to the universe of discourse (e.g., the fact that the font on a check can be changed is not relevant in a banking system).
- Cohesive: An operation must do only one thing at any one time.
- Encompassing: An operation must be characteristic of the entire object, not a component of it (e.g., change diameter is an attribute of a tire, not of a car).

Specific Object-Oriented Model (UML) Considerations

1. Does the class diagram contain all necessary classes?
2. Does each class have a correctly filled:
   a. Name compartment?
   b. Attributes compartment?
   c. Operations compartment?
3. Are all attributes correctly marked by their respective types?
4. Are all attributes marked by their respective visibility scopes?
5. Are all creator/constructor operations available?
6. Are all destructor operations (if designed for) available?
7. Are all operations clearly either strict procedures or strict functions? Do all functions have a clearly identified return type?

8. Are all functions cohesive? That is, do they each only perform one simple task?

9. Does the class contain a routine that does not or cannot be named as *create_x, destroy_x, get_y, set_y,* or *do_w,* where *x* is the class name, *y* is an attribute of the class, and *w* is an algorithmic description for a routine belonging to that class?

10. Is there a *create_x, destroy_x* routine that (excluding assertions) exceeds five lines of pseudocode description or equivalent?

11. Is there a *get_y* or *set_y* routine that (excluding assertions) exceeds three lines of pseudocode or equivalent?

12. Is there a *do_w* that (excluding assertions) exceeds 12 lines of pseudocode or equivalent?

13. Are all return types of functions and types of attributes, and parameters defined and available in the design?

14. Are there any *out* parameters?

15. Have all assertions been operationalized (i.e., nothing in the fourth compartment of a class or any business rules explicit on the design diagram)?

16. Have all notes and comments on the diagram been absorbed?

17. Have all abstract classes and operations been italicized?

18. Have all required associations been declared and clearly drawn?

19. Have all associations been named and do all names have an arrowhead indicating the direction in which the name should be read?

20. Have all roles been identified and those adding clarity marked on the diagram (particularly in the case of unary associations)?

21. Have all association multiplicities been identified and clearly marked?

22. Are all associations directional? If not, do the ones that show mapping clearly model mappings and not a path of a message?

23. Are there any higher than binary associations?

24. Are there any link attributes not yet promoted to a class?

25. Are all aggregations identified?

26. Have they been resolved as either composition or a weak attribute?

27. Are there any containment relationships incorrectly defined as aggregation?

28. Are there any *is_defined_through_a number_of* associations incorrectly modeled as aggregation?

29. Has all inheritance been identified and modeled?

30. Is there an inheritance hierarchy that is deeper than five levels?

31. Is there inheritance other than subtyping that can be modeled alternatively?

32. Is there multiple inheritance that can be modeled alternatively?

33. Is there a specification inheritance instance that can but has not been alternatively modeled using aggregation?

34. Is there a superclass initialization that has been unintentionally omitted?

35. Is there a subclass that is incorrectly placed in a hierarchy to which it cannot belong?

36. Is there a superclass attribute that is visible and can be directly manipulated by subclass routines?

37. Are all name scopes unambiguously resolved?

38. Can a subclass accept a message that violates the parent's class invariant?

39. Are there any operations or methods that are redundant?

40. Are there any subclasses that relax the preconditions of the parent?

41. Can all objects that participate in the sequence diagram be legitimately instantiated from an existing class?

42. Are all objects on a sequence diagram clearly and correctly marked in a rectangle with their type indicated?

43. Is there a lifeline for each object on a sequence diagram?

44. Does each event emanate from only one object lifeline?

45. Does each event land on only one object's lifeline? If not so, is there simultaneity? Has it been correctly understood and modeled?

46. Do events that land on and emanate from a lifeline alternate? Can the model be resolved to satisfy this condition?

47. If more than one arrow lands on a lifeline without an interleaving event departing, are they all coming from the same object? If so, review the design, as there may be too much decomposition. If not, look for design omissions and resolve.

48. Are all activation regions correctly drawn? If there is parallelism, has it been correctly understood and modeled?

49. Have all events been correctly labeled (named)?

50. Have all objects that need to be destroyed been so marked?

51. Are there any repetition conditions that have not been marked?

52. Are there any continuation conditions that have not been marked?

53. Are there any conditionals? (There should not be, or at least their use should be minimized.)

54. Is the sequence diagram organized following the MVC convention (e.g., from left to right, actors and views, then controllers, the model objects, then controllers again, and then views and actors on the right)?

55. Is there a collaboration diagram?

56. Is there an equivalent sequence diagram for the collaboration diagram? If so, are they compatible and do they convey the same design message?

57. Are all simultaneous events on the collaboration diagram marked by the same number followed by the letters of the alphabet (e.g., 6a, 6b, 6c)?

58. Is there at least one state diagram per each "model" element of the design?

59. Does each arrow represent an identifiable event pertinent to that object?

60. Does each bubble represent an identifiable, valid, and unique state that object can assume?

61. Are all the states in the analysis state model included in the design state model of the same object?

62. Are the transitions out of a state mutually exclusive?

63. Does each state have at least one *do/* statement?

64. Does the state diagram consist of a set of closed loops? If not, is there any design reason why this is not the case?

65. Are there any substates and have they been correctly declared?

66. Is there concurrency and has it been correctly modeled?

67. Are all guards and conditionals correctly marked?

68. Is there a transformational description for each routine of each class?

69. Does each sequence diagram have a corresponding usecase at the same level of granularity?

70. Does each sequence diagram show the interaction of objects from the class diagram?

71. Does each aggregation relationship in the class diagram imply going down one level of granularity in the corresponding dynamic model, as shown by a set of sequence diagrams?

72. Conversely, does this lower level of interactions just mentioned correspond to an extant set of usecases?

73. Do the public operations of the class correspond to the events of relevant sequence diagrams at the same level of granularity? In other words, there should be no aggregate and aggregand objects on the same sequence diagram.

74. Do all private methods of the class correspond to the events of relevant sequence diagrams at a lower level of granularity?

75. Is the client–server model established by the interactions of each and every sequence diagram?

76. Do all client objects observe all the preconditions of the server object?

77. Are all servers compatible with the postconditions of the client?

78. Is each event on a sequence diagram incident on a given object shown as an arrow on the state diagram drawn for that object?

79. Is each event on a sequence diagram incident from a given object shown as an activity (do/x) for that object?

80. Are multiple events incident on the lifeline of an object without an interleaving arrow departing modeled as multiple activities for the corresponding state?

81. Are the most detailed (at the lowest level of granularity) sequence diagrams defined in terms of events that correspond to the lowest level of granularity aggregations on the class diagram?

82. Are the lowest level objects and sequence diagrams composed of routines and events, respectively, that are more than a few (maximum of 12–15) lines of code each?

83. Whenever possible, has there been polymorphism used instead of branching and conditionals?

84. Have all polymorphic name and scope problems been resolved?

85. Is polymorphism implemented on a hierarchy that is strictly subtyped?

86. Are design patterns used whenever practical?

87. Are classes that are logically or operationally cohesive placed in a package and named?

88. Is cohesion within each package maximized?

89. Is coupling between packages minimized?

90. Is there at least one deployment model?

Script 17-C
Code Inspection Checklist

General Programming Defects

1. Global Variables

There exists an externally declared variable that is referenced within a function but has not been passed in as a parameter.

2. Poor Naming Conventions

2.1. There exist identifiers with names that are too long (> 15 characters long).

2.2. There exist identifiers consisting of single-character representations (excepting loop indexes).

2.3. There exist identifiers that resemble a keyword (regardless of case).

3. Redundant Declarations

3.1. There exist external variables and functions that are declared in one source file but never actually used in that source file.

3.2. There exist formal parameters that are declared in the function heading but never used within the function.

3.3. There are variables that are declared in a compound statement but never actually used within the compound statement.

4. Input Coupling

There exists a variable that is assigned a value via an input, but is not modified or referenced before being passed to a user-defined function as a function call argument.

5. Magic Numbers

There exist numbers other than –1, 0, or 1 in a program statement.

6. Hidden Loops

6.1. There exists a guarded variable from a loop guard that is modified once within a single branch of a guarded statement.

6.2. There exists a guarded variable from a loop guard, or a branch guard within a loop, that is modified within the loop body, or assigned a value independent of itself within an "if" statement branch (if this variable is not a loop guard variable, it must occur in the guard of the branch).

7. Uninitialized Variables

There exists a variable that has not been explicitly initialized prior to its first use in an expression.

8. Lax Grouping

There are identical subexpressions in each conditional expression of two conditional (*if*) statements, but there are no statements between the guards of the two "*if*" statements that modify the variables occurring in the aforementioned identical subexpressions.

9. Zero Iteration Defect

There exists a variable that occurs in a loop body (not in a guard), that:

- is not initialized before the loop, and
- is assigned but not referenced within the loop body, and
- after being assigned, does not appear in an inner loop.

10. Superfluous Variables in Loop: (Does Not Apply to Loop Control Variable)

10.1. There exist temporary variables in a loop that do not save time in computation.

10.2. There exists a nonaccumulative assignment to a variable in a loop that appears (just once) in the right-hand side of a subsequent assignment statement.

11. Loops That May Make No Progress

There exist no variables from the loop guard of a loop that are updated within the body, except inside another guarded command.

12. Redundant Loop Computations

There exists a subexpression that is evaluated within a loop and involves variables that are not changed within the loop (these variables are global to the loop body scope).

13. Loop Guard Too Complex

There exists a loop statement that contains more than two conditional constructs within its loop guard.

14. Loop Contains Posttermination Structure

There exists a loop body that contains a conditional (*if*) statement, whose block's last statement breaks out (e.g., a *break* statement) that has an afore nonempty batch of code.

15. Redundant Conditional Assignment

There exists an equality guard component for a conditional statement that matches an assignment statement that it guards, but the variables in the guard are not modified prior to the execution of the matching assignment.

16. Self-Assignment

There exists an assignment statement in which the left-hand side and right-hand side are identical.

17. Dispersed Initialization

There exists a variable that is a control variable of a loop, initialized more than five statements away from where it is employed in the loop, not referenced or modified after the initialization and before the loop.

18. Premature Initialization

There exists a loop control variable for an inner nested loop that is initialized twice: once before entering the external loop and once before entering or on leaving the inner loop.

19. Redundant Accumulation

There exist two or more congruent accumulative statements within a loop that are of the form $i = i + c1$ and $j = j + c2$, where $c1 = c2$.

20. Redundant Test on Loop Exit

There exists an extra guard to test the exit condition of the guarded loop after a loop statement. Between the guard and the loop exit, there exist no statements to change the variables that occur in the guard. (Note: If there are control statements in the loop passing control outside of the loop, then the destination of those control statements should be after the external guard.)

21. Redundant Guard

There exists a subexpression within a loop of a conditional statement that has previously been established for the given execution path. (The variables that occur in the subexpression are not changed between the outer and enclosed guards.)

22. Readjustment of Loop Variable on Exit

There exists an expression or statement that readjusts a loop variable on exit from a loop.

23. Redundant Internal Guard

There exists a guard component that is applied more than once in a loop body without changing its component variables.

24. Statement Duplication

There exists a statement that occurs more than once within a loop body, although between these duplicated statements, the variables they contain are not changed.

25. Duplicate Output

There exists a variable that is output via an output function and unmodified before being output again by another output function.

26. Function Comments

There are no comments describing the class, attribute, or function's job, either before or after the function heading.

27. Multiple Exits from a Function

There exists more than one exit statement within a function body.

28. Unassigned Address Parameter

There exists an address parameter that is not assigned a value within a function.

29. Function Side Effects

There exists a function that returns a value; and there exists:

- An address parameter that may be used to change the contents of a corresponding actual parameter, or
- An external variable that is changed inside this function.

30. Amended Nonaddress Parameter

There exists a nonaddress parameter that is amended inside the body of a function.

31. Redundant Guard Test

There exists a variable that occurs in two relational expressions joined by the (AND) logical operator. The pair of relational operators involved in either of these expressions can be one of the following: (equal, not equal), (equal, greater than), (equal, less than).

32. Indirectly Terminated Loops

There exists a single variable that is used as a guard of an iterative statement, assigned within a guarded statement (selection or iterative statements) within the loop body.

33. Dual-Purpose Variable Usage

There exists a variable that is modified in the body of a loop, then reassigned after the loop.

34. Double Initialization

There exists a loop variable that is initialized more than once prior to its use in a loop, although the offending variable is not referenced between the statements in which it is initialized.

35. Subscript Within Bounds

There exists an array the subscripts for which exceed the bounds.

36. Noninteger Subscript

Subscripts of an array should always be integers.

37. Incorrect Initialization

Arrays and strings are usually required to be set to default values.

38. Procedure That Returns a Value as a Parameter

There exists a procedure that has been specified to return no value before its heading or has no return statement with a return value. This procedure has only one address parameter that is assigned within the body.

39. Operation with No Visible Effect

There exists an operation that has no effect.

40. Overloaded Loop Index

There exists an inner loop that changes an outer loop control variable.

41. Mixed-Mode Computation

Types do not conform for correct computation.

42. Division by Zero

The denominator of operation has not been guarded against evaluating to zero.

43. Integer Division

Integer division truncates the remainder.

44. External Object Attribute Hard-Coded

The attributes of external objects (e.g., a file) have been explicitly hard-coded.

45. Function Has No Return Value

There exists a (nonvoid) function that contains a return statement with no return value.

46. Unused Input

There exists a variable that is assigned a value via an input function, not used or referenced until being assigned another value by another input function.

47. Unmodified Output

There exists a variable that is assigned a value from an input function, unmodified before being output again by an output function.

48. Identifiers in Scope Are Character Similar

- There exist two function names that are character similar.
- There exist two global variable identifiers that are character similar.
- There exist a function name and a global identifier that are character similar.
- There exist a function name and a parameter identifier that are character similar.
- There exist a global identifier and a parameter name that are character similar.
- There exist two parameters that are character similar.
- There exist two local variables defined within the same scope and their identifiers are character similar.
- There exist a function name and a local variable identifier that are character similar.
- There exist a global variable identifier and a local identifier that differ in case.
- There exist a parameter identifier and a local identifier, both declared within the same function, that are character similar.
- There exist two local identifiers; one is declared in a scope enclosing the other's declaration. Both identifiers are character similar.

49. Identifiers in Scope Differing in Case

- There exist two function names that differ only in case.
- There exist two global variable identifiers that differ only in case.
- There exist a function name and a global identifier that differ in case.

- There exist a function name and a parameter identifier that differ in case.
- There exist a global identifier and a parameter name that differ in case.
- There exist two parameters that differ in case.
- There exist two local variables defined within the same scope and their identifiers differ in case.
- There exist a function name and a local variable identifier that differ in case.
- There exist a global variable identifier and a local identifier that differ in case.
- There exist a parameter identifier and a local identifier, both declared within the same function, that differ in case.
- There exist two local identifiers; one is declared in a scope enclosing the other's declaration. Both identifiers differ in case.

50. McCabe's Cyclomatic Complexity

A cyclomatic complexity value of more than 5 indicates that the function is too complex and should be reduced, if possible.

51. Unacceptable Initialization of Global Variables

There exists a global variable that is initialized in its variable declaration without the use of the appropriate keyword. (Volatile variables are the only exception to this.)

52. Local Variables Not Declared within Their Minimal Scope

There exist local variables that are declared for a block, not referenced at the top level of that block, but within an inner block (at a lower level).

53. Unintentional Empty Loop

There exists a loop within an empty body.

54. Inconsistent Use of Delimiters

There exists a body within a conditional (*if–else*) statement that is enclosed in delimiters (e.g., a compound statement), whereas the other body counterpart is not a compound statement.

55. Multiple Breaks in Loop

There exists more than one break statement within the body of an iterative statement.

56. Redeclaration of Identifiers

56.1. The name of some global variable is declared as a local variable in some block, or a formal parameter for some function; or

56.2. The name of some function is declared as a local variable in some block, or a formal parameter for some function; or

56.3. The name of some formal parameter is declared as a local variable in some block; or

56.4. The name of some variable in a block is declared as a local variable in some enclosing block.

57. No Break at End of Multiple Branching (*case*) Statement

The last statement in the body of a multiple branching statement is not a break statement, when the last case label in that body is not a default label.

58. Default Is Not the Last Label in a Multiple Branch

There exists a multiple branch statement that contains a default label and that default label does not occur as the last label within this switch statement.

59. Noncompound Multiple Branch Body

There exists a multiple branch statement where its body statement is not a compound statement.

60. Multiple Branch Statement Fall-Through

There exists a top-level case (or default) labeled statement within the body of a multiple branch statement, which is not the first case (or default) labeled statement in the body, and is not preceded by a break statement.

61. Goto Statements Considered Harmful

There exists a *goto* statement within the body of a function.

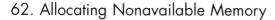

62. Allocating Nonavailable Memory

Memory has been allocated where system memory has been exhausted.

Object-Oriented Programming Defects

1. Memory Is Deallocated Improperly

Memory has been deallocated:

- Not using a removal (e.g., destructor) routine,
- Not using the proper removal (e.g., destructor) routine, or
- In an object by another object.

2. The Assignment Operator Returns Unexpected Type

The type of the object and that of the return type of the assignment operator do not match.

3. Assignment Operator Attribute Missing

Attributes have been omitted while overloading the assignment operator.

4. Passing Derived Class Objects by Value

A derived class passed by value is not treated as a base class (it should be).

5. Out-of-Order Initialization of Base Classes

In most multiple-inheritance situations, the order of declaration of base classes matters.

6. Inheriting the Same Feature from More Than One Class

The branch from which the feature is to be inherited in a multiple-inheritance situation has not been made explicit.

7. Improper Exception Management

- Exception propagates beyond the scope.

- Exception is ignored, resulting in process to halt.
- Exception is passed from a server to a client improperly.
- Exception-handling mechanism is missing.
- Exception-handling mechanism is incorrect.
- The wrong exception is thrown.
- The exception-handling mechanism falls into an infinite loop.

8. Improper Inheritance Implementation

- An unnecessary or inappropriate feature has been inherited by a subclass.
- Subclass violates the invariant of its superclass.
- Subclass violates the precondition of the superclass.
- Subclass implements specification or restriction.
- A feature that is supposed to be implemented in a subclass is missing.
- Superclass is not initialized.
- Superclass initialization is incorrect.
- Visibility rules have been violated.

9. Improper Assertion

- Precondition not checked at entry.
- Postcondition not ensured at exit.
- Class invariant not checked at construction, at entering a precondition, and at exit.
- Modal assertions not checked (for modal classes).

Java-Specific Programming Defects

1. Use of Instance Operators with Expanded Types

An instance operator has been used with an expanded type (primitive type).

2. The \ Character Misrepresented

The \ character has not been represented as string \\.

3. Substring Extraction Offsets Used Incorrectly

The substring offsets have been used in a relative fashion, as opposed to two zero-based offsets: one pointing to the start, the other to the character one past the end.

4. Strings Have Been Compared Using Incorrect Operator

Strings not intern( )ed have been compared using the == operator.

5. Static Method Assumed Dynamic

Static method has been assumed to be selected dynamically.

6. Incorrect Overriding of Methods in Constructor

A constructor overridden in a subclass contains a method that uses the subclasses fields that have not been initialized in that constructor.

7. Default Logical Value Assumed

A statement has assumed return of logical value without comparison.

8. A Reference to a Final Feature Misused

A feature declared as final allows change of data values in an object because it is called by reference and not by value.

9. Expanded Type Overflow

An overflow without warning occurred with respect to a type such as *int, long, float,* or *double*.

10. Return Type Declared for Constructor

A constructor has been declared with a return type.

11. *void* Type Declared for Constructor

A constructor has been declared with a *void* return type.

12. The + Operator

The + operator has mistakenly been used by the system to imply concatenation when addition was intended or vice versa.

13. Array Problems

- No space has been allocated for array.
- No objects assigned to each array location.
- The type of array object and type of array element incompatible.

14. Casting Over Nonexpanded Types

Casting has been used to work over nonexpanded types (objects other than primitives).

REFERENCES

Abdel-Hamid, T.K.; Madnick, S.E.; "Lessons Learned from Modelling the Dynamics of Software Development"; *Communications of the ACM*, Vol. 32, No. 12; December 1989; pp. 1426–1438.

Ackerman, A.F.; Buchwald, L.S.; Lewiski, F.H.; "Software Inspections: An Effective Verification Process"; *IEEE Software*; May 1989; pp. 31–39.

Ackerman, A.F.; Fowler, P.J.; Ebenau, R.G.; "Software Inspections and the Industrial Production of Software"; in: *Software Validation*; Hausen, H.L. ed.; Elsevier; Netherlands; 1984.

Allen, M.J.; Yen, W.M.; *"Introduction to Measurement Theory"*; Brooks; Mountainview, CA; 1979.

Aristotle; *"Metaphysics"*; Trans. W.D. Ross; Oxford University Press; Oxford, UK; 1924.

Bach, J.; "Enough About Process: What We Need Are Heroes"; *IEEE Software*; March 1995; pp. 96–98.

Bashir, I.; Goel, A.; *Testing Object-Oriented Software: Life-Cycle Solutions*; Springer; 2000.

Basili, V.R.; "Viewing Maintenance as Reuse-Oriented Software Development"; *IEEE Software*; January 1990.

Basili V.R.; Rombach, H.D.; "The TAME Project: Towards Improvement Oriented Software Environments"; *IEEE Transactions on Software Engineering*, Vol. 14, No. 6; June 1988; pp. 758–773.

Basili, V.R.; Selby, Jr., R.W.; "Comparing the Effectiveness of Software Testing Strategies"; *IEEE Transactions on Software Engineering*, Vol. 13, No. 12; December 1987; pp. 1278–1296.

Basili, V.R.; Selby, Jr., R.W.; Philips, T.Y.; "Metric Analysis and Data Validation Across Fortran Projects"; *IEEE Transactions on Software Engineering*, Vol. 9, No. 6; November 1983; pp. 652–663.

Beck, K.; Cunningham, W.; "A Laboratory for Teaching Object-Oriented Thinking"; in: Proceedings of OOPSLA; Addison-Wesley; Reading, MA; 1989.

Beizer, B.; *Software Testing Techniques*, 2nd ed.; Van Nostrand Reinhold; New York; 1991.

Bently, J.L.; "Programming Pearls: Confessions of a Coder"; *Communications of the ACM*, Vol. 28, No. 7; July 1985; pp. 671–679.

Bicevskis, J.; Borzovos, J.; Staujmus, U.; Zarins, A.; Miller, E.; "SMOTL—A System to Construct Samples for Data Processing and Program Debugging"; *IEEE Transactions on Software Engineering*, Vol. 5, No. 8; August 1990; pp. 60–66.

Binder, R.V.; "State-Based Testing"; *Object Magazine*, Vol. 5, No. 5; July–August 1995a; pp. 75–78.

Binder, R.V.; "State-Based Testing: Sneak Paths and Conditional Transitions"; *Object Magazine*, Vol. 5, No. 6; October 1995b; pp. 87–89.

Binder, R.V.; "Testing Object-Oriented Software: A Survey"; *Journal of Software Testing, Verification and Reliability*, Vol. 6; December 1996; pp. 125–252.

Bisant, D.B.; Lyle, J.R.; "A Two-Person Inspection Method to Improve Programming Productivity"; *IEEE Transactions on Software Engineering*, Vol. 19, No. 10; October 1989; pp. 1294–1304.

Bjorner, D.; "The Vienna Development Method: Software Abstraction and Program Synthesis"; Lecture Notes in Computer Science, Vol. 75: *Mathematical Studies of Information Processing*; Springer-Verlag; New York; 1979.

Boehm, B.W.; "Software Engineering Economics"; *IEEE Transactions on Software Engineering*, Vol. 10, No. 1; January 1984; pp. 4–21.

Boehm, B.; Egyed, A.; "Tele-cooperation Experience with the Win-Win System"; Proceedings 15th IFIP; 1998.

Boehm, B.W.; Papaccio, P.N.; "Understanding and Controlling Software Costs"; *IEEE Transactions on Software Engineering*, Vol. 14, No. 10; October 1988; pp. 1462–1477.

Booch, G.; *Object-Oriented Analysis and Design with Applications*, 2nd ed.; Benjamin–Cummings; San Francisco, CA; 1994.

Bruegge, B.; Dutoit, A.; *Object-Oriented Software Engineering: Conquering Complex and Changing Systems*; Prentice-Hall; Upper Saddle River, NJ; 2000.

Bruner, J.S.; "On Perceptual Readiness"; *Psychological Review*, Vol. 64; 1957; pp. 123–152.

Brykczynski, W.; Meeson, R.; Wheeler, D.A.; "Software Inspection Insertion Efforts for the Ballistic Missile Defense Organization"; IDA P-2876; Institute for Defense Analyses; Alexandria, VA; September 1993.

Budd, T.A.; "Mutation Analysis of Program Test Data"; Doctoral thesis; Yale University; New Haven, CT; 1980.

Bush, M.; "Improving Software Quality: The Use of Formal Inspections at the Jet Propulsion Laboratory"; Proceedings of the 12th ICSE; Los Alamitos, CA; 1990.

Butler, R.W.; Finelli, G.B.; "The Infeasibility of Quantifying the Reliability of Life-Critical Real-Time Software"; *IEEE Transactions on Software Engineering*, Vol. 19, No. 1; January 1993; pp. 3–12.

Chaar, J.K.; "In-Process Evaluation for Software Inspection and Test"; *IEEE Transactions on Software Engineering*, Vol. 19, No. 11; November 1993; pp. 1055–1070.

Checkland, P.B.; Scholes, J.; *Soft Systems Methodology in Action*; Wiley; New York; 1990.

Checkland, P.B.; *Systems Thinking, Systems Practice*; Wiley; Chichester, UK; 1981.

Chen, T.Y.; Yu, Y.T.; "On the Expected Number of Failures Detected by Subdomain Testing and Random Testing"; *IEEE Transactions on Software Engineering*, Vol. 22, No. 2; February 1996; pp. 109–119.

Chen, T.Y.; Yu, Y.T.; "On the Relationship Between Partition and Random Testing"; *IEEE Transactions on Software Engineering*, Vol. 20, No. 12; December 1994; pp. 977–980.

Chilenski, J.J.; Miller, S.P.; "Applicability of Modified Condition/Decision Coverage to Software Testing"; Boeing Company and Rockwell International Corporation; Seattle, WA; 1993.

Clarke, L.A.; "A System to Generate Test Data and Symbolically Execute Programs"; *IEEE Transactions on Software Engineering*, Vol. 2, No. 3; September 1976; pp. 215–222.

Clarke, L.A.; Podgursky, A.; Richardson, D.J.; Zeil, S.J.; "A Formal Evaluation of Data Flow Path Selection Criteria"; *IEEE Transactions on Software Engineering*, Vol. 15, No. 11; November 1989; pp. 1318–1332.

Clarke, L.A.; Richardson, D.J.; Zeil, S.J.; "TEAM: A Support Environment for Testing, Evaluation, and Analysis"; in: Proceedings of the ACM SIGSOFT/SIGPLAN Software Engineering Symposium of Practical Software Development; November 1988; pp. 153–162.

Cobb, R.H.; Mills, H.D.; "Engineering Software Under Statistical Quality Control"; *IEEE Software*; November 1990; pp. 44–54.

Constantine, L.; Yourdon, E.; *Structured Design: Fundamentals of a Discipline of Computer Program and Systems Design*; Prentice-Hall; Englewood Cliffs, NJ; 1979.

Crosby, P.B.; *Quality Is Free*; McGraw-Hill; New York; 1979.

Curtis, G.; *Business Information Systems*; Addison-Wesley; London; 1989.

Dahl, O.J.; Dijkstra, E.W.; Hoare, C.A.R.; *Structured Programming*; Academic Press; New York; 1972.

Davis, A.; "Fifteen Principles of Software Engineering"; *IEEE Software*; November 1994; p. 94.

Davis, G.B.; "Strategies for Information Requirements Determination"; *IBM Systems Journal*, Vol. 21, No. 1; 1982.

DeMillo, R.A.; Lipton, R.J.; Sayward, F.G.; "Hints on Test Data Selection: Help for the Practicing Programmer"; *IEEE Computer*, Vol. 11, No. 4; April 1978; pp. 34–41.

DeMillo, R.A.; Offutt, A.J.; "Constraint-Based Automatic Test Data Generation"; *IEEE Transactions on Software Engineering*, Vol. 17, No. 9; September 1991; pp. 900–910.

Descartes, R.; "Discourse on Method"; in: *The Philosophical Works of Descartes*; Trans. E. Haldane; G.R.T. Ross; Cambridge University Press; Cambridge, UK; 1911.

Dichter, J.H.; "Inspections as an Up-Front Quality Technique"; in: *Handbook of Software Quality Assurance*; Schulmeyer, G.G.; McManus, J.I., eds.; Van Nostrand Reinhold; New York; 1992.

Ditlersen, O.; Madsen, H.O.; *Structural Reliability Methods*; Wiley; New York; 1996.

Dromey, R.G.: *Program Derivation: The Development of Programs from Specification*; Addison-Wesley; London; 1989.

Dromey, R.G.; "A Model for Software Product Quality"; *IEEE Transactions on Software Engineering*, Vol. 21, No. 2; February 1995; pp. 146–162.

Dromey, R.G.; "Cornering the Chimera"; *IEEE Software*; January 1996; pp. 33–48.

Dromey, R.G.; McGettrick, A.D.; "On Specifying Software Quality"; *Software Quality Journal*, Vol. 1, No. 1; 1992; pp. 45–74.

D'Souza, D.; Wills, A.C.; *Objects, Components and Frameworks with UML: The Catalysis Approach*; Addison-Wesley; Reading, MA; 1999.

Duke, R.; Rose, G.; *Formal Object-Oriented Specification and Design Using Object-Z*; Software Verication Research Centre; University of Queensland, Australia; 1998.

Durnota, B.; Mingins, C.; "Tree-Based Coherence Metrics in Object-Oriented Design"; in: *Proceedings of TOOLS 12*; Prentice-Hall; Englewood Cliffs, NJ; 1993.

Dyer, M.; *The Cleanroom Approach to Quality Software Development*; Wiley; New York; 1992.

Dyer, M.; "Verification Based Inspection"; in: Proceedings of the 25th Hawaii International Conference on System Sciences Vol. 2; 1991; pp. 418–427.

Easterbrook, S.; "Elicitation of Requirements from Multiple Perspectives"; Doctoral thesis; Department of Computing, Imperial College; London; 1991.

El-Emam, K.; SPICE: *The Theory and Practice of Software Process Improvement and Capability Determination*; IEEE Computer Society Press; 1997.

El-Emam, K.; Briand, L.; Smith, R.; "Assessor Agreement in Rating Spice Processes"; International Software Engineering Research Network; Report No. ISERN-96-09; 1996.

Elmendorf, W.R.; "Functional Analysis Using Cause-Effect Graphs"; in: Proceedings of SHARE XLIII; 1974; pp. 567–577.

Endres, A.; "An Analysis of Errors and Their Causes in System Programs"; *IEEE Transactions on Software Engineering*, Vol. 1, No. 2; 1975; pp. 140–149.

Eysenck, M.W.; Keane, M.T.; *Cognitive Psychology*; Lawrence Erlbaum Associates; Hove, UK; 1990.

Fagan, M.E.; "Advances in Inspections"; *IEEE Transactions on Software Engineering*, Vol. 12, No. 7; July 1986; pp. 744–751.

Fagan, M.E.; "Design and Code Inspections to Reduce Errors in Program Development"; *IBM Systems Journal*, Vol. 15, No. 3; 1976; pp. 182–211.

Fenton, N.; *Software Metrics: A Rigorous Approach*; Chapman-Hall; London; 1991.

Fenton, N.E.; Pfleeger, S.L.; *Software Metrics: A Rigorous and Practical Approach, 2nd ed.*; International Thomson Press; London; 1996.

Frankl, P.; Hamlet, R.; Littlewood, B.; Strigini, L.; "Choosing a Testing Method to Deliver Reliability"; in: Proceedings of the 19th ICSE; Boston; 1997; pp. 68–78.

Frankl, P.G.; Weyuker, E.J.; "An Applicable Family of Data Flow Testing Criteria"; *IEEE Transactions on Software Engineering*, Vol. 14, No. 10; October 1988; pp. 1483–1498.

Frankl, P.G.; Weyuker, E.J.; "Assessing the Fault-Detecting Ability of Testing Methods"; *ACM Software Engineering Notes*, Vol. 16, No. 5; December 1993; pp. 202–213.

Freedman, D.P.; Weinberg, G.M.; *Handbook of Walkthroughs, Inspections and Technical Reviews: Evaluating Programs, Projects and Products, 3rd ed.*; Little, Brown; Boston; 1982.

Fury, S.; Kitchenham, B.; "Point/Counterpoint: Function Points"; *IEEE Software*; March–April 1997; pp. 28–33.

Gamma, E.; Helm, R.; Johnson, R.; Vlissides, J.; *Design Patterns: Elements of Reusable Object-Oriented Design*; Addison-Wesley; Reading, MA; 1995.

Garvin, D.; *Managing Quality: The Strategic and Competitive Edge*; Free Press; New York; 1988.

Ghezzi, C.; Jazayeri, M.; Manderioli, D.; *Fundamentals of Software Engineering*; Prentice-Hall; Englewood Cliffs, NJ; 1992.

Gibson, J.J.; *The Senses Considered as Perceptual Systems*; Houghton-Mifflin; Boston; 1966.

Gilb, T.; Graham, D.; *Software Inspection*; Addison-Wesley; London; 1993.

Gillies, A.; *Software Quality—Theory and Management*; Chapman & Hall; London; 1992.

Goldberg, A.; Zimmerman, D.; Wang, T.C.; "Applications of Feasible Path Analysis to Program Testing"; International Symposium on Software Testing and Analysis; Seattle, WA; 1994.

Goodenough, J.B.; Gerhart, S.L.; "Toward a Theory of Test Data Selection"; *IEEE Transactions on Software Engineering*, Vol. 1, No. 2; June 1975; pp. 156–173.

Graden, M.E.; Horsley, P.S.; "The Effects of Software Inspections on a Major Telecommunications Project"; *AT&T Technical Journal*, Vol. 65, No. 3; May–June 1989; pp. 32–40.

Graham, I., Henderson-Sellers, B.; Younessi, H.; *OPEN Process Specification*; Addison-Wesley; London; 1997.

Gregory, R.L.; "Perceptions as Hypotheses"; *Philosophical Transactions of the Royal Society of London, Series B*, Vol. 290; 1980; pp. 181–197.

Haas, V.; Messnarz, R.; Koch, G.; Kugler, H.J.; Decrinis, P.; "Bootstrap: Fine Tuning Process Assessment"; *IEEE Software*; July 1994; pp. 67–76.

Hamlet, R.; Taylor, R.; "Partition Testing Does Not Inspire Confidence"; *IEEE Transactions on Software Engineering*, Vol. 16, No. 12; December 1990; pp. 1402–1411.

Haung, J.C.; "An Approach to Program Testing"; ACM Computing Surveys Vol. 7, No. 3; September 1975.

Henderson-Sellers, B.; *Object-Oriented Metrics*; Prentice-Hall; Englewood Cliffs, NJ; 1996.

Henderson-Sellers, B.; Simons, A.J.; Younessi, H.; *The OPEN Toolbox of Techniques*; Addison-Wesley; London; 1998.

Hetzel, W.C.; *The Complete Guide to Software Testing, 2nd ed.*; QED Information Sciences; Boston; 1988.

Higashino, T; von Bochman, G.; "Automated Analysis and Test Case Derivation for a Restricted Class of LOTOS Expressions with Data Parameters"; *IEEE Transactions on Software Engineering*, Vol. 20, No. 1; January 1994; pp. 29–42.

Hinchley, M.G.; Bowen, J.P.; *Applications of Formal Methods*; Prentice-Hall; Englewood Cliffs, NJ; 1995.

Howden, W.E.; "Validation of Scientific Programs"; *ACM Computing Surveys*, Vol. 14, No. 2; June 1982.

Humphrey, W.S.; *Managing the Software Process*; Addison-Wesley; Reading, MA; 1989.

Humphrey, W.S.; *A Discipline for Software Engineering*; Addison-Wesley; Reading, MA; 1995.

Hutchins, M.; "Experiments on the Effectiveness of Dataflow and Controlflow Based Test Adequacy Criteria"; in: Proceedings of 16th ICSE; Sorrento, Italy; 1994; pp. 191–200.

Jacobson, I; Booch, G.; Rumbaugh, J.; *The Unified Software Development Process*; Addison-Wesley; Reading, MA; 1999.

Jones, C.L.; "A Process-Integrated Approach to Defect Prevention"; *IBM Systems Journal*, Vol. 24, No. 2; 1985; pp. 150–167.

Jones, C.; *The Economics of Object-Oriented Software; Software Productivity Research*; Burlington, MA; 1997.

Jüttner, P., Kolb, S.; Zimmerer, P.; "Experiences in Testing Object-Oriented Software"; Proceedings of EuroSTAR'94; Jacksonville, FL; October, 1994.

Kelly, J.C.; Sherif, J.S.; Hops, J.; "An Analysis of Defect Densities Found During Software Inspections"; *Journal of Systems and Software*, Vol. 17, No. 2; February 1992; pp. 111–117.

Kemmerer, R.A.; "Testing Formal Specifications to Detect Design Errors"; *IEEE Transactions on Software Engineering*, Vol. SE11, No 1; January 1985; pp. 32–43.

Kitchenham, B.A.; Kitchenham, A.P.; Fellows, J.P.; "The Effects of Inspections on the Software Quality and Productivity"; *ICL Technical Journal*, Vol. 5, No. 1; May 1986; pp. 112–122.

Kitchenham, B.; Linkman, S.J.; "Validation, Verification, and Testing: Diversity Rules"; *IEEE Software*; July–August, 1998; pp. 46–49.

Kitchenham, B.; Pfleeger, S.L.; "Software Quality: The Elusive Target"; *IEEE Software*; January 1996; pp. 12–21.

Knight, J.C.; Myers, E.A.; "An Improved Inspection Technique"; *Communications of the ACM*, Vol. 36, No. 11; November 1993; pp. 51–61.

Koch, G.R.; "Process Assessment: The BOOTSTRAP Approach"; *Journal of Information and Software Technology*, Vol. 35, No. 6–7; June–July 1993; pp. 387–403.

Kotler, P.; *Marketing Management: Analysis, Planning, Implementation, and Control, 9th ed.*; Prentice-Hall; Englewood Cliffs, NJ; 1997.

Lano, K.; Haughton, H.; *Reverse Engineering and Software Maintenance*; McGraw-Hill; New York; 1994.

Larson, R.R.; "Test Plan and Test Case Inspection Specification"; Technical Report TR21.585; IBM Corp.; New York; April 1975.

Lauesen, S.; Younessi, H.; "Is Software Quality Visible in the Code?"; *IEEE Software*; July–August 1998; pp. 69–74.

Leveson, N.G.; "Software Safety: What, Why, and How"; *ACM Computing Surveys*, Vol. 18, No. 2; June 1986; pp. 125–164.

Lewis, L., Sprich, R.; "Principled Negotiation, Evolutionary Systems Design, and Group Support Systems: A Suggested Integration of Three Approaches to Improving Negotiations"; in: Proceedings of the 25th Annual Hawaii International Conference on Systems Sciences; IEEE; 1991.

Lientz, B.P.; Swanson, E.B.; *Software Maintenance Management*; Addison-Wesley; Reading, MA; 1980.

Lindquist, T.E.; Jenkins, J.R.; "Test-Case Generation with IOGem"; *IEEE Software*; January 1988; pp. 72–79.

Littlewood, B.; "Software Reliability Growth Models"; in: *Software Reliability Handbook*; Rook, P., ed.; Elsevier; London; 1990.

Luo, G.; Das, A.; von Bochman, G.; "Software Testing Based on SDL Specifications with Save"; *IEEE Transactions on Software Engineering*, Vol. 20, No. 1; January 1994; pp. 72–87.

Luqi; Gougen, J.; "Formal Methods: Promises and Problems"; *IEEE Software*; January 1997; pp. 73–85.

Macro, A.; Buxton, J.; *The Craft of Software Engineering*; Addison-Wesley; Reading, MA; 1987.

Martin, J.; Odell, J.J.; *Object-Oriented Methods: A Foundation*; Prentice-Hall; Englewood Cliffs, NJ; 1995.

McCabe, T.J.; "A Complexity Measure"; *IEEE Transactions on Software Engineering*, Vol. 2, No. 4; December 1976; pp. 308–320.

McDowell, C.E.; Helmbold, D.P.; "Debugging Concurrent Programs"; *ACM Computing Surveys*, Vol. 21, No. 4; December 1989; pp. 593–622.

Meyer, B.; *Object-Oriented Software Construction*; Prentice-Hall; London; 1988.

Meyer, B.; Eiffel: *The Language*; Prentice-Hall; Englewood Cliffs, NJ; 1992.

Meyer, B.; "Design by Contract"; in: *Advances in Object-Oriented Software Engineering*; Manderioli, D.; Meyer, B., eds.; Prentice-Hall; Englewood Cliffs, NJ; 1992.

Mills, H.D.; "On the Statistical Validation of Computer Programs"; Technical Report No. FSC 72-6015; IBM Corporation; New York; 1972.

Mills, H.D.; Dyer, M.; Linger, R.; "Cleanroom Software Engineering"; *IEEE Software*; September 1987; pp. 19–25.

Minkowitz, C.; Henderson, P.; "A Formal Description of Object-Oriented Programming Using VDM"; in: VDM-Europe Symposium on VDM—A Formal Method at Work, LNCS 252; Mac an Airchinnigh, M.; Bjorner, D.; Jones, C.; Neuhold, E., eds.; Springer-Verlag; Berlin; 1987.

Morell, L.J.; "Theoretical Insights Into Fault-Based Testing"; in: Proceedings of the Second Workshop on Software Testing, Verification, and Analysis; Banff, Canada; July 1988.

Mumford, E.; "Defining System Requirements to Meet Business Needs: A Case Study"; *The Computer Journal*, Vol. 28, No. 2; 1985; pp. 148–156.

Murphy, G.; Townsend, P.; Wong, P.; "Experience and Class Testing"; *Communications of the ACM*, Vol. 37, No. 9; September 1994; pp. 39–47.

Myers, G.J.; "A Controlled Experiment in Program Testing and Code Walkthrough/Inspections"; *Communications of the ACM*, Vol. 21, No. 9; September 1978; pp. 760–768.

Myers, G.J.; *The Art of Software Testing*; Wiley; New York; 1979.

Neisser, U.; *Cognition and Reality*; Freeman; San Francisco, CA; 1976.

Ntafos, S.C.; Hakimi, S.L.; "On Path Cover Problem in Digraphs and Applications"; *IEEE Transactions on Software Engineering*, Vol. 5, No. 5; September 1979.

Nuseibeh, B; Easterbrook, S; *"Requirements Engineering: A Roadmap"*; in: Proceedings of International Conference on Software Engineering (ICSE-2000); Ireland; June 2000.

Offutt, J.A.; "Investigations of the Software Testing Coupling Effect"; *ACM Transactions on Software Engineering and Methodology*, Vol. 1, No. 1; January 1992; pp. 5–20.

Omar, A.A.; Mohammed, F.A.; A Survey of Software Functional Testing Methods; *ACM SIGSOFT Software Engineering Notes*, Vol. 16, No. 2; April 1991; pp. 75–82.

Ostrand, T.J.; Balcer, M.J.; "The Category Partition Method for Specifying and Generating Functional Tests"; *Communications of the ACM*, Vol. 31, No. 6; June 1988; pp. 676–686.

Parnas, D.L.; Weiss, D.M.; "Active Design Reviews: Principles and Practices"; *Journal of Systems and Software*, Vol. 12, No. 7; 1987; pp. 259–269.

PASS-C; PASS-C: Program Analysis and Style System, User Manual; Software Quality Institute; Griffith University; Brisbane, Australia; 1993.

Paulk, M.C.; Curtis, B.; Chrissis, M.B.; Weber, C.V.; "Capability Maturity Model for Software, Version 1.1"; *IEEE Software*; July 1993; pp. 18–27.

Perry, D.; Kaiser, G.E.; "Adequate Testing and Object-Oriented Programming"; *Journal of Object-Oriented Programming*, Vol. 2, No. 5; January–February 1990; pp. 13–19.

Pfleeger, S.L.: "Investigating the Influence of Formal Methods"; *IEEE Computer,* Vol. 30, No. 2; February 1997; pp. 33–43.

Pfleeger, S.L.; Jeffery, R.; Curtis, B.; Kitchenham, B.; "Status Report on Software Measurement"; *IEEE Software*; March–April 1997; pp. 33–45.

Plato; "The Republic"; Trans. G.M.A. Grube; Hackett; Indianapolis, IN; 1974.

Plato; "The Symposium"; Trans. P. Woodruff; A. Nehamas; Hackett; Indianapolis, IN; 1989.

Preece, J.; Rogers, Y.; Sharp, H.; Benyon, D.; Holland, S.; Carey, T.; *Human Computer Interaction*; Addison-Wesley; Reading, MA; 1995.

Pressman, R.S.; *Software Engineering: A Practitioner's Approach, 4th ed.*; McGraw-Hill; New York; 1995.

Ramesh, B.; Bui, T.; "Negotiation in Network Based Requirement Analysis"; in: Proceedings of 32nd Annual Hawaii International Conference on System Sciences; IEEE; New York; 1998.

Rapps, S.; Weyuker, E.J.; "Selecting Software Test Data Using Data Flow Information"; *IEEE Transactions on Software Engineering,* Vol. 14, No. 4; April 1985; pp. 367–375.

Redmill, F.J.; "Fagan's Inspection"; *Managing System Development,* Vol. 13, No. 3; March 1993; pp. 1–5.

Redmill, F.J.; Johnson, E.A.; Runge, B.A.; "Document Quality–Inspection"; *British Telecom Telecommunication Engineering,* Vol. 6; January 1988; pp. 250–256.

Reeve, J.T.; "Applying the Fagan Inspection Technique"; *Quality Forum,* Vol. 17, No. 1; March 1991; pp. 40–47.

Remus, H.; "Integrated Software Validation in the View of Inspections and Reviews"; in: *Software Validation*; Hausen, H.L., ed.; Elsevier; Amsterdam; 1984.

Richardson, D.J.; Thompson, M.C.; "The Relay Model for Error Detection and Its Application"; in: Proceedings of the Second Workshop on Software Testing, Verification, and Analysis; Banff, Canada; July 1988.

Ross, K.A.; Wright, C.R.B.; *Discrete Mathematics, 3rd ed.*; Prentice-Hall; Englewood Cliffs, NJ; 1992.

RTCA; "Software Considerations in Airborne Systems and Equipment Certification"; Doc. No. RTCA/DO-178B; RTCA; Springfield, VA; December 1992.

Rumbaugh, J.; et al.; *Object-Oriented Modeling and Design*; Prentice-Hall; Englewood Cliffs, NJ; 1990.

Rumbaugh, J.; Jacobson, I.; Booch, G.; *The Unified Modeling Language Reference Manual*; Addison-Wesley; Reading, MA; 1999.

Russell, G.W.; "Experience with Inspection in Ultralarge-Scale Development"; *IEEE Software*, Vol. 8, No. 1; January 1991; pp. 25–31.

Sanders, J.; "Product, Not Process: A Parable"; *IEEE Software*; March–April 1997; pp. 6–10.

Sauer, C.; Lau, C.; "The Adoption of Information Systems Methodologies— An Analytical Framework and a Case Study"; in: Proceedings of the Fifth Australasian Conference on Information Systems, ACIS94 Vol. 1; Shanks, G.; Arnott, D., eds.; Monash University, Australia; 1994; pp. 87–97.

Schuman, S.A.; Pitt, D.H.; "Object-Oriented Sub-System Specification"; in: *Program Specification and Transformation*; Meertens, G.L.T., ed.; Elsevier Science Publishers; Amsterdam; 1987.

Sommerville, I.; *Software Engineering*, 5th ed.; Addison-Wesley; London; 1995.

Strauss, S.; Ebenau, R.G.; *Software Inspection Process*; McGraw-Hill; New York; 1995.

Stroustroup, B.; *The C++ Programming Language, 2nd ed.*; Addison-Wesley; Reading, MA; 1992.

Taylor, F.W.; *Principles of Scientific Management*; Harper; New York; 1911.

Thevenod-Fosse, P.; Waeselynck, H.; "An Investigation of Statistical Software Testing"; *Journal of Software Testing, Verification and Reliability*, Vol. 1, No. 2; July 1991; pp. 5–25.

Travassos, G.; Shull, F.; Fredricks, M; Basili, V.; "Detecting Defects in Object-Oriented Designs: Using Reading Techniques to Improve Software Quality"; in: Proceedings of OOPSLA; Denver, CO; 1999.

Van Emden, M.H.; "Structured Inspection of Code"; *Software Testing, Verification and Reliability*, Vol. 2, No. 3; September 1992; pp. 133–153.

Viller, S.; Sommerville, I.; "Coherence: Social Analysis for Software Engineers"; Cooperative Systems Engineering Group Technical Report Ref: CSEG/6/98; 1998.

Voas, J; Kassab, L.; "Using Assertions to Make Untestable Software More Testable"; *Software Quality Professional Journal*, Vol. 1, No. 4; March 1999.

Votta, L.G.; "Does Every Inspection Need a Meeting?"; *ACM Software Engineering Notes*, Vol. 18, No. 5; December 1993; pp. 107–114.

Wallace, D.R.; Fujii, R.U.; "Software Verification and Validation: An Overview"; *IEEE Software*; May 1989; pp. 10–18.

Weatherall, A.; "Structured Negotiation Using GroupSystems Electronic Meetings"; in: Proceedings of the 32nd Annual Hawaii International Conference on System Sciences; IEEE; New York; 1998.

Weiser, M.; "Program Slicing"; *IEEE Transactions on Software Engineering,* Vol. 10, No. 4; July 1984; pp. 352–357.

Weller, E.F.; "Lessons Learned from Two Years of Inspection Data"; in: Proceedings of the 3rd International Conference Applications of Software Measurement; 1992; pp. 2.57–2.69.

Weyuker, E.J.; "Assessing Test Data Adequacy Through Program Interface"; ACM Transactions on Programming Languages and Systems Vol. 5, No. 4; October 1983; pp. 641–655.

Weyuker, E.J.; Jeng, B.; "Analyzing Partition Testing Strategies"; *IEEE Transactions on Software Engineering,* Vol. 17, No. 7; July 1994; pp. 703–711.

Weyuker, E.J.; Ostrand, T.J.; "Theories of Program Testing and the Application of Revealing Subdomains"; *IEEE Transactions on Software Engineering,* Vol. 6, No. 3; May 1980; pp. 236–246.

Whittaker, J.A.; Thomason, M.G.; "A Markov Chain Model for Statistical Software Testing"; *IEEE Transactions on Software Engineering,* Vol. 20, No. 10; October 1994; pp. 812–824.

Wilson, B.; Systems, *Concepts and Methodologies*; Wiley; Chichester, UK; 1989.

Woit, D.M.; "Realistic Expectations of Random Testing"; CRL Rep. 246; McMaster University; Hamilton, Canada; May 1992.

Younessi, H.; Grant, D.D.; "A Framework for Development of a Predictive Model for Software Process Quality"; in: *Quality Management*; Ross, M.; Brebbia, C.A.; Staples, G.; Stapleton, J., eds.; Computational Mechanics Publications; Southampton, UK; 1995.

Younessi, H.; Henderson-Sellers, B.; "Cooking Up Quality Software"; *Object Magazine*; October 1997; pp. 38–42.

Younessi, H.; Smith, R.; "Towards a Systemic Approach to Object-Oriented Analysis"; in: Proceedings of Australasian Conference on Information Systems (ACIS'95); Perth, Australia; September 1995.

Younessi, H.; Zeephongsekul, P.; Bodhisuwan, W.; "A General Model of Dynamic Testing Efficacy"; *Software Quality Journal*; (accepted for publication 2002).

Yourdon, E.; *Structured Walkthroughs, 5th ed.*; Prentice-Hall; Englewood Cliffs, NJ; 1989.

INDEX

A

abstraction, 42–44, 110, 126
access control mechanisms and policies, 159–160
accessor routines, 236
activity diagrams, 196–199
adaptive maintenance, 113
analyzing strategy, 78
architectural design styles
    comparison of, 140–141
    encapsulated architecture style, 138
    layered architecture style, 135–137
    overview, 134–135
    partitioned architecture style, 137–138
    pipes and filters architecture style, 139
    repository architecture style, 138–139
architectural (system) design documentation,
    162–163
architecture
    blackboards for polling, 147
    centralized topology, 131
    design, steps for basic. *See* basic steps for
    architectural design
    design styles. *See* architectural design styles
    feedback/feedforward for process control,
    145–147

    logical topology, 131
    MVC partitioning for user-interface
    independence, 147–148
    overview, 130–131
    parallelism for fault tolerance, 144–145
    physical topology, 131
    problems, solving specific architectural,
    143–148
asking strategy, 78
aspect, inspection by, 214
assertion-based testing of a class
    class invariants, 230–231
    constraint-based testing, 231
    loop invariants, 231
    loop variants, 231
    overview, 227–229
    postconditions, 231
    preconditions, 230
assessing product quality
    bug, 25
    defect, 25
    defect management as means of ensuring
    quality, 22–23
    defects of functionality, 26
    defects of usability, 28
    determination of product quality attributes, 34

D

E

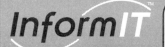
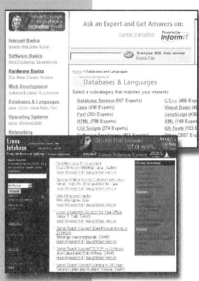

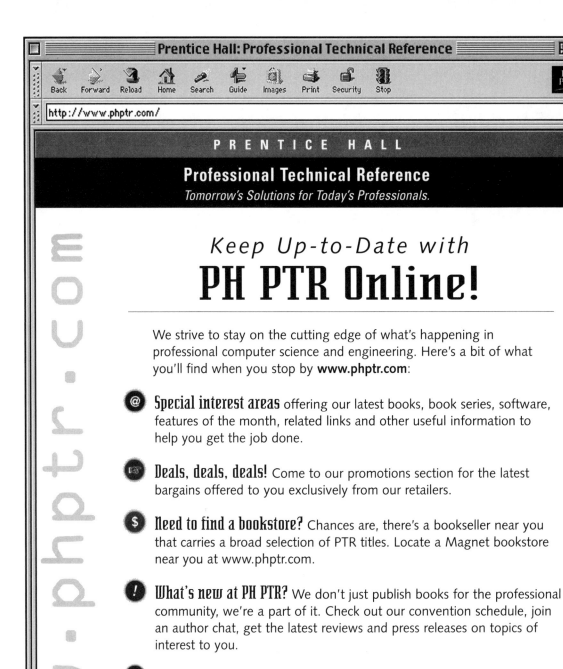